IMAGES
of America

NORTH RIDGEVILLE

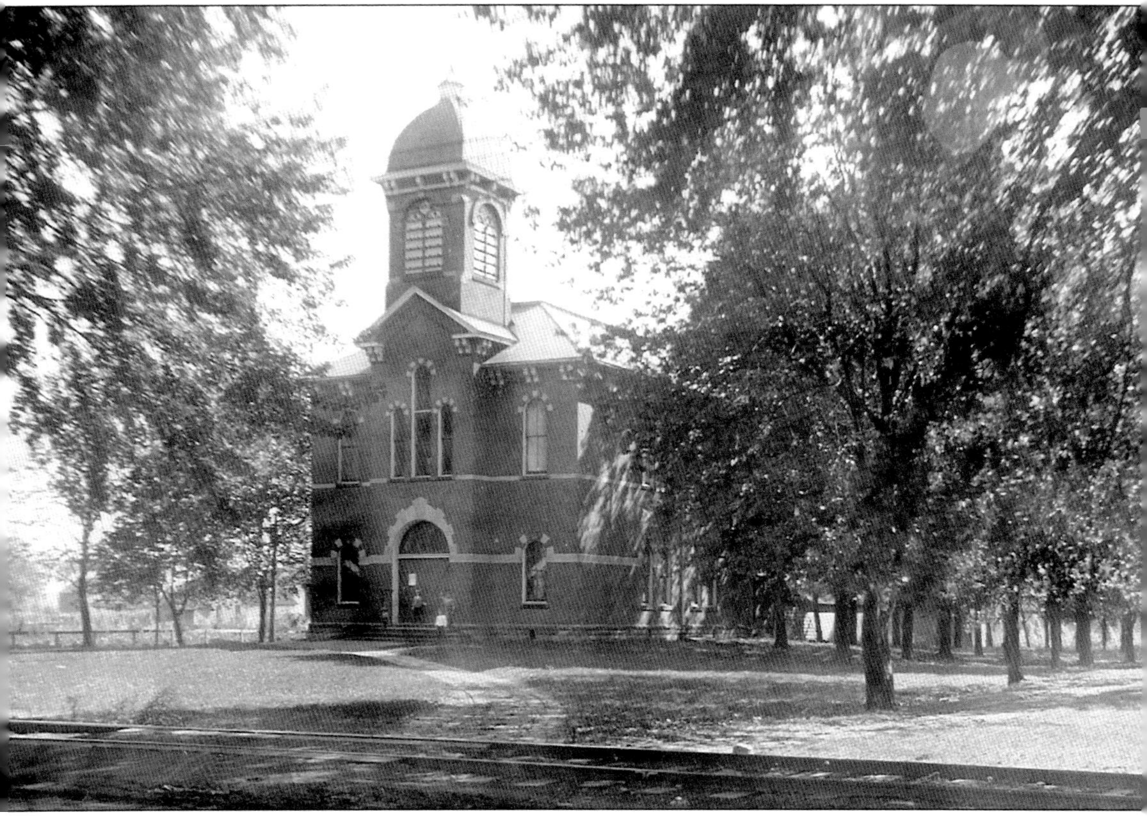

North Ridgeville's landmark, the Old Town Hall, was built in 1882 and 1883, replacing the 1850 frame structure on Center Ridge Road west of Avon Belden Road (Route 83). The total cost of the two-story brick structure was approximately $12,000. It was dedicated during a celebration ceremony held on December 20, 1883. The event included band music, speeches, and a large dinner. Since it was constructed, the building has served the community in many ways. It was used as the township hall, the village hall, and the city hall. The North Ridgeville Branch Library was housed on the first floor from 1977 to 1989. Currently the stately building is the site of the North Ridgeville Historical Society Museum. The second floor is the home of the Olde Towne Hall Theatre, which holds both dramatic and musical productions on stage, while the audience enjoys them from the comfort of the refurbished opera seats. (Courtesy of North Ridgeville Historical Society.)

On the cover: Ridgeville Township in the 19th and early 20th centuries was essentially a farming town. There was a small assortment of other businesses, but tilling the soil and growing crops was the mainstay of the township. The face of this hardworking community is clearly depicted in this photograph taken on threshing day at Christian Thome's farm on Stoney Ridge Road about 1910. (Courtesy of North Ridgeville Historical Society.)

IMAGES
of America

NORTH RIDGEVILLE

Carol G. Klear

ARCADIA
PUBLISHING

Copyright © 2008 by Carol G. Klear
ISBN 978-0-7385-5246-0

Published by Arcadia Publishing
Charleston, South Carolina

Printed in the United States of America

Library of Congress Catalog Card Number: 2008920692

For all general information contact Arcadia Publishing at:
Telephone 843-853-2070
Fax 843-853-0044
E-mail sales@arcadiapublishing.com
For customer service and orders:
Toll-Free 1-888-313-2665

Visit us on the Internet at www.arcadiapublishing.com

To Electa Wilmot Terrell, the first woman to settle in Ridgeville. She not only exemplified the courage of a true pioneer, but the memory of her spirit guided the writing of this book.

Contents

ACKNOWLEDGMENTS

This book would not have been possible had it not been for the courage of the early families like the Terrells and the Beebes, who left their homes in Connecticut to begin new lives. The yesterdays of those pioneers helped to create the North Ridgeville of today.

Although one name is listed as the author, the completed book took the talents and generosity of many people, and I want to acknowledge the roles they played. Karen and Jeff Sigsworth, who are the city's historians and guide the historical society in remembering the community's ancestors, spent countless hours helping to research vintage photographs and the histories behind the faces and places. They also lent their valuable expertise in editing the book as it neared completion to ensure that every name and date was accurate. A special thank-you to Gene Kleinholz, whose enthusiasm for the book from its beginning and the photographs he provided were invaluable. To all the people who shared photographs or stories or helped in any way, you are more appreciated than you know.

To my editor, Melissa Basilone, thank you for always being there to answer questions and offer words of encouragement.

Unless otherwise noted, all photographs have been contributed by the North Ridgeville Historical Society. My gratitude goes to the historical society, the Lorain County Historical Society, Mayor Dave Gillock, North Ridgeville Police detective Larry Swenk, the First Congregational United Church of Christ, Shepherd of the Ridge Lutheran Church, St. Julie Billiart Catholic Church, the R. W. Beckett Corporation, the Ridge Tool Company, the Mould family, the Don Pitts family, the Worcester family, Marcella Baldauf, Ron Bauer, Kathy Bly, Tina Bright, Ken Buescher, Loyola Diederich, Ray Diederich, Bob Gilder, Tom Guggenbiller, Jim Hales, Bill Hall, Bill Laubenthal, Marge Lesnick, former mayor Dick Noll, Mary Ann Poff, Russell and Jane Sigsworth, Tissy Simon, Lois Sullivan, and Marian Taylor.

Finally, I thank my husband, Tom, for his patience in allowing me the time I needed to work on this book and also, on occasion, for being my personal courier. A special thank-you also goes to my family for their support.

INTRODUCTION

It was a bold and daring idea for that small band of men from Waterbury, Connecticut, but the more they discussed it, the more excited they became with the prospect of heading west. They had heard there was some public land in Ohio that lay west of Pennsylvania, and the men were more than a little anxious to blaze a trail to what could be a new life.

The territory, which included both Pennsylvania and Ohio, had originally been deeded by England to the Connecticut Colony and was known as the Connecticut Western Reserve. After the Revolutionary War, Connecticut held fast to the land in Ohio but in 1795 sold the portion now known as the Western Reserve to a group called the Connecticut Land Company. The owners had the property surveyed, and by the early 1800s, the western part was apportioned into townships.

In 1810, 17 men, many of them from the Terrell and Beebe families, set out. As they trudged westward from Connecticut, the pioneers undoubtedly faced what lie ahead with some trepidation and apprehension. After all, they may not have been rich or well known in Connecticut, but it had been home, and they were leaving it for the unknown. But they would not turn back. The decision had been made.

The journey was long and not at all easy, but the men were determined. As they made their way along, they encountered wildlife that was not always friendly and weather that was sometimes harsh. As they rode their horses or directed their wagons, the men talked about what they were going to do when they reached their destination. On May 10, 1810, they reached the end of their journey and established the first permanent settlement in what became known as North Ridgeville.

Within a few weeks, the word got back to Connecticut, and additional pioneers arrived, including the first woman, Electa Wilmot Terrell, who joined the others living in the wilderness, at least until there was time to clear land and build a community. In some parts of the settlers' new home, the land was ridged, the result of Lake Erie receding many years before. The ridges added to the settlers' difficulties, making the land harder to till and the soil less workable, but those early people were courageous and determined in purpose.

Today there are five roads in North Ridgeville named for those ridges—Center Ridge, Stoney Ridge, Sugar Ridge, Chestnut Ridge, and Butternut Ridge.

Center Ridge Road ran east and west and became the main thoroughfare, extending from Buffalo to Detroit. It was where the first homes were built and perhaps the first farms were established. Within a few decades, rows of maple trees were planted along the main road. As they grew tall and stately, they provided beautiful, arched shelters for those traveling from one end of the community to the other. Today Center Ridge Road continues to be the prime artery of North Ridgeville, and although the appearance has changed dramatically from the time of the first settlers, some parts of the road are still recalled as the area of the Pitts farm or the Diederich farm.

After building places to live, the pioneers set about providing for their children's education, and in 1812, a log schoolhouse was constructed, which served for three years until it burned down. Again, undeterred, they built another school, and in time, the area was divided into school districts.

As time went on, a few smaller settlements developed, including what was known as Fields Corners, which was located at Butternut Ridge and Root Roads and was served by a general store and a post office. Near the railroad tracks on Avon Belden Road, now Route 83, a band of German, English, and Irish immigrants gathered and built homes at what was called Shawville.

All the while, those first people strived to take their places in a new life, but they never forgot the Creator who guided their lives. The first church was organized in 1822 and eventually became what is now known as the First Congregational United Church of Christ, located on Center Ridge Road at Stoney Ridge. It was followed by what is now called the Fields United Methodist Church and then by St. Peter Catholic Church.

Over time, small businesses sprang up out of a necessity to serve the people. There were gristmills, blacksmith shops, cheese factories, and general stores; however, farms were the mainstays in those times. Tilling the soil and working the crops kept entire farming families busy from sunup to sundown, but they were happy and, for the most part, healthy.

Today North Ridgeville is a very different place from what it was in 1810. From the first 17 men who set out to carve niches in a new territory, the population has grown to nearly 27,000, and Ridgeville Township is now the city of North Ridgeville. There is one school district with several elementary schools, a middle school, and a high school. There are also two private schools. The three original houses of worship have been expanded to approximately two dozen churches of various denominations. The former farms have been replaced by numerous housing developments. The dirt roads are now paved streets. There are stores, restaurants, gas stations, motels, and other businesses to serve the residents.

North Ridgeville has undergone many changes over the years, but one thing that remains constant is the courageous and sometimes feisty spirit of its people, all in the name of the city they call home.

One

FAITH OF OUR FATHERS

The journey from Waterbury, Connecticut, to Ohio was long and perilous. With every step the pioneers took, or with each turn of the wagon wheels, there was the fear of the unknown. Wild and unfamiliar animals seemed to lurk everywhere. Native Americans were also a concern, although by the time the settlers arrived in Ridgeville, Moses Cleaveland had already reached the Western Reserve, met with Native American chiefs and pledged friendship, which quelled the uprisings. The small band of men and one woman hoped and prayed that they would survive the trek and reach their intended destination without incident. After arriving in what is now known as North Ridgeville on May 10, 1810, so far from their native Connecticut, the immigrants held a thanksgiving service in gratitude to their God for guiding them safely to their new home. For a number of years many of the settlers continued to hold religious services in houses until 1822, when the present First Congregational United Church of Christ was founded, followed a few years later by Fields United Methodist Church and St. Peter Catholic Church. Today there are nearly two dozen houses of worship in North Ridgeville.

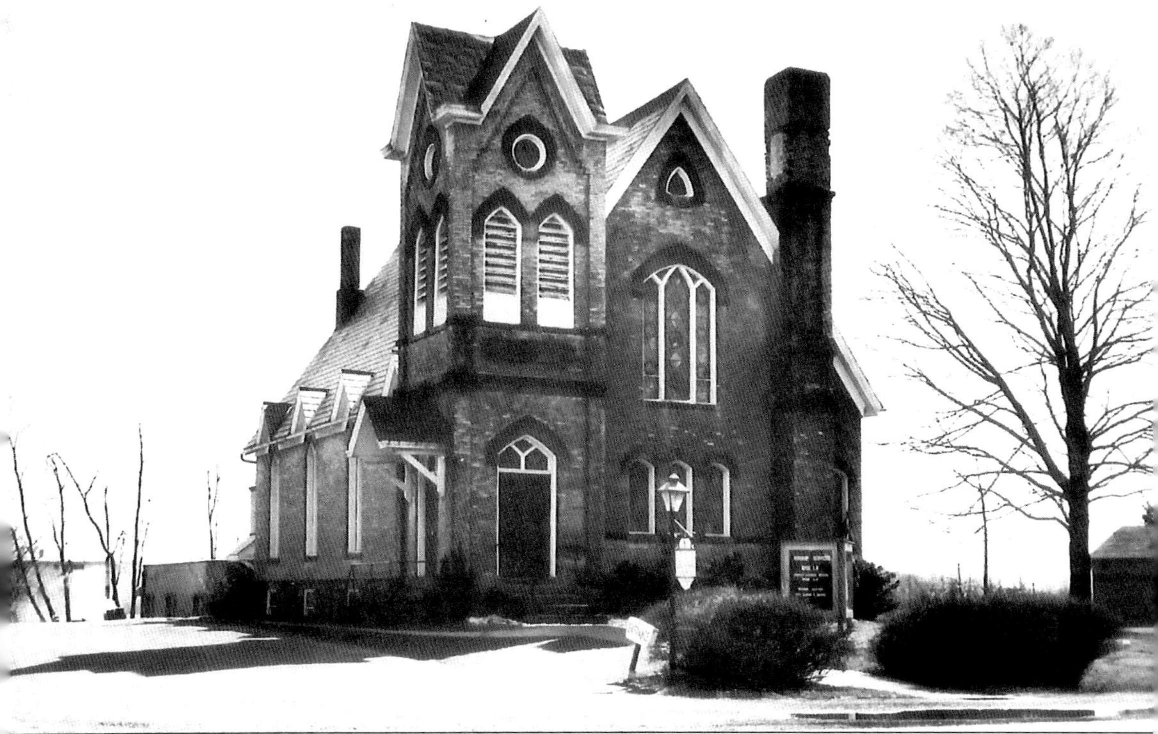

The First Presbyterian Church was the first church organized in Ridgeville Township as the result of people migrating from New England to the Western Reserve. Worshipers met in homes for the first 12 years until the First Congregational United Church of Christ was founded in 1822. There were six charter members 185 years ago, and they assembled in a log schoolhouse at Route 76 (now Route 83) and Route 20. The first members were Chester Beebe and his wife, Marcia, Hezekiah Case, Samuel Eldred, Seth R. Alcott, and Lucinda Cahoon. On December 27, 1822, a week after the founding, four more members were received: Hezekiah Case's wife; Marcus Case and his wife, Laura; and Ora Case. Truman Case, the son of Marcus and Laura, was the first recorded baptism.

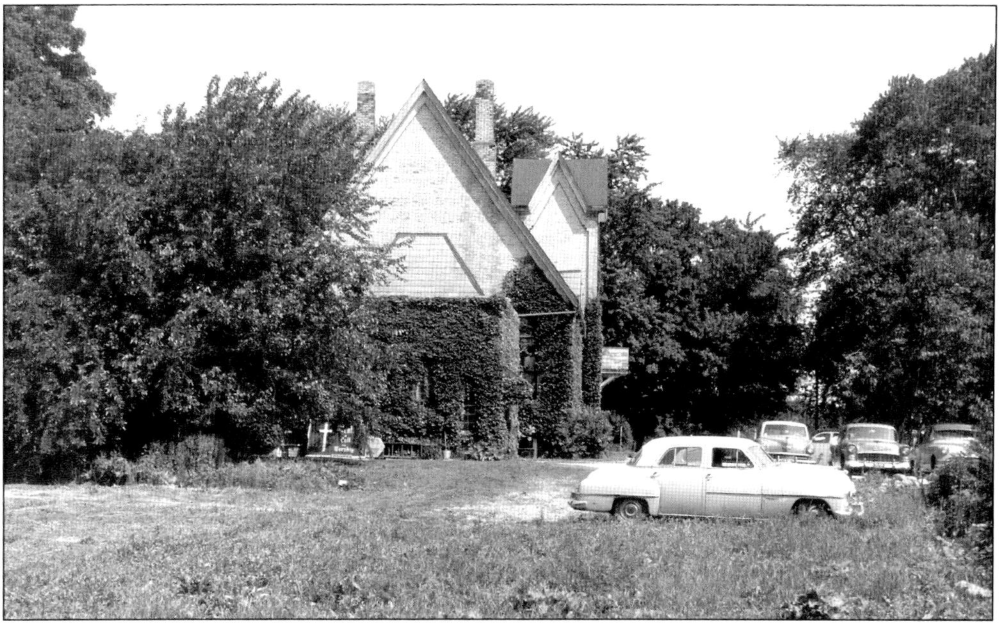

The present brick structure of the First Congregational United Church of Christ on Center Ridge Road near Stoney Ridge was completed in 1875 and replaced an earlier frame structure. The building was expanded in 1931 and again in 1956, when a church hall was added. The photograph of the rear of the church is from the mid-1950s. (Courtesy of the First Congregational United Church of Christ.)

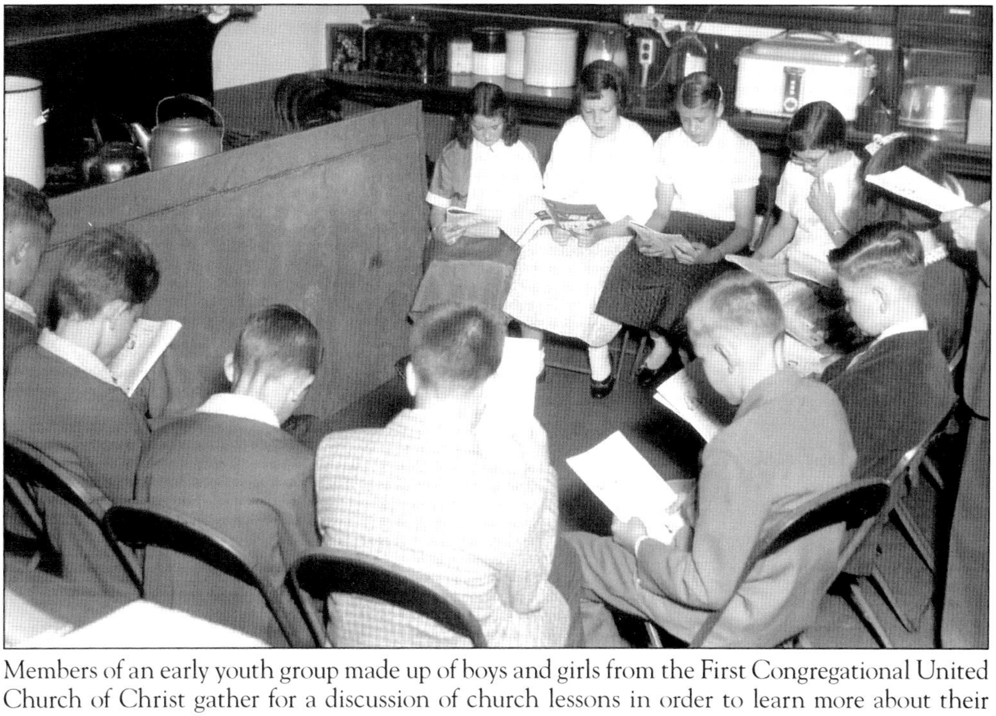

Members of an early youth group made up of boys and girls from the First Congregational United Church of Christ gather for a discussion of church lessons in order to learn more about their religious beliefs and become better members of the church. (Courtesy of the First Congregational United Church of Christ.)

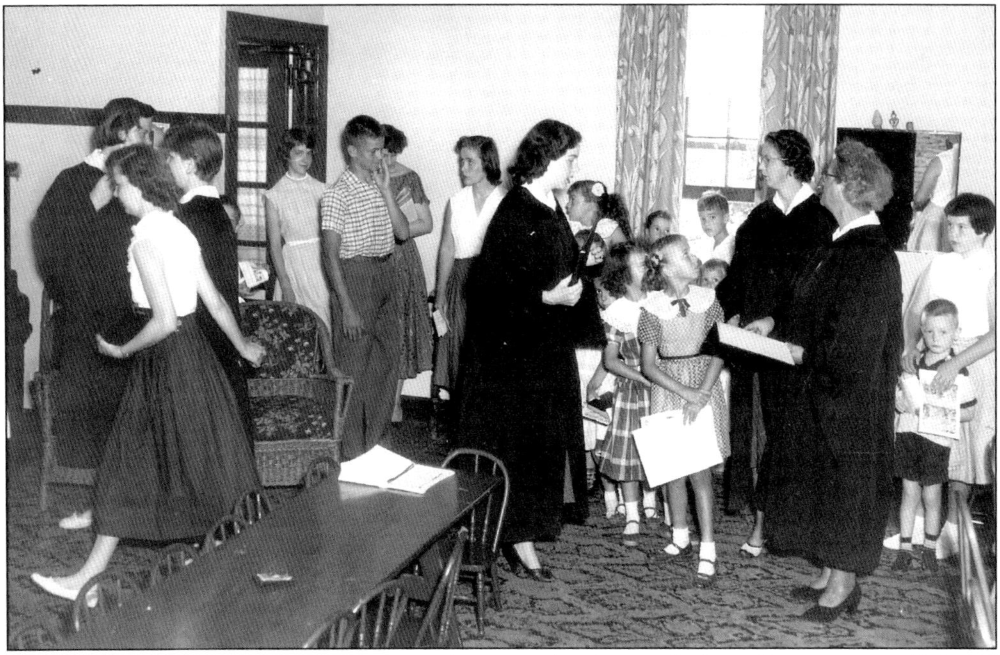

There must have been an important event about to take place at the First Congregational United Church of Christ. It appears that a number of women are scurrying around and donning choir robes, while the boys and girls in their Sunday best prepare for a special service. (Courtesy of the First Congregational United Church of Christ.)

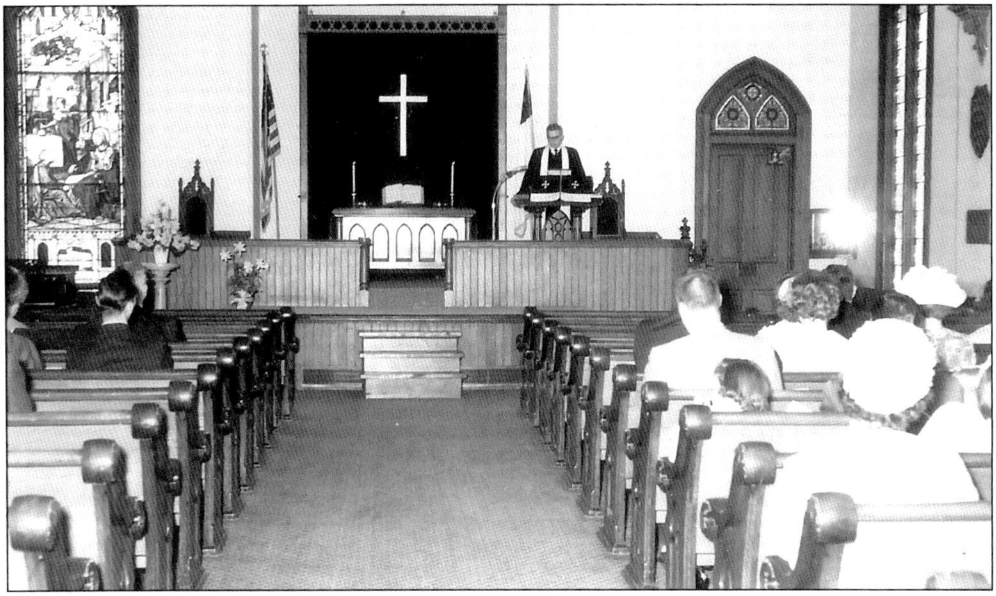

The church celebrated its 185th anniversary in 2007. The first leader was D. W. Lathrop, who served from 1825 to 1832. The Reverend John Fairweather is the present pastor. The following persons were honored for being members for more than 45 years: Eleanor Wood, Laura Long, Edith Fitts, Mary Jane Dreger, Jean Gilder, Robert Gilder, Evelyn Kearney, William Wood, Billie Bier, Kenneth Bier, Mary Stuart, Betty Noland, June Yost, and James Yost. (Courtesy of the First Congregational United Church of Christ.)

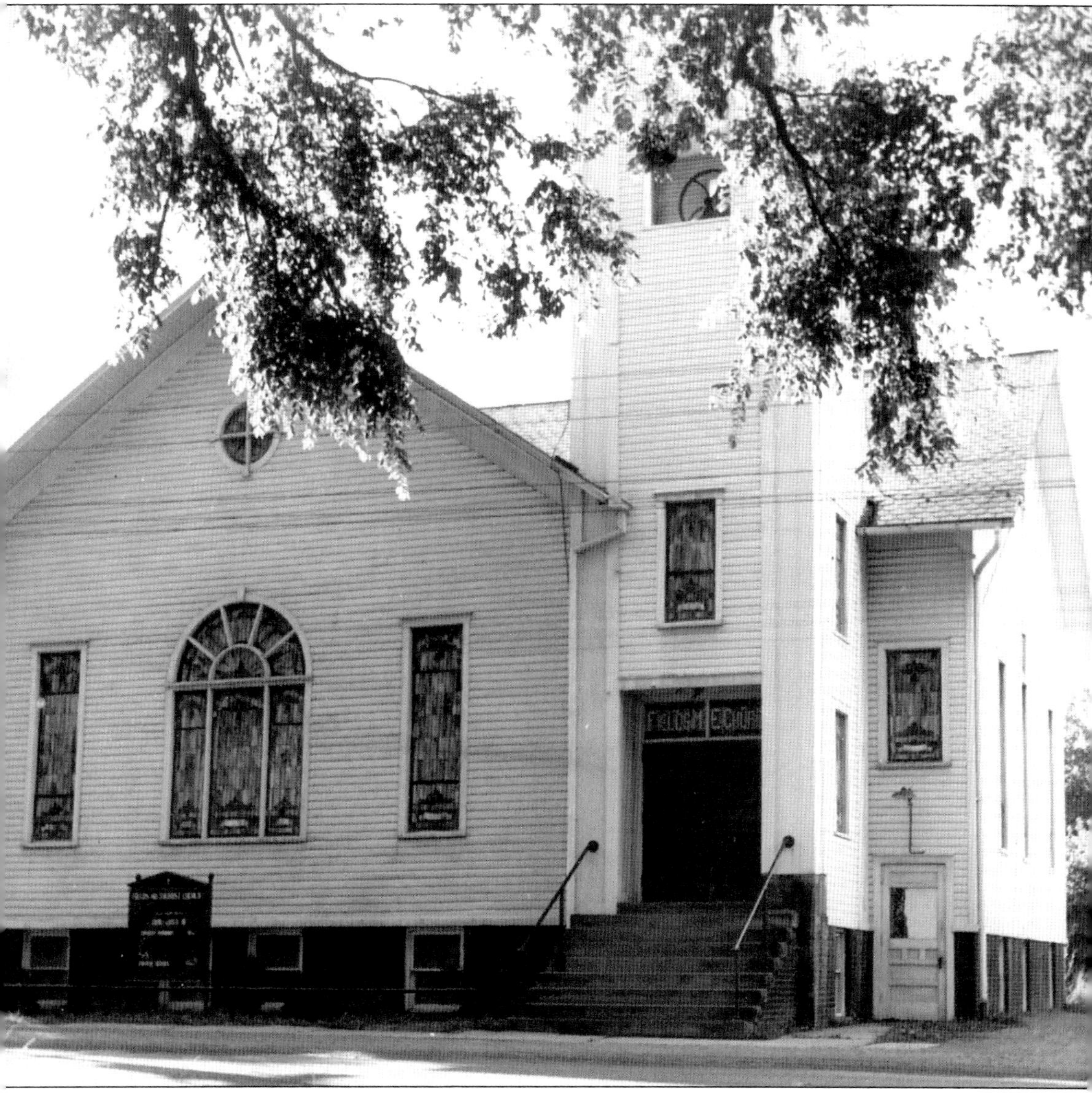

The second church in Ridgeville Township is now called Fields United Methodist Church. It was started by a small group of pioneer families in 1825, the year after Lorain County was organized. The earliest members included Wilson and Hannah Blaine, Elijah and Eliza Rigby, and the Harris Emmons family. The members met in the Blains' log cabin on Butternut Ridge near Bagley Road. For 80 years, they were served by Methodist Episcopal circuit riders. The building shown was built in 1836 by the Avon Congregational Church and moved to the southwest corner of Butternut Ridge and Root Road (formerly Fields Corners) in 1882, replacing an earlier building destroyed by fire. The church was remodeled in 1916 and was sold to Faith Baptist Temple after the Methodist church relocated to its present site across from Fields Cemetery in 1968. The following have been members for more than 60 years: Alice Smith Vanek, Delbert Worcester, Russell Sigsworth, Joyce Henson Reinhart, Margaret Ritsko Sigsworth, Bob and Norma Fortune, and Jean Gaydash Williams. (Courtesy of Jeff Sigsworth.)

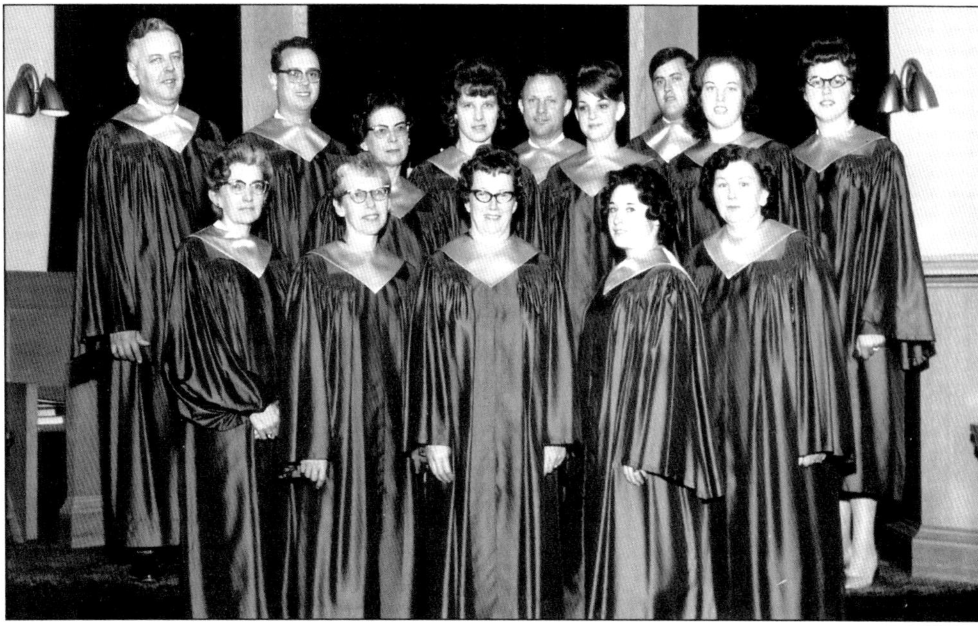

Members of Fields United Methodist Church Chancel Choir prepare for a performance in this early 1960s photograph. From left to right are (first row) Velma Bainbridge, Lorna Sweet, Cleo Myers, unidentified, and Charlotte Morgan; (second row) Bert Bridge, unidentified, Mary Rofe, Norma Fortune, Harry Chalmers, Cheryl Huene, Dwight Bridge, Jennifer (Henson) Smith, and Marge Sigsworth. (Courtesy of Jeff Sigsworth.)

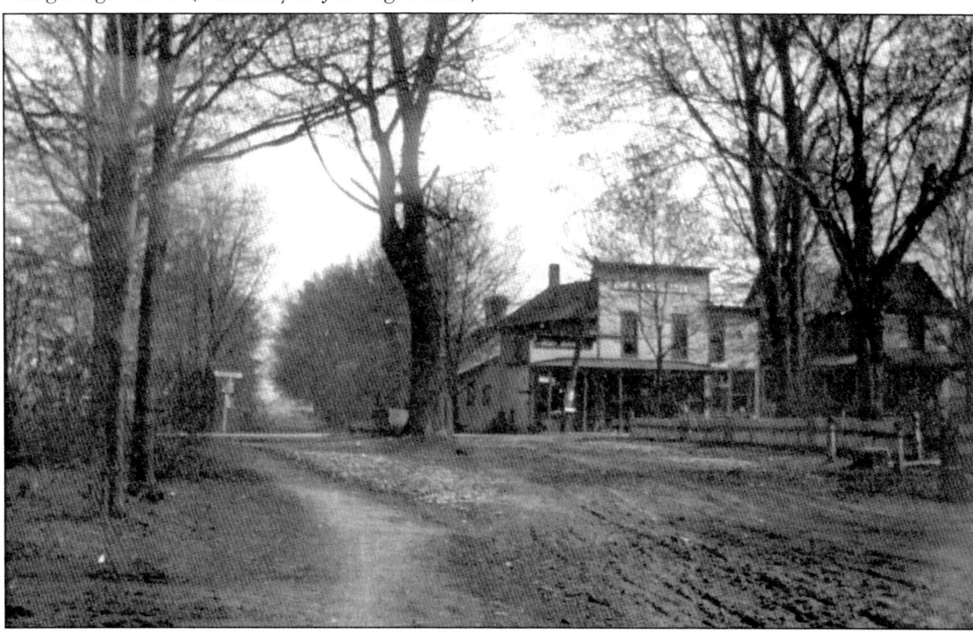

Root Road was one of the main roads in Ridgeville Township and was used for foot travel or horses and buggies. This early photograph is looking south on Root Road toward Butternut Ridge, now known as Lorain Road. The C. C. Benjamin General Store and the Fields post office were located on the southwest corner of the road crossing, between the road and the Methodist church. (Courtesy of Jeff Sigsworth.)

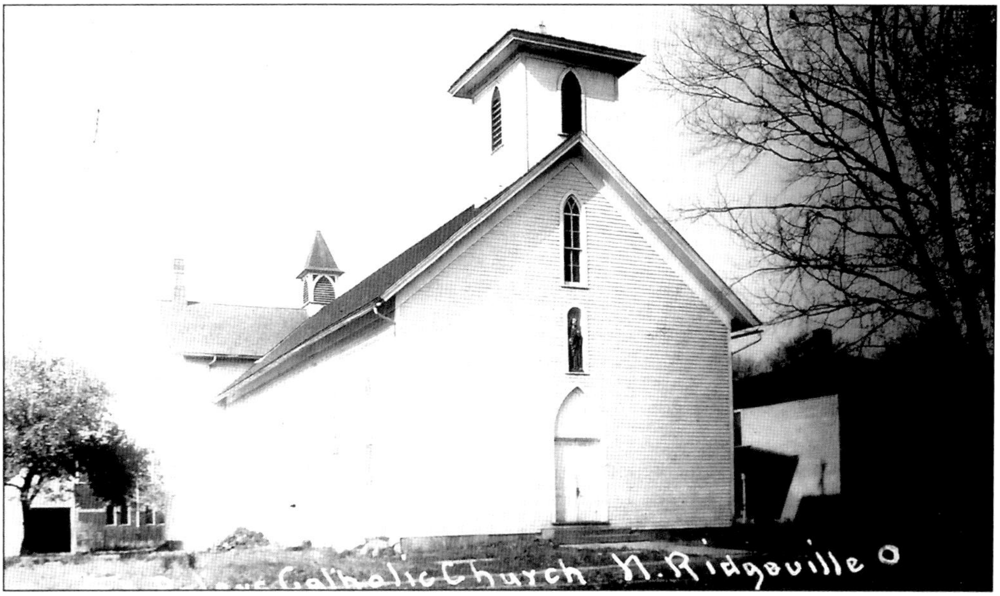

The first Catholic settlers arrived in Ridgeville in 1838, and over the next three decades, Louis Schwartz, Jacob Schmitz, Nicholas and Mathias Klein, Mathias Pitts, Joseph Diehn, Phillip Bauer, Mathias Myers, Leopold Dusendank, Peter Schmitz, John Hollander, Andrew Meyer, Peter Nuhn, Mathias Diederich, and Adam Barres moved into the area, primarily in the northern half of the township. St. Peter Roman Catholic Church was organized in Ridgeville Township in 1875 with many of the early parish families of German or Irish descent. The first building, shown in this 1910 photograph, was dedicated on Christmas Day in 1875 and was located on present-day Avon Belden Road (Route 83) near the current fire station. The Reverend Jacob Heidegger said the first Mass and led the parish from 1875 to 1879. Fire destroyed the structure on January 15, 1914, and a new church was completed in 1923 at the present site on Center Ridge Road.

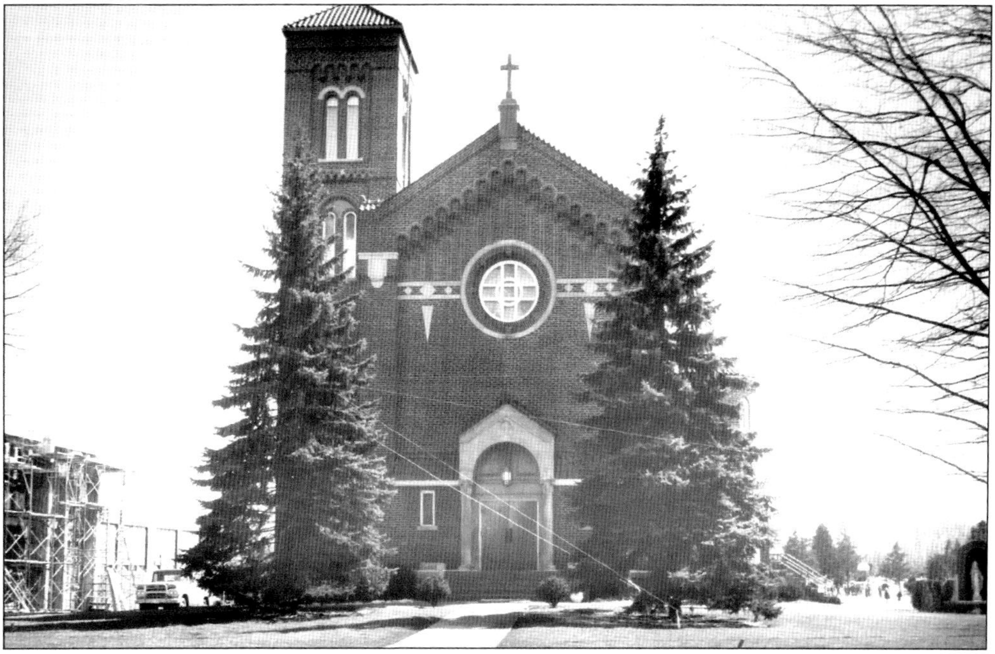

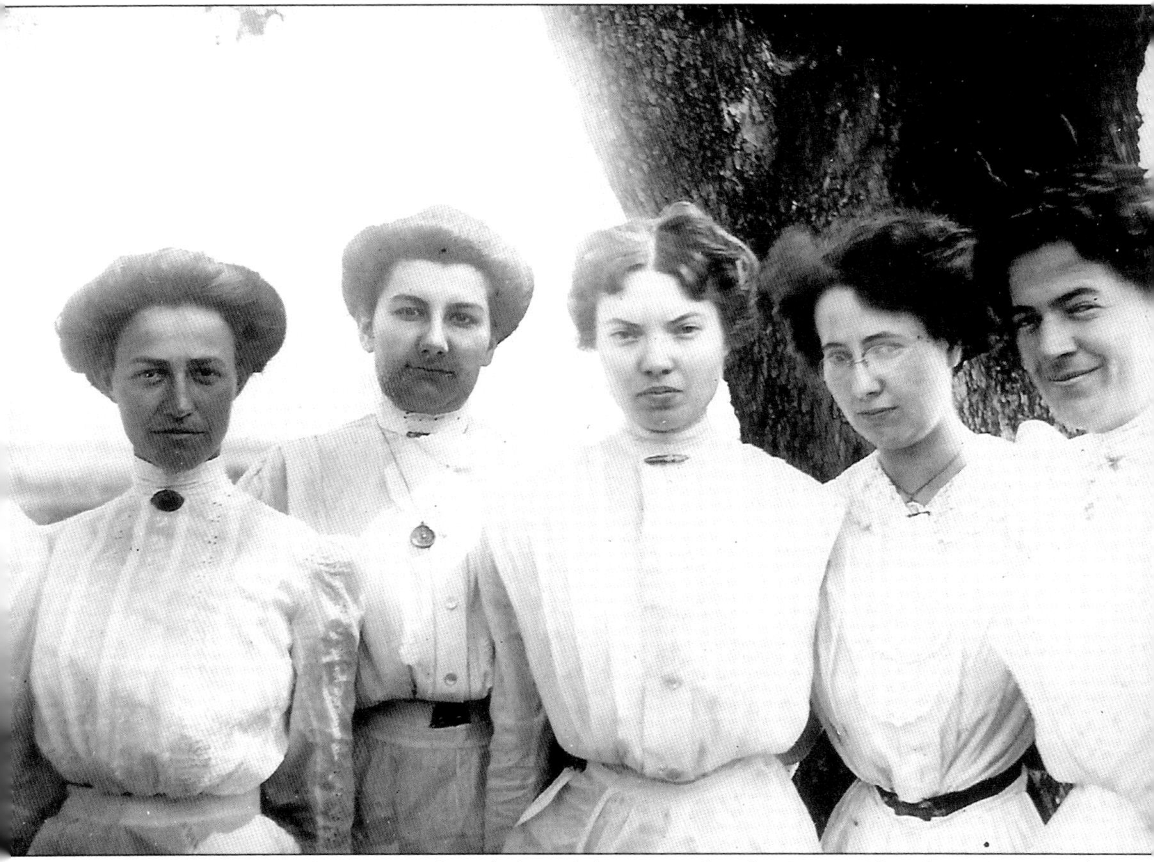

In February 1887, the Reverend Nicholas Pfeil, pastor of Holy Trinity Church in Avon, took charge of St. Peter Parish as a mission. He took over his new duties with enthusiasm and founded both the church and the school. He first directed his attention to obtaining a school and purchased the property for it at a cost of $900, which included a two-story frame dwelling. Benches were secured, and the parish had two classrooms. Pfeil also hired Mary Diederich to be the schoolteacher. In addition to his main goals of providing a church and school, the priest later set about organizing a Young Ladies Sodality with a starting enrollment of 25 members. Pictured from let to right are Hannah Meyer, Barbara Schneider, Alma Moore, Anna Moore, and Clara Meyer, five of the first members of the organization.

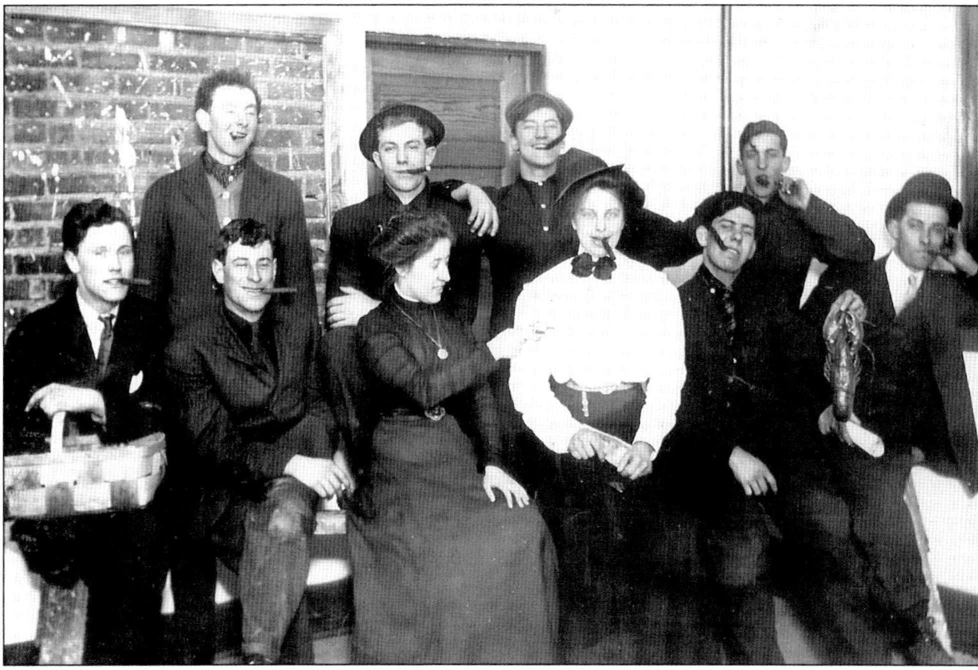

St. Peter Parish organized a drama club that required many rehearsals in order to present a production. A group of members from the St. Peter Drama Club are shown above as they practice for a play. From left to right, they are (first row) Clarence Alflen, Carl Lehman, Clara Sheak, Kate Schneider, Carl Bommer, and unidentified; (second row) unidentified, Leo Sheak, Frank Diederich, and Frank Fischer. In the photograph below, a group of club members assemble on the stage at the Old Town Hall for a play. Elizabeth Myers is in the center; the others are unidentified.

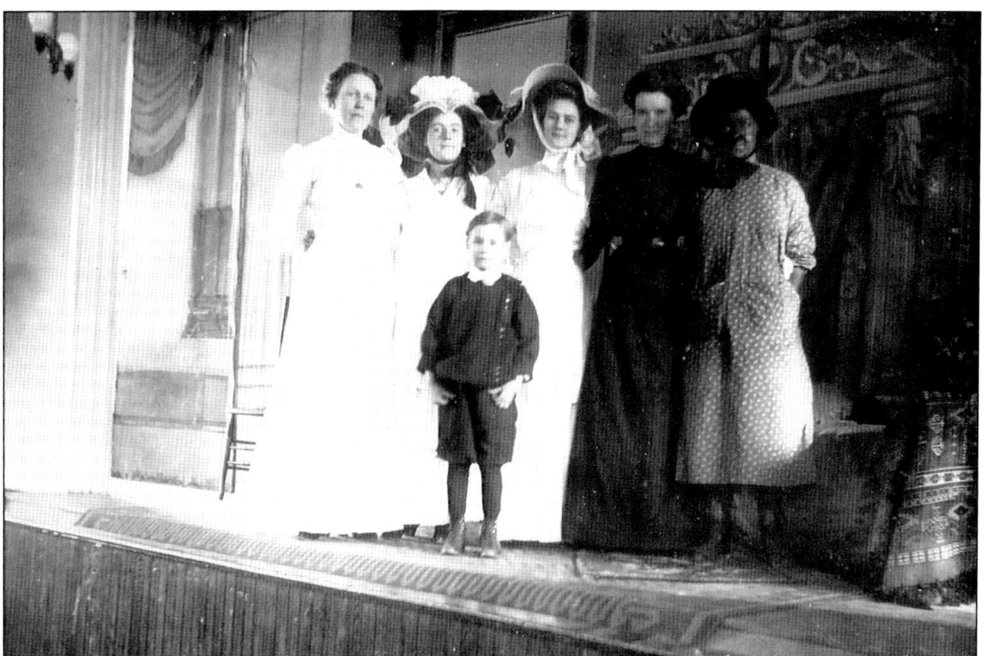

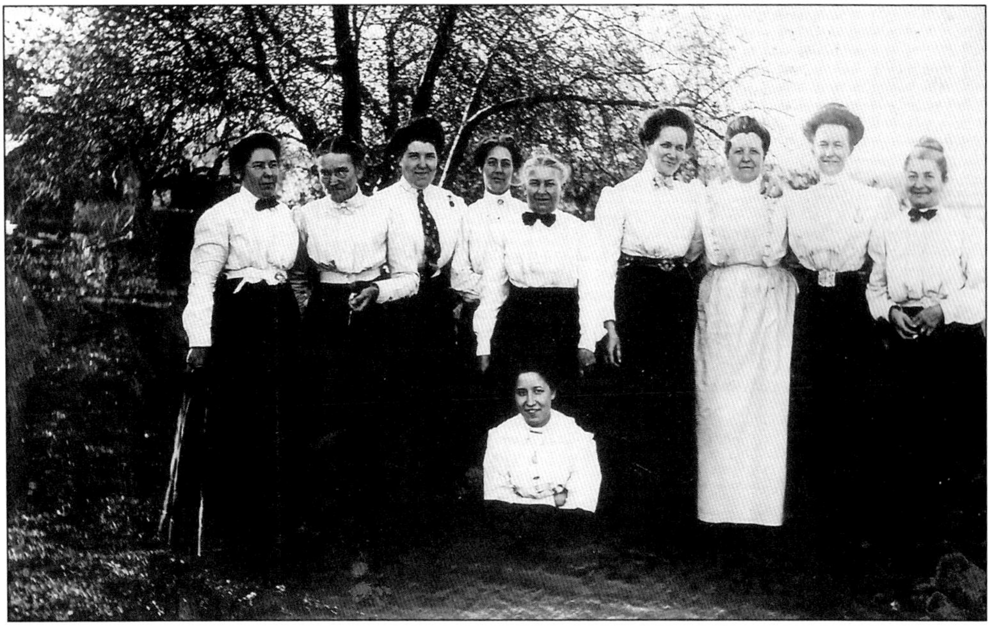

In St. Peter Parish's second year of existence, the Reverend John Heidegger organized the Altar Society and invited all women, married and unmarried, to join. A total of 54 members enrolled. Members of the group include, from left to right, Anna Bacher, Anna Barres, Louise Pitts, Rose Loescher, Kate Bouer, Rose Pitts, Mary Bommer, Emma Otten, Maggie Myers, and Clara Sheak (seated).

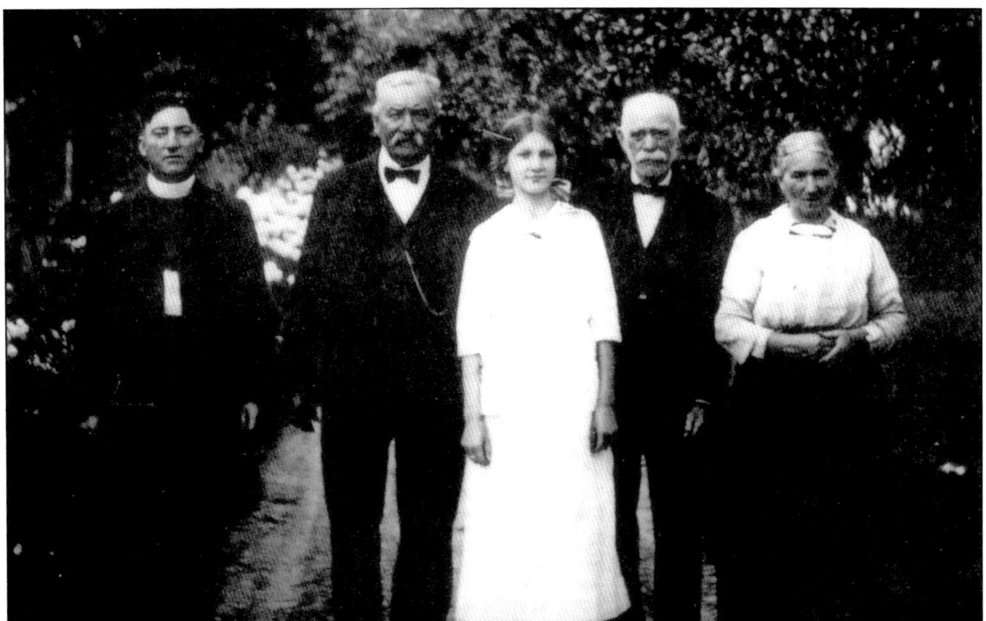

The Reverend Joseph Trapp, previously an assistant at St. Stephen Church in Cleveland, was appointed resident pastor of St. Peter Parish on June 9, 1909. Pictured in this 1914 photograph from left to right are Trapp, an unidentified man who was probably his uncle, Gertrude Trapp Worcester, and her grandparents Frank X. and Barbara Trapp.

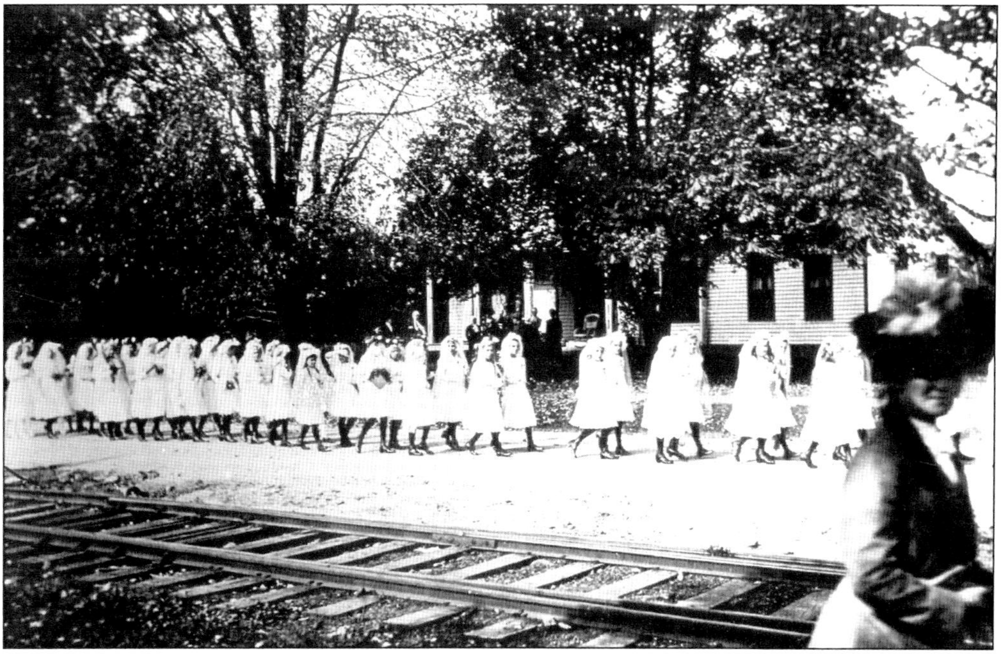

On first communion day in 1912, a photograph taken by Trapp shows St. Peter School students, who assembled at the school on Center Ridge Road, walking alongside the Green Line tracks to the church on Station Road, which is now known as Avon Belden Road. The parish house is in the background.

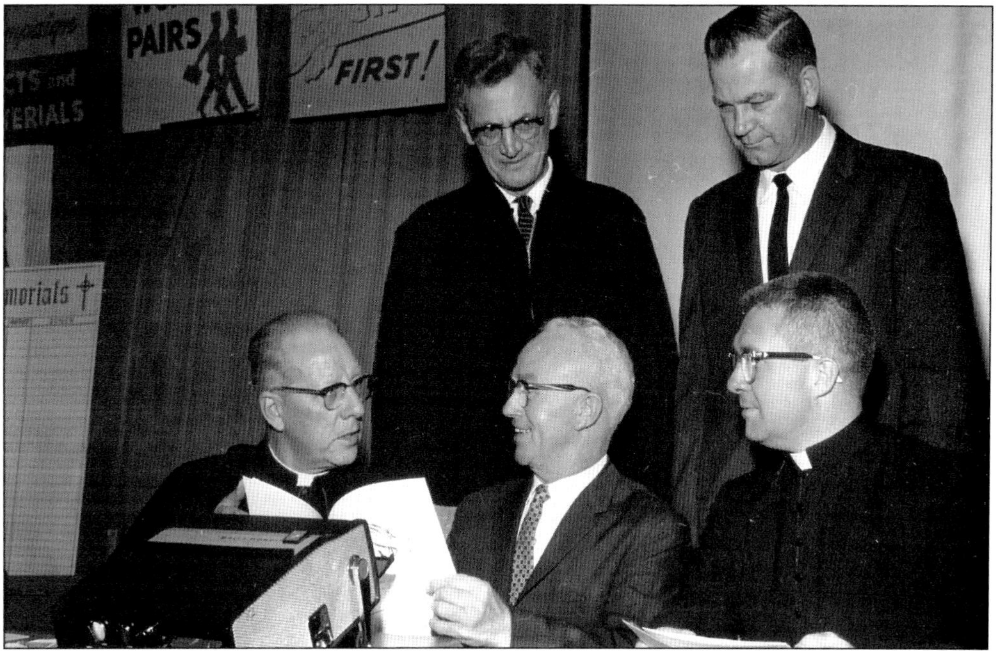

As the membership grew, St. Peter Parish organized council to help with the church events. This 1960s photograph shows a meeting of the council members. From left to right are (first row) Msgr. Edward Halloran, the pastor; Otto Laubenthal; and the Reverend John Jacoby, assistant pastor; (second row) unidentified and Al Gerhart. (Courtesy of Bill Laubenthal.)

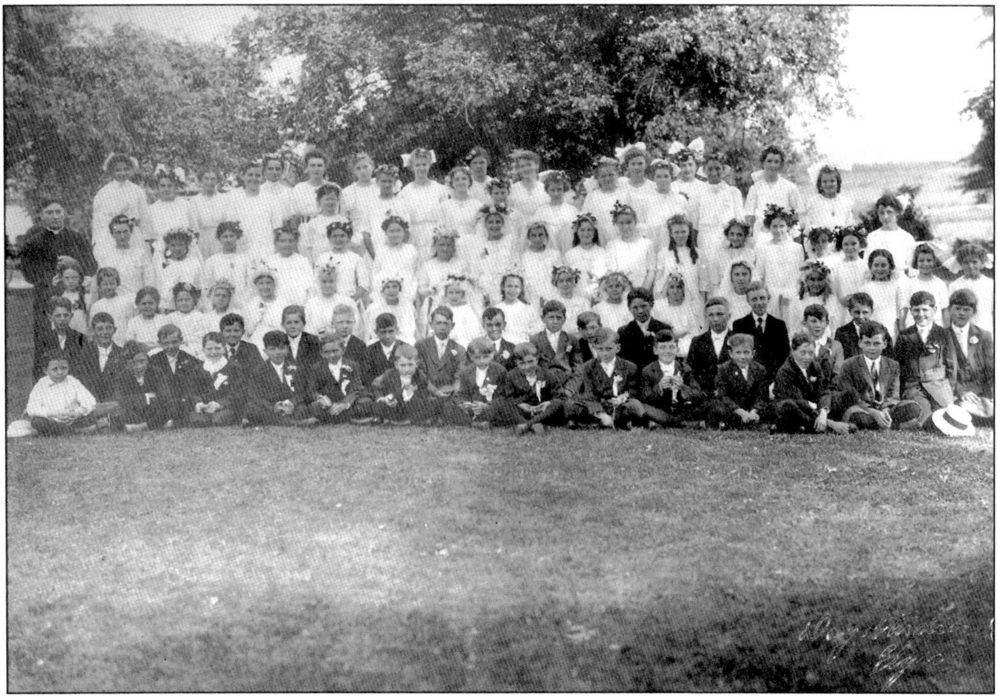

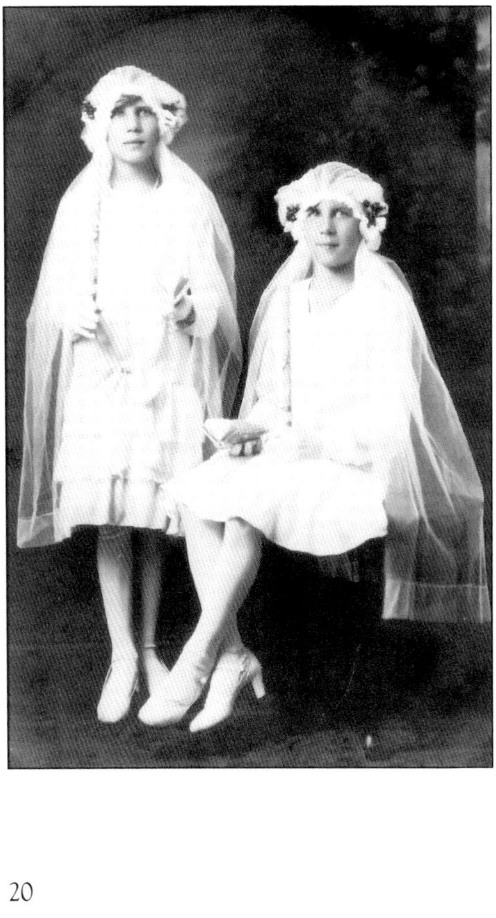

This large class of boys and girls celebrated its first communion at St. Peter Parish (above). The girls wore white dresses and flowers or crowns in their hair, and the boys were dressed in suits. This early-1920s photograph shows them in the apple orchard on the church grounds in front of a horse shed where the present church now stands. The Reverend Joseph Trapp is standing at the far left. He was pastor of St. Peter's from 1909 to 1920. At left, sisters Rita and Ruth Barnes are pictured in their first communion dresses. Rita Barnes is the mother of former North Ridgeville police chief Ron Bauer. (Courtesy of Loyola Diederich and Ron Bauer.)

The Reverend John H. Rhein became pastor of St. Peter Church in 1921. While Rhein was pastor, the present church and rectory were built. He also renovated the parish school. After serving for 17 years, Rhein died unexpectedly at the age of 62. He is buried in St. Peter Cemetery. (Courtesy of Loyola Diederich.)

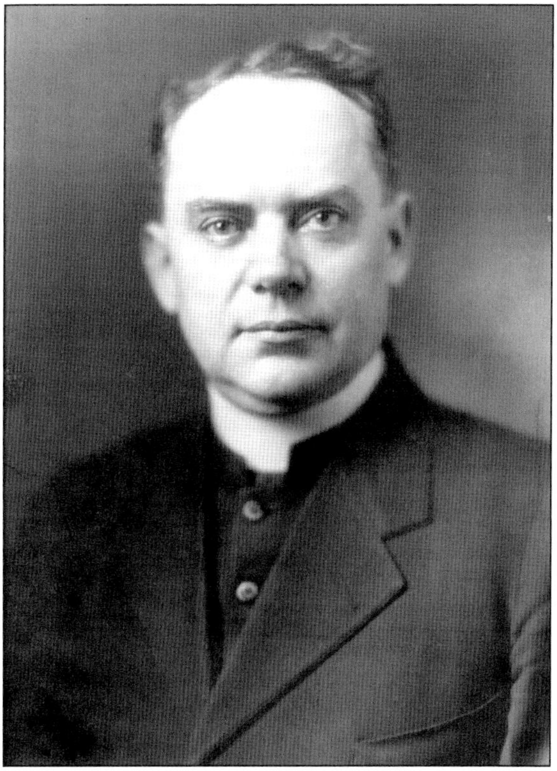

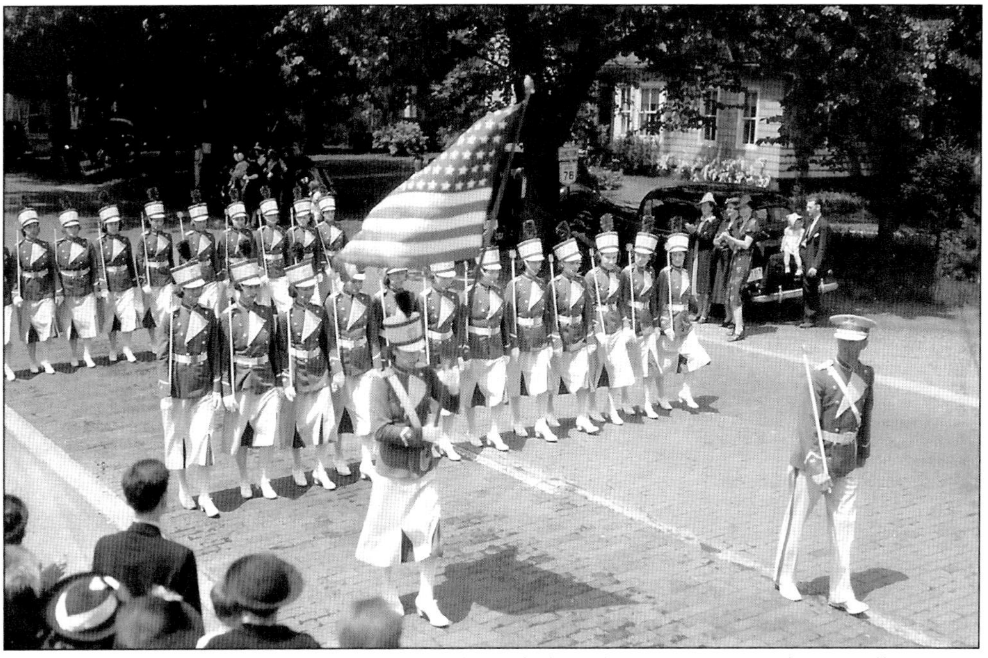

On May 21, 1939, members of St. Peter Parish, including the Women's Auxiliary Drill Team of the Knights of St. John, walked in procession from Stoney Ridge Road to the front lawn of the church where a new flagpole was dedicated. From there, everyone went into church where a Mass was celebrated in memory of Rhein. (Courtesy of Lois Sullivan.)

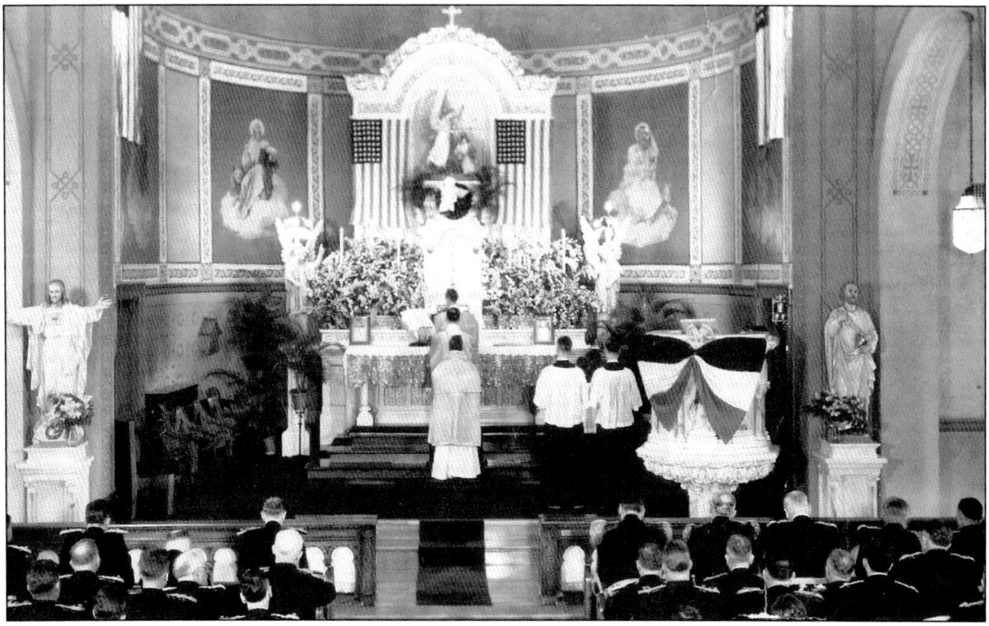

The Reverend John H. Rhein was one of St. Peter's most beloved pastors, and parishioners were saddened by his unexpected death. He not only built the church and rectory and renovated the school, but he also graded the grounds and cemetery. On May 21, 1939, the Reverend Joseph R. Buescher sang a solemn High Mass in his honor assisted by the Reverend George F. Martin, Rhein's successor, and the Reverend Leo Warth of Avon. Following the Mass, Buescher, who was serving his first assignment since being ordained, led the congregation, including the Knights of St. John, parishioners, and friends of the late pastor, from the church to St. Peter Cemetery, located behind the church. When everyone was assembled, a large stone monument that was in the shape of a Celtic cross was unveiled at Rhein's grave. It had been purchased with donations from parishioners and friends and presented to the church that day. (Courtesy of Loyola Diederich and Ken Buescher.)

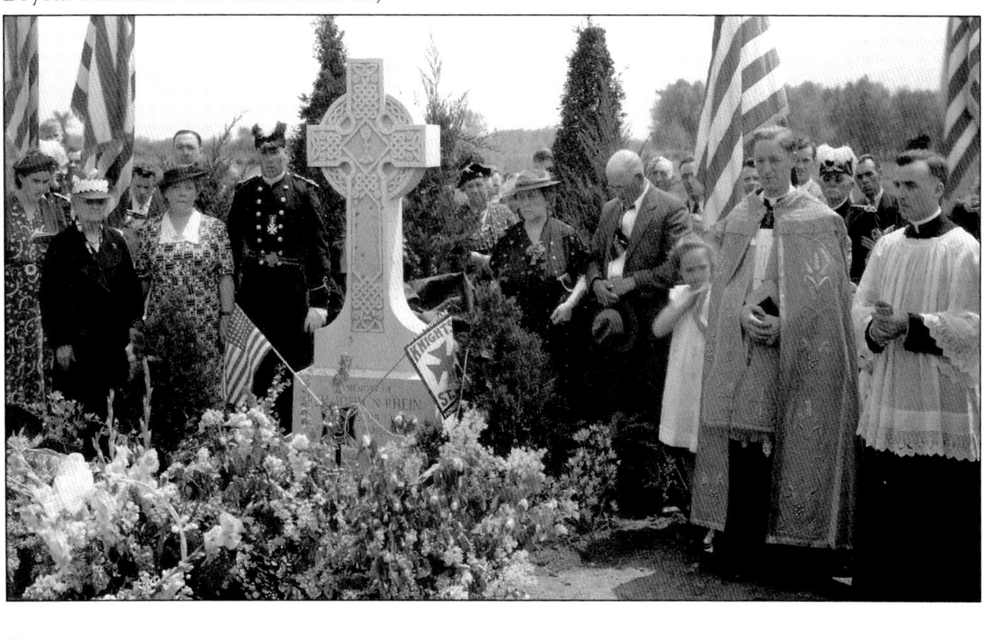

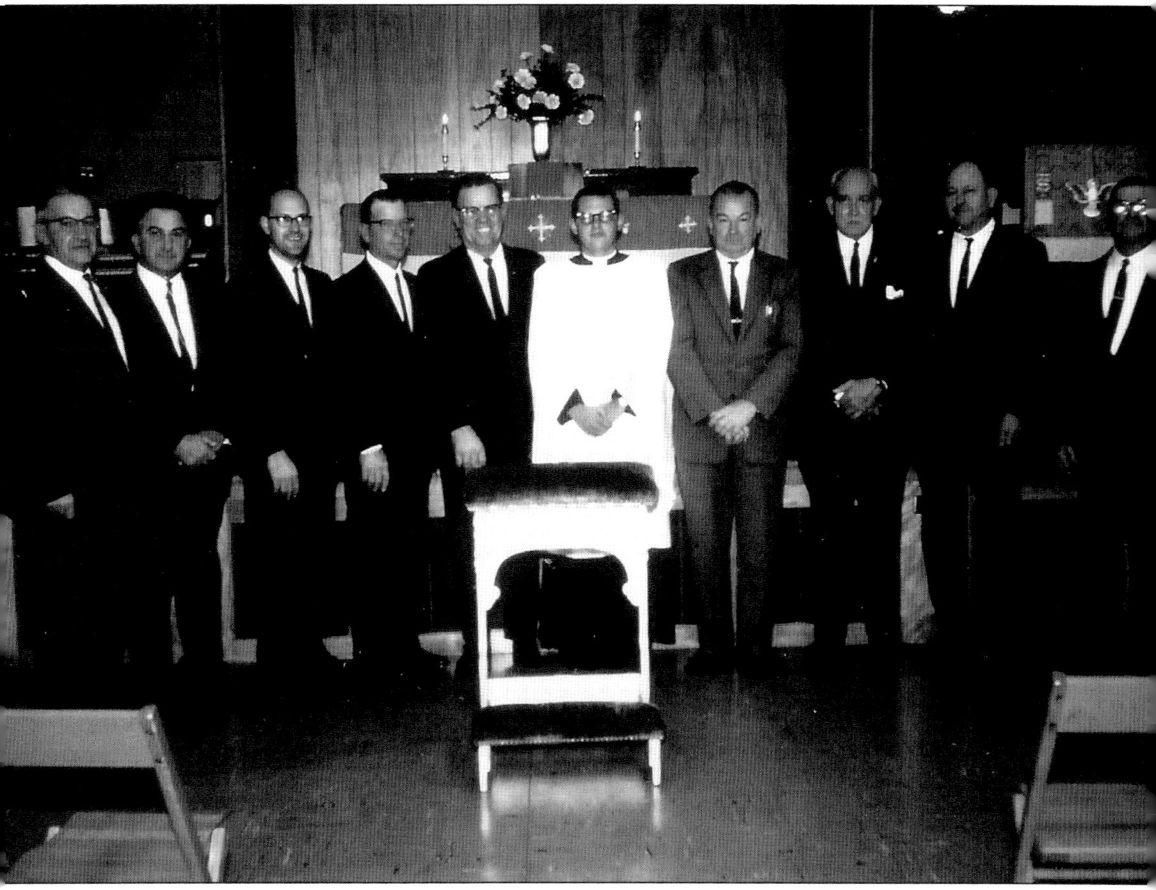

Shepherd of the Ridge Lutheran Church is located on Center Ridge Road west of Pitts Boulevard. In 1965, the Reverend David Albertin was called by the mission board of the Ohio district to begin organizing people who were interested in starting a Lutheran church in North Ridgeville. He arrived from St. Louis to begin his assignment. The first worship service was held at Fields School on September 9, 1965, with 169 worshipers attending. The first Sunday school classes began on October 7, 1965, and Charter Day was held on January 30, 1966. Services continued to be held at Fields School until the new church was built. Albertin is pictured in the September 25, 1966, photograph, following his installation as the first pastor called by the congregation to guide them in their faith. (Courtesy of Shepherd of the Ridge Lutheran Church.)

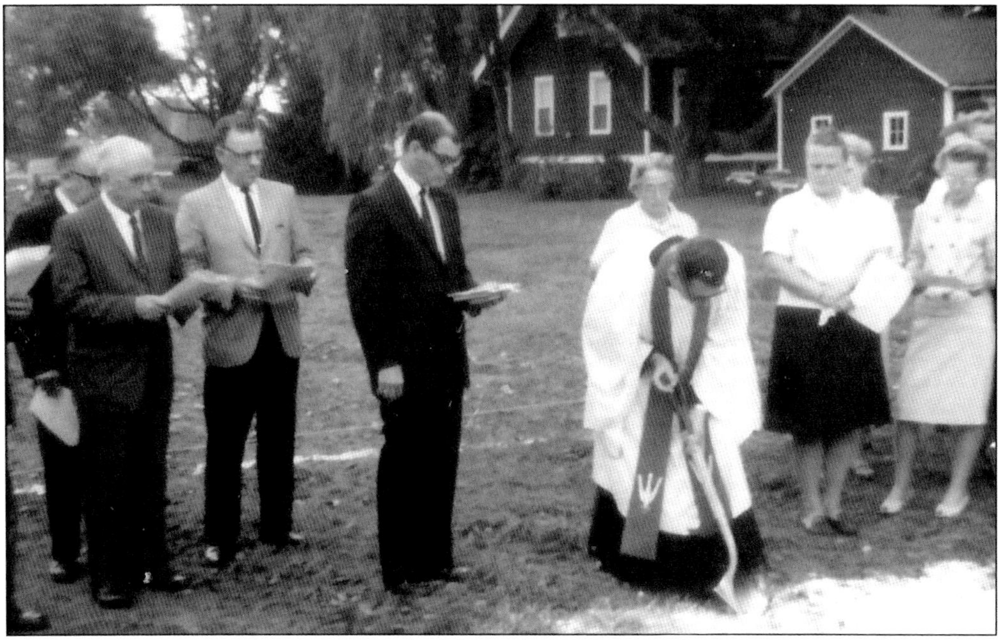

On May 21, 1967, members of Shepherd of the Ridge Lutheran Church purchased a five-acre lot on Center Ridge Road as a building site for the congregation's worship facilities. On August 18, 1968, ground was broken for the new church building. On April 6, 1969, Easter Sunday, the first service of worship was held in the basement of the new church and the cornerstone was also laid. On June 29, 1969, Pastor Henry Fry was installed as the second pastor. A new sanctuary was dedicated to the glory of God on March 1, 1970. Since then, a weekday school was begun for children in grades 1 to 6 and the Christina Nursery School for four year olds was held three days each week. The Reverend Paul Oberhaus was the most recent pastor. (Courtesy of Shepherd of the Ridge Lutheran Church.)

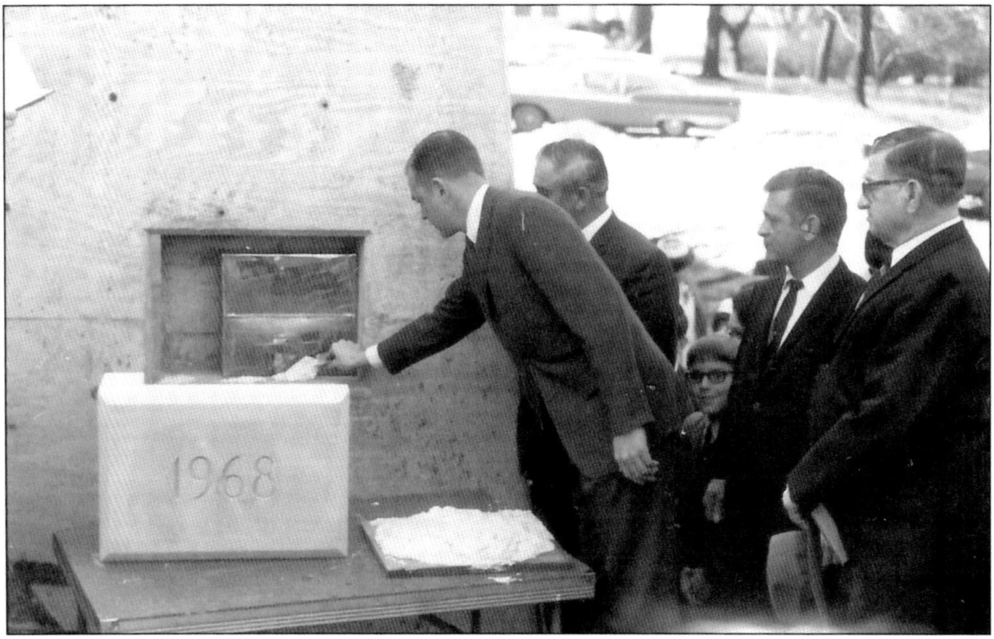

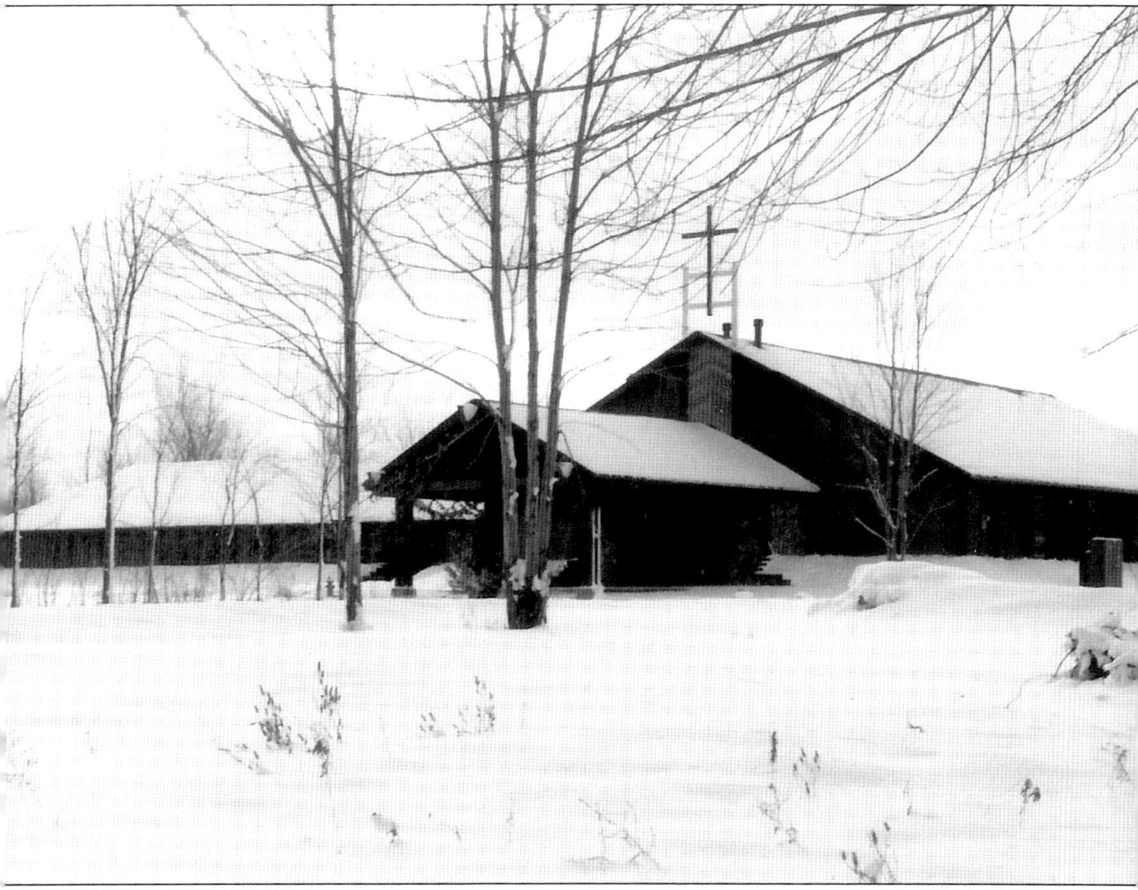

St. Julie Billiart Catholic Church was established on August 15, 1978. Bishop James Hickey, head of the Cleveland Catholic Diocese at that time, appointed the Reverend Dr. Richard A. Gonser as founding pastor of the church. The church grounds are located between Lear Nagle Road and Opal Drive. After moving into the parish administration center on Opal Drive in the summer of 1980, Gonser began making plans for the construction of a church and catechetical center. The church is situated off Lear Nagle Road, and construction on the facility began in July 1981. Members of the new parish came together in order to complete the new church within a short time. Since that early beginning, Gonser has continued to serve as the parish pastor, and with the help of the ever-growing faith community, he has begun many programs and activities. (Courtesy of St. Julie Billiart Catholic Church.)

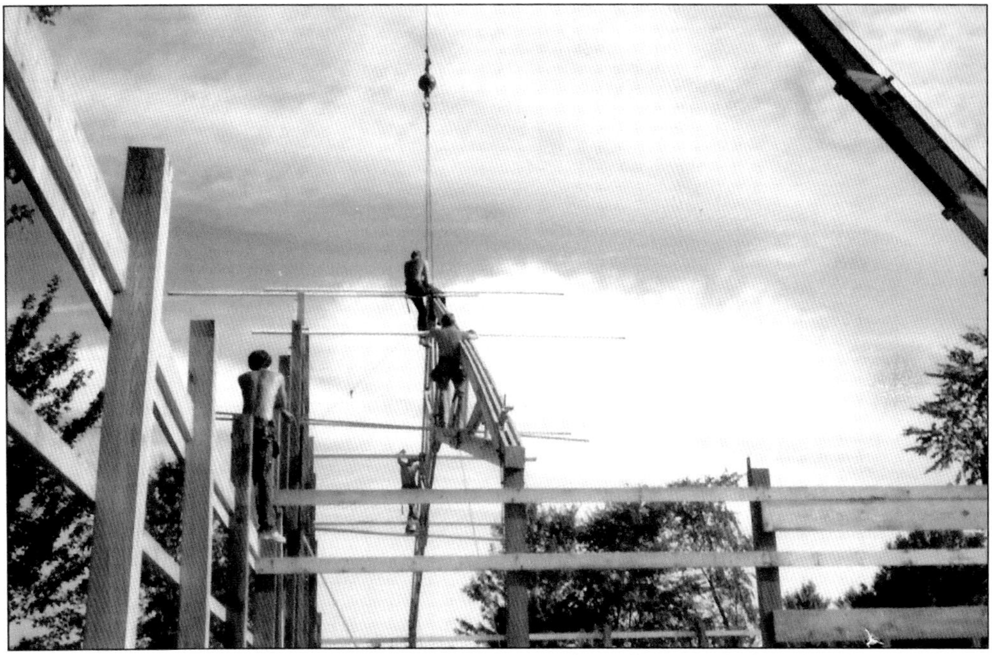

The summer season allowed the construction of St. Julie Billiart Catholic Church to continue rapidly before cold weather began. This photograph shows one of the workers high up in the air, while others complete the construction on the lower part of the church. (Courtesy of St. Julie Billiart Catholic Church.)

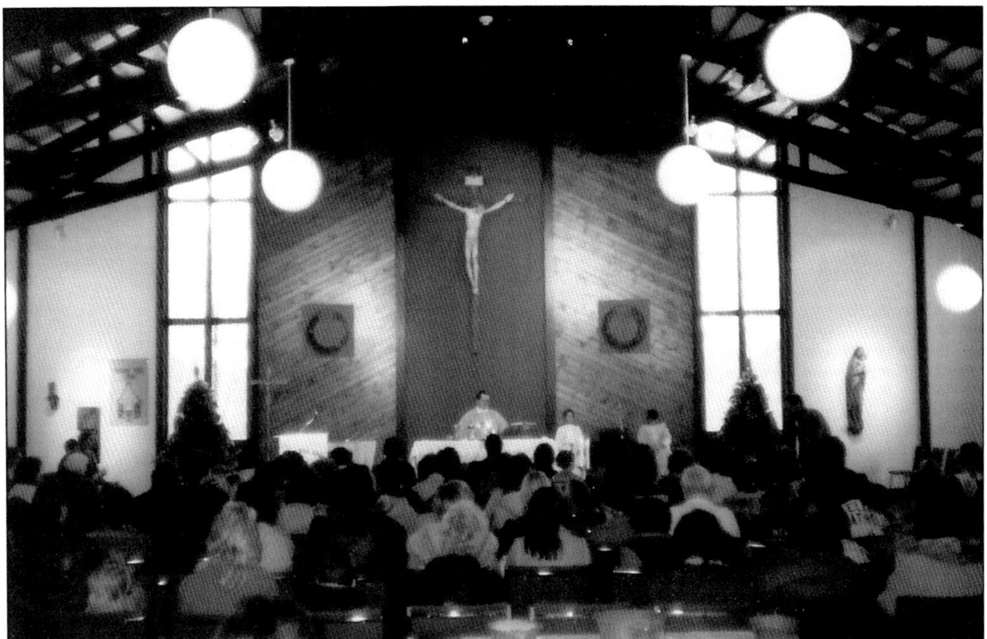

The first Mass in St. Julie Billiart Catholic Church was celebrated on Christmas Eve in 1981. The geographical boundaries of the parish are approximately three square miles of the northeast corner of North Ridgeville. Membership has grown from the original 200 families to 535 families in 2007. (Courtesy of St. Julie Billiart Catholic Church.)

Two

Sunup to Sundown

Out of necessity, the early settlers set about building log cabins for protection from the elements, like the wind that swirled out of control at times, the rains that deluged the land, and the heat of the sun that often burned the skin. To construct shelters, the pioneers began to cut through the dense forests in hopes of clearing the land for houses and also to till the soil and grow enough food on which to survive. The weather in what was first known as Rootstown was not what they were accustomed to in their eastern home, and the first attempts at farming were no doubt a combination of trial and error. Eventually they called upon their instincts and began adding barns to their cabins along with livestock. There were cows for milk, chickens for eggs, and horses for transportation. Little by little, some of the men purchased large tracts of land, and the new region became known as a thriving rural community. Although farming was the primary means of earning a livelihood, it gave rise to a number of other occupations, such as blacksmith shops, general stores, and cheese factories. Most of the early farms are now gone, but the community has continued to grow and a number of businesses that opened their doors in the early to mid-1900s have remained part of the fabric of the city.

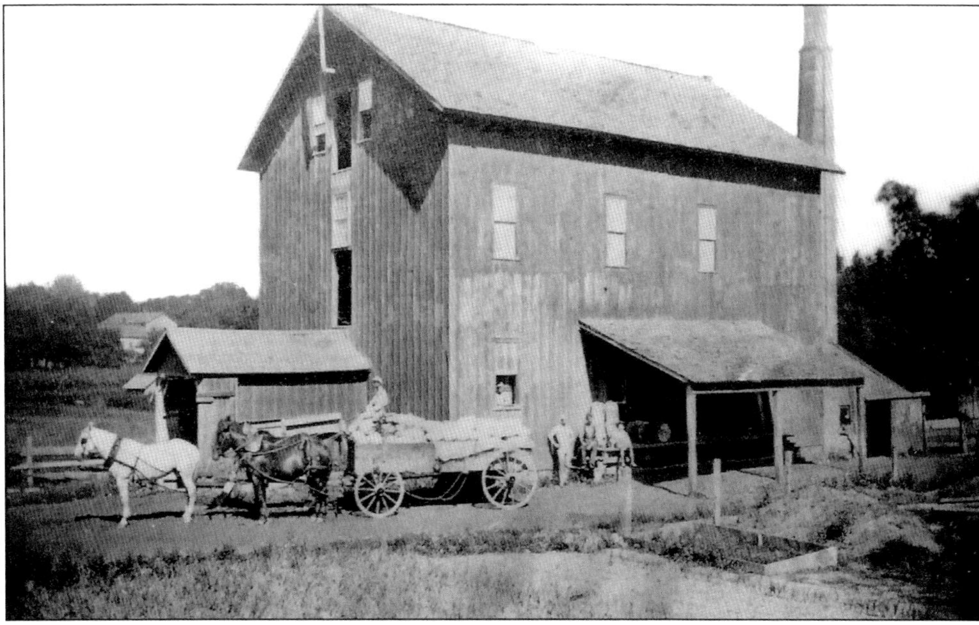

Townships and villages built several mills to handle the business of local farmers, including sawmills, gristmills, and fanning mills. The early mills were animal powered or located on a river, stream, or creek and were operated by a large waterwheel. In later years, they were steam powered. This steam-driven mill in the late 1800s may be the Terrell mill on Center Ridge Road near Stoney Ridge. (Courtesy of the Lorain County Historical Society.)

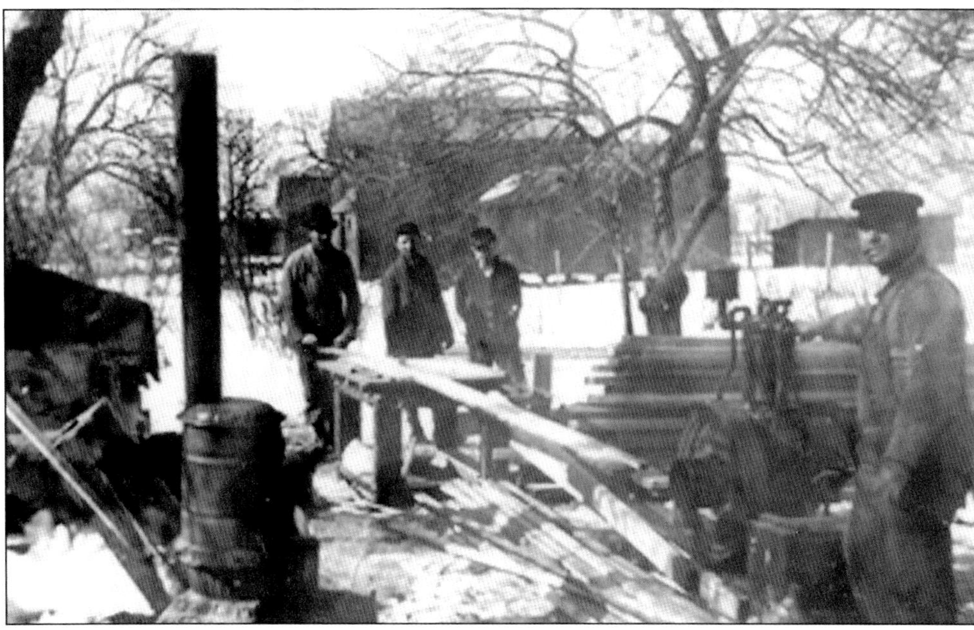

This photograph from about 1900 shows Ridgeville's farming community, which thrived until the township became a city in 1960. By that time, most of the area farms were gone. Many 19th- and early-20th-century farmers shared equipment with one another. The men in this photograph are cutting their own lumber on a sawmill powered by a stationary engine. (Courtesy of Tom Guggenbiller.)

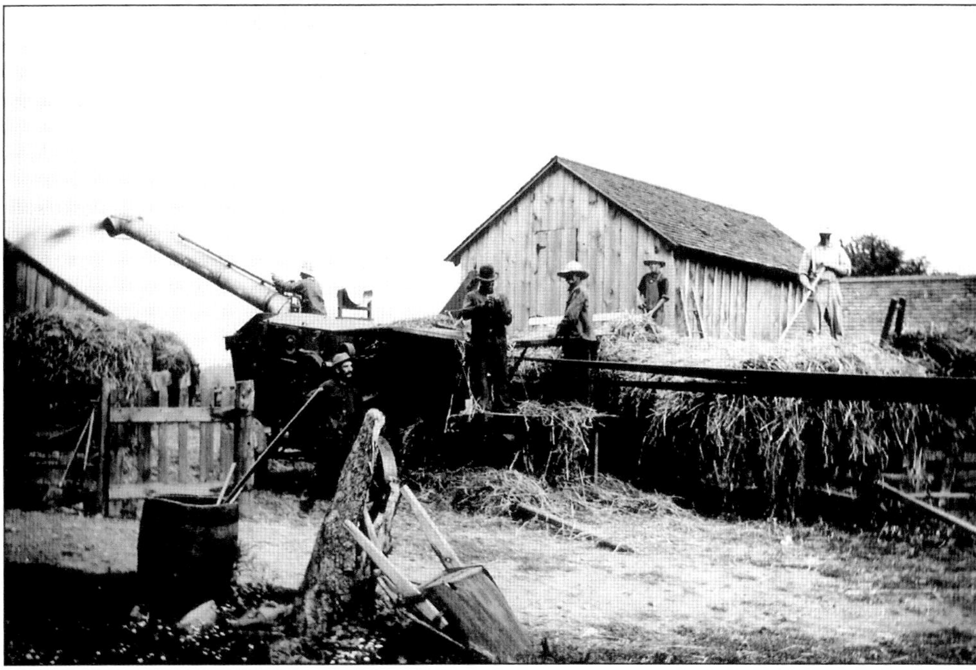

Threshing day at the Christian Thome Farm on Stoney Ridge Road meant many days of hard but careful work in order to separate the grain from the crops of wheat. The belts that can be seen stretching across the middle portion of the photograph lead to the coal-fired steam engine. They were always placed at a good distance to lessen the danger of sparks igniting the dry straw and causing a fire. On another Stoney Ridge Road farm (below), from left to right, Joseph Pitts and his sons Ralph and Bernard are seen laying tile, which was also a hard job, especially in the heat of the summer sun.

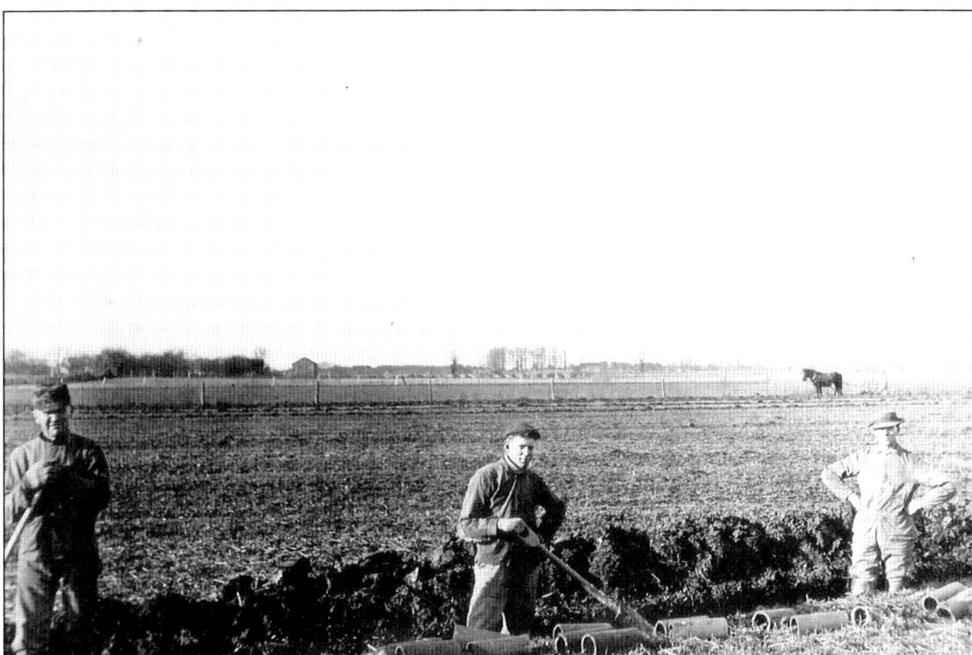

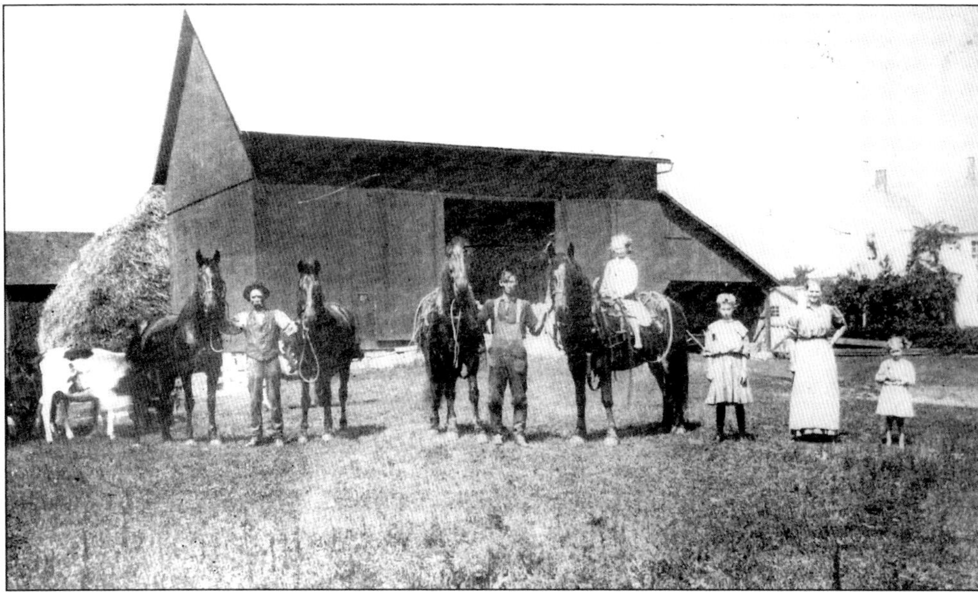

Lois Sullivan's grandfather Joseph Myers owned a farm on Stoney Ridge Road in the early 1900s. Shown in this photograph from left to right are Joseph Myers (holding onto two horses), John Myers, Gertrude Myers (on a horse), Cecilia Myers, grandmother Katherine Myers, and her daughter Kathryn Myers. (Courtesy of Lois Sullivan.)

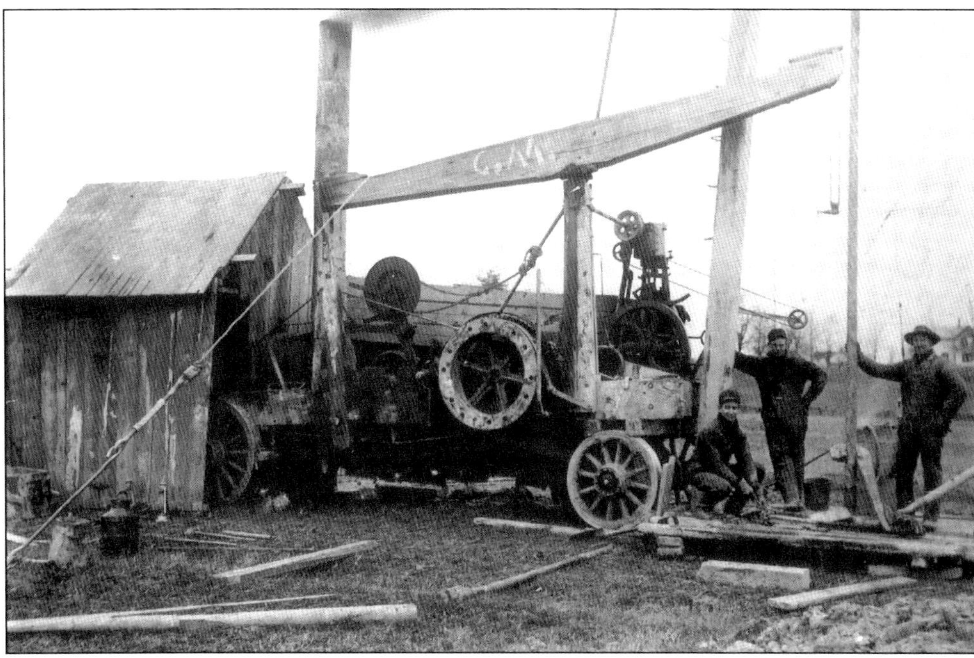

Many gas wells were drilled with this rig in Lorain and Cuyahoga Counties during the early 1900s. From left to right are Phillip Gerhart of Avon; George Myers, the owner of the rig; and William Diederich. Depending on road conditions, up to 16 horses were used to move the rig to various locations, including to Alexander Winton's home in Cleveland. Winton produced the first automobile in Cleveland in 1896. (Courtesy of Lois Sullivan.)

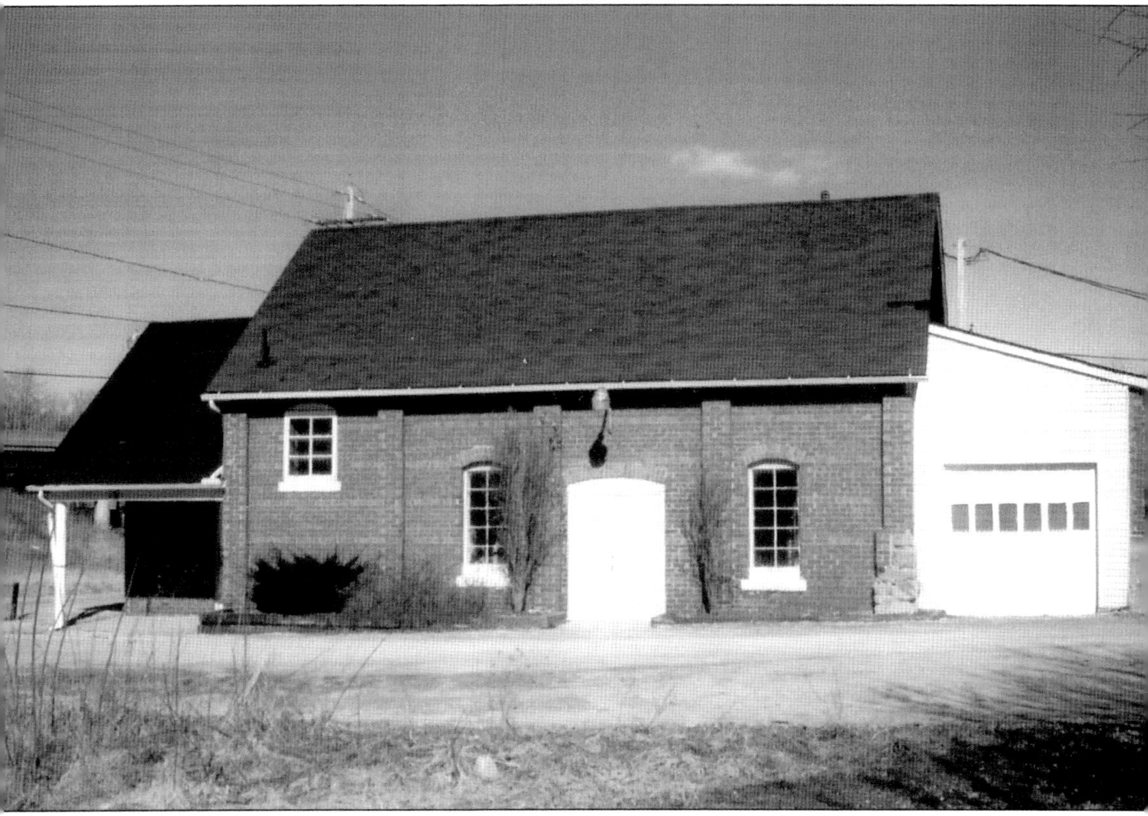

The brick building in the photograph is on Avon Belden Road, just north of Butternut Ridge Road. It was constructed in 1871 as a cheese factory, replacing the original structure that was built in 1869 and destroyed by fire. Francis Eldred, son of Ridgeville pioneer and War of 1812 veteran Moses Eldred (1774–1857), along with his son William H. Eldred (1841–1906), operated the Excelsior Cheese Factory with men named Adams and Jackson. Using the milk from Ridgeville farmers' dairy cows, they produced Cheshire Cheese, which was shipped to England. Through the years, the building has been used by various businesses. There were a total of four cheese factories in Ridgeville Township in the late 1800s. The Ridgeville cheese was sold not only in the township but also some of it was put on trains at the Shawville Station and sent to other places.

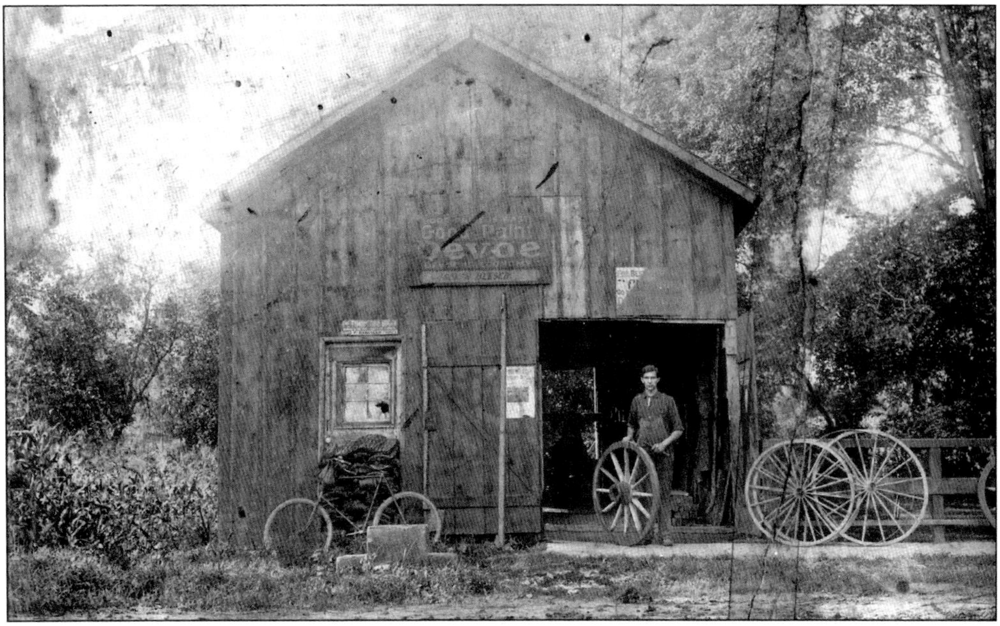

Charles Gilder operated one of the few blacksmith shops in Ridgeville Township. In those days many blacksmiths' duties included shoeing horses, fixing wagons, and sometimes even sharpening a plow blade. Gilder began his business at Fields Corners on Butternut Ridge Road near Root Road, as shown in the 1898 photograph above. When Gilder's son Ralph was ready to enter the business, he relocated to a building on Center Ridge Road alongside the creek across from the present middle school in 1918. He also contracted to service Ford automobiles and later any type of automobile along with horseshoeing and general blacksmithing. Gilder's Garage, shown in the photograph below, later specialized in towing and welding and flourished at that site until 1968. The Gilder shop is one of the many businesses that began in the late 1800s or early 1900s in Ridgeville.

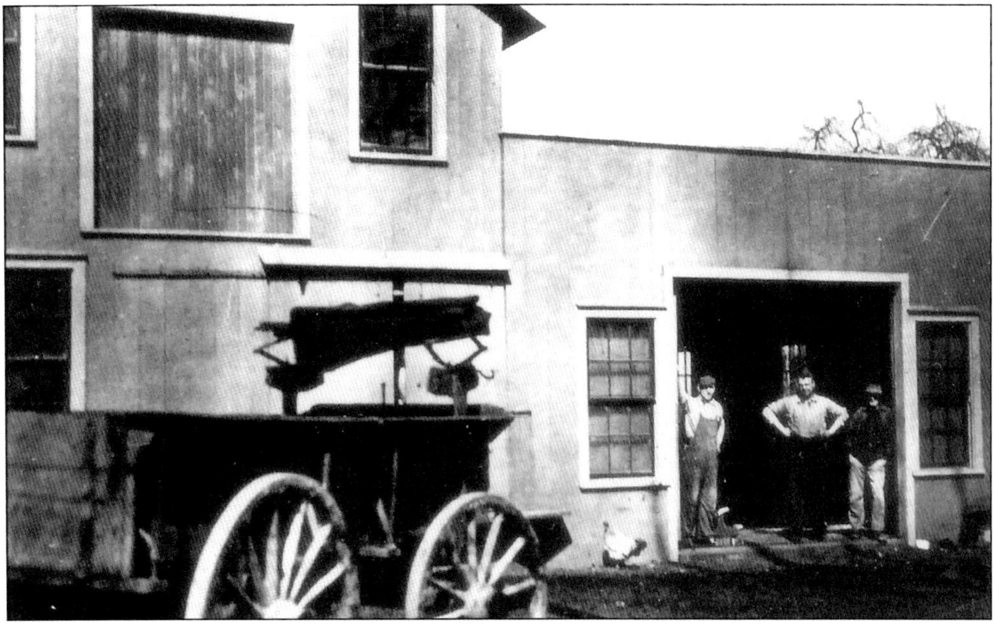

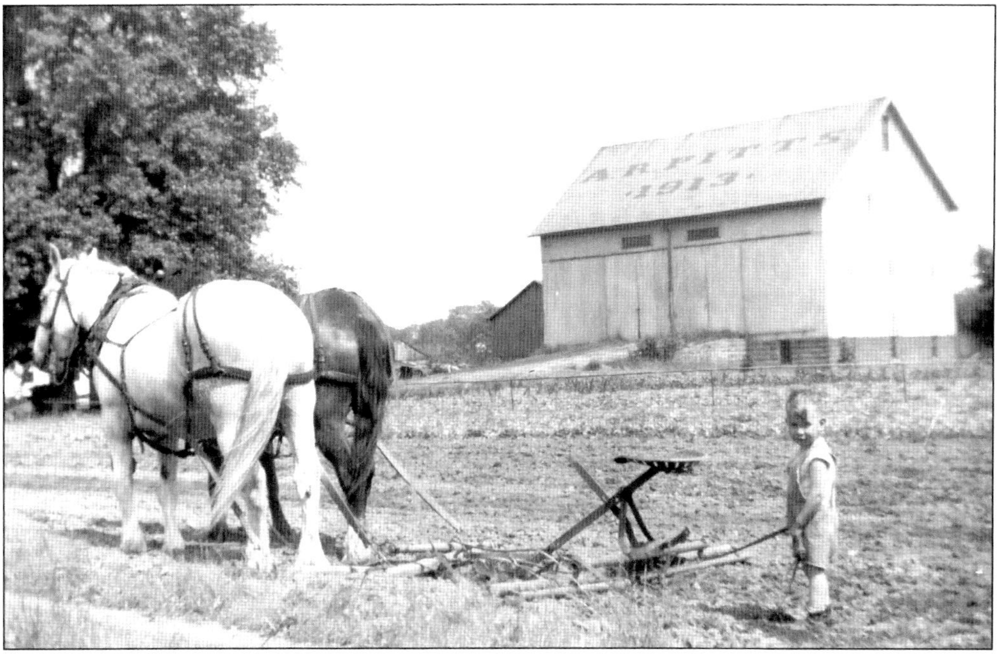

The Pitts family wanted everyone to get started in the farming business at an early age, and although he was just four years old, Don Pitts tried to lend a hand with the work. He seemed to enjoy working with Tom and Jerry, the family team of horses. He is seen on the Pitts farm on Center Ridge Road in this early-1930s photograph.

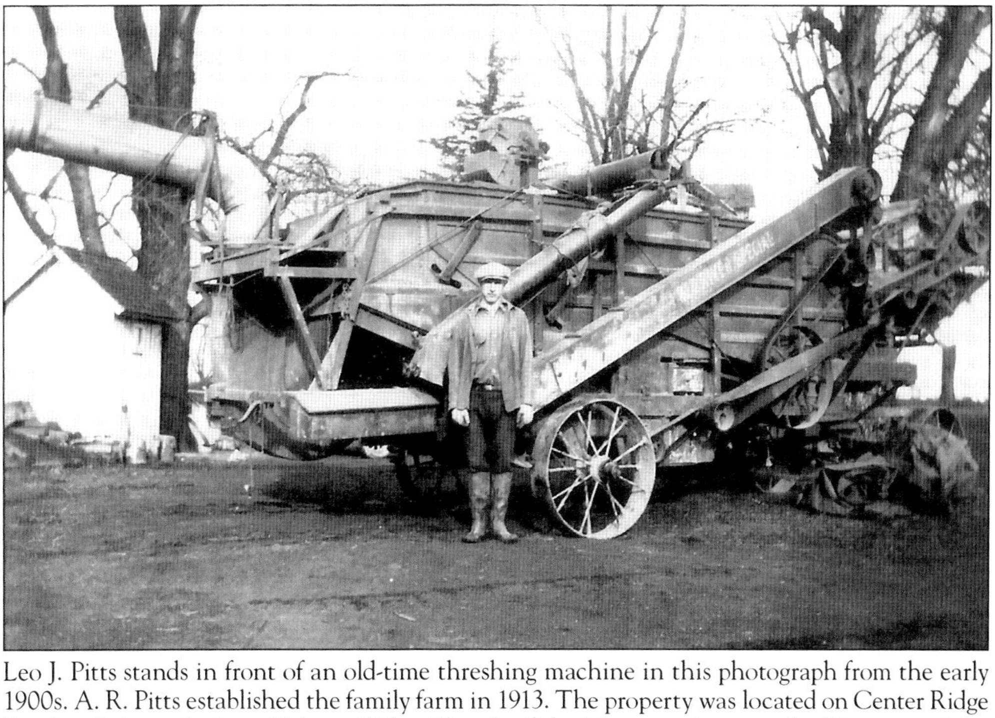

Leo J. Pitts stands in front of an old-time threshing machine in this photograph from the early 1900s. A. R. Pitts established the family farm in 1913. The property was located on Center Ridge Road and situated where Calvary Ridge Church of the Nazarene is presently. (Courtesy of the Don Pitts family.)

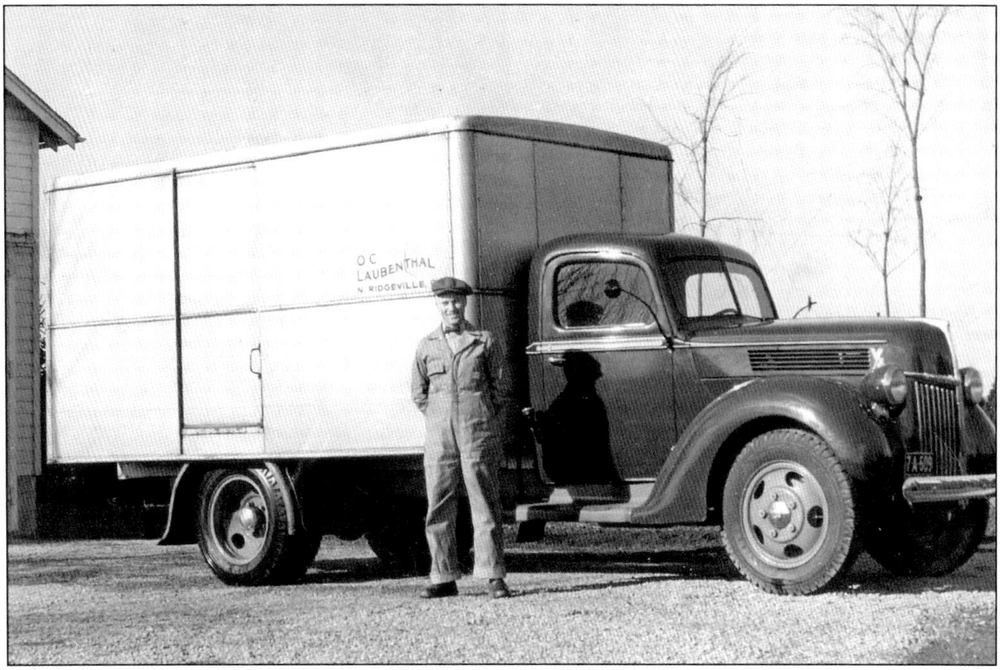

Joseph Laubenthal began the milk-hauling business in the late 1920s, and around 1940, his son Otto Laubenthal took over the business. For a time, it was known as O. C. Laubenthal and eventually was named Otto Laubenthal Milk Cartage. Otto's son, William Laubenthal, began working with his father and is currently in his 48th year in the business, hauling milk to various cities, including Cleveland. In the 1940 photograph above, Otto stands in front of one of his trucks. The 1952 photograph below shows a fleet of milk-hauling trucks from different years. From left to right are a model from 1941, a model from 1946, a model from 1945, and a 1948 truck. (Courtesy of Bill Laubenthal.)

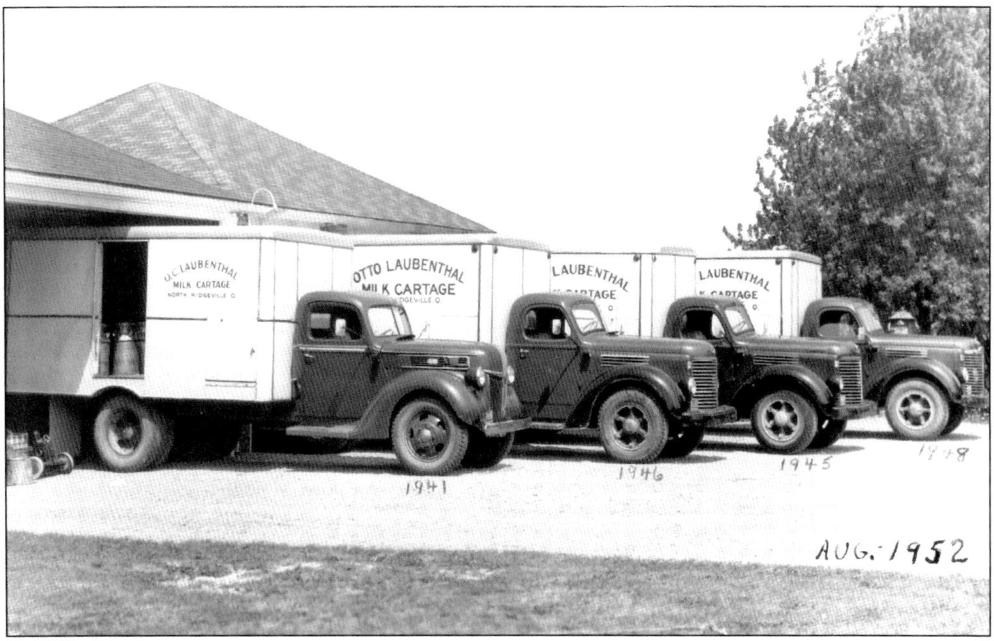

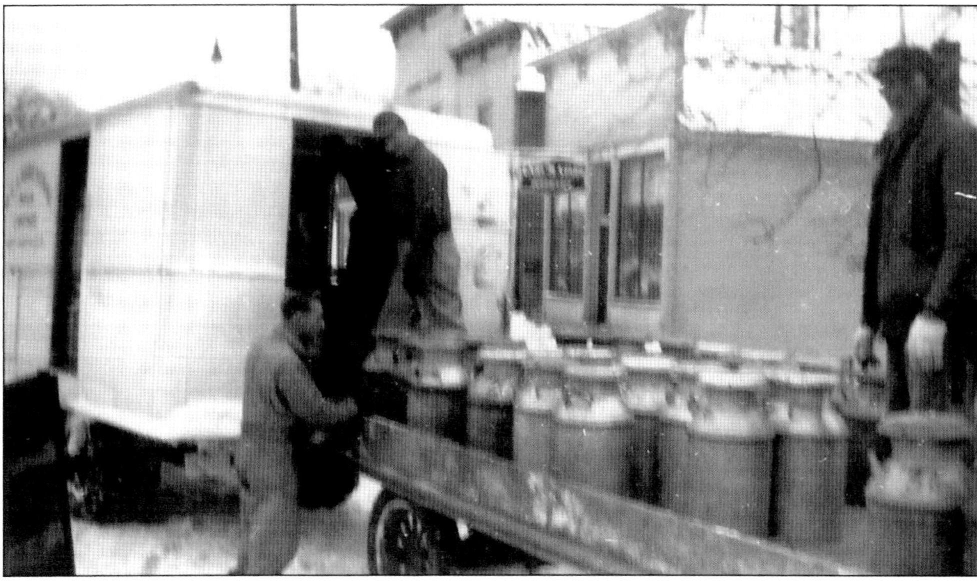

In the early days of the Laubenthal milk-hauling company, horse-drawn wagons filled with large metal milk cans could be seen traveling through towns delivering the milk. It was quite a different way of handling milk than the plastic bottles or cartons used for today's consumers. (Courtesy of Tina Bright.)

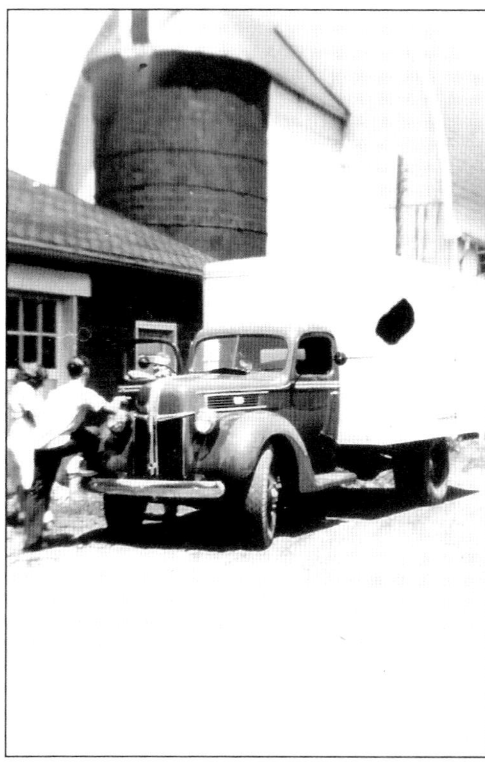

The Laubenthal milk-hauling company made stops at the Mills Dairy Farm at the east end of North Ridgeville on Center Ridge Road (Route 20). The milk was taken to the Dairyman's Company in Cleveland to be processed and bottled. In the old days of the Mills Dairy Farm, automobile traffic was sometimes stopped so the farm's cows could cross the road. (Courtesy of Bill Laubenthal.)

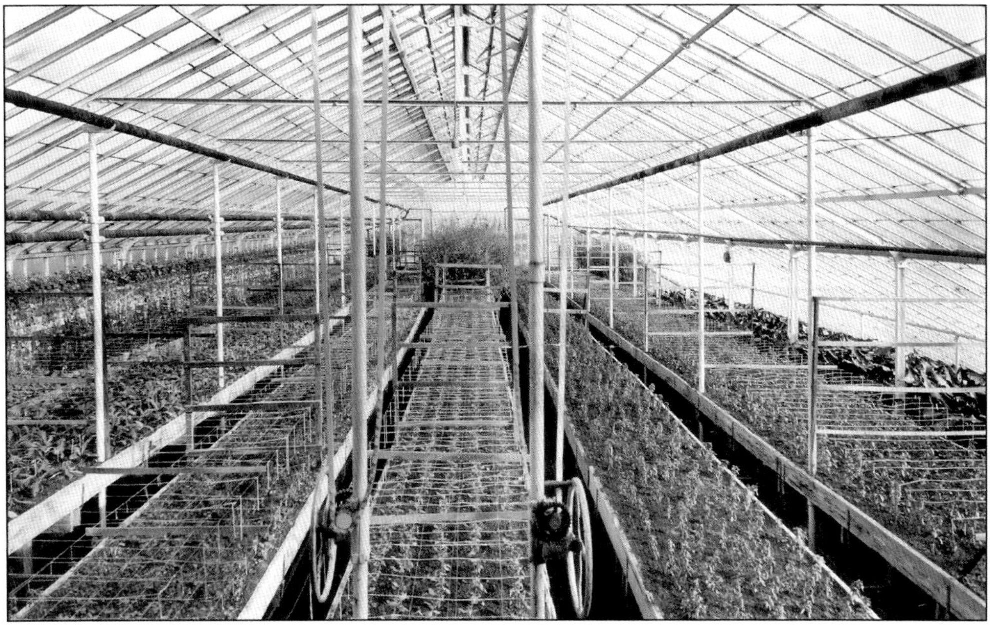

In 1924, John Peter Diederich and his sons Audoen and Justin built a greenhouse in Ridgeville as a hobby. The following year, Audoen married Aurelia Pitts, and together they founded the Diederich family greenhouse business on Center Ridge Road, which was located just east of the former Ridgeview Shopping Center site. At one time, the couple lived in what is now the main floral shop. The large family home was built in 1928, and additional greenhouses were added as the business grew. J. P. Diederich Sons is now operated by the children and grandchildren of Audoen and Aurelia and includes 80,000 square feet of growing area with outside acreage for summer crops. It is one of the oldest continuously run businesses in the city. In a 1950s photograph, Ray Diederich is seen working in the family greenhouse. (Courtesy of Loyola Diederich.)

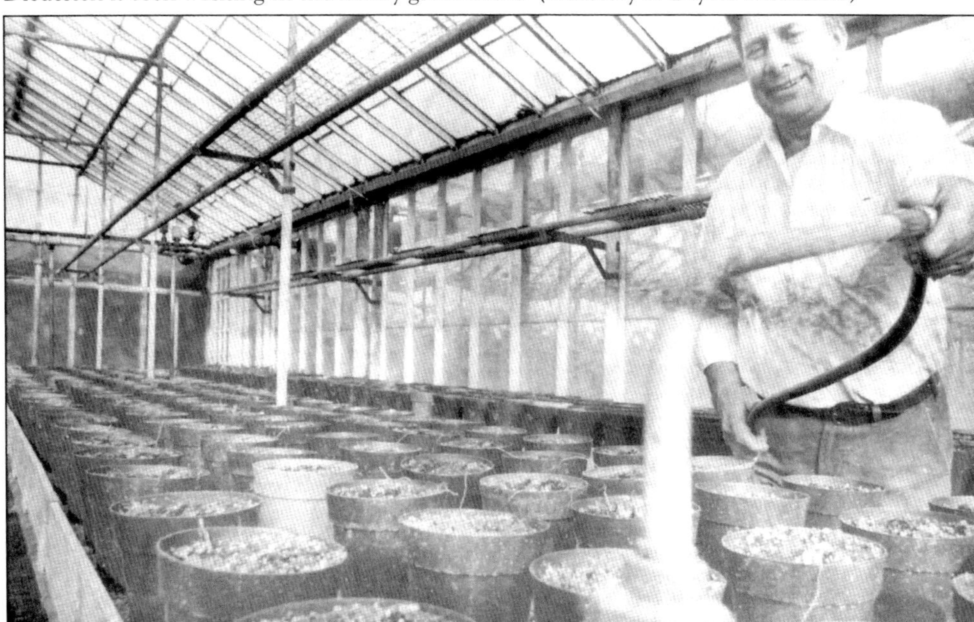

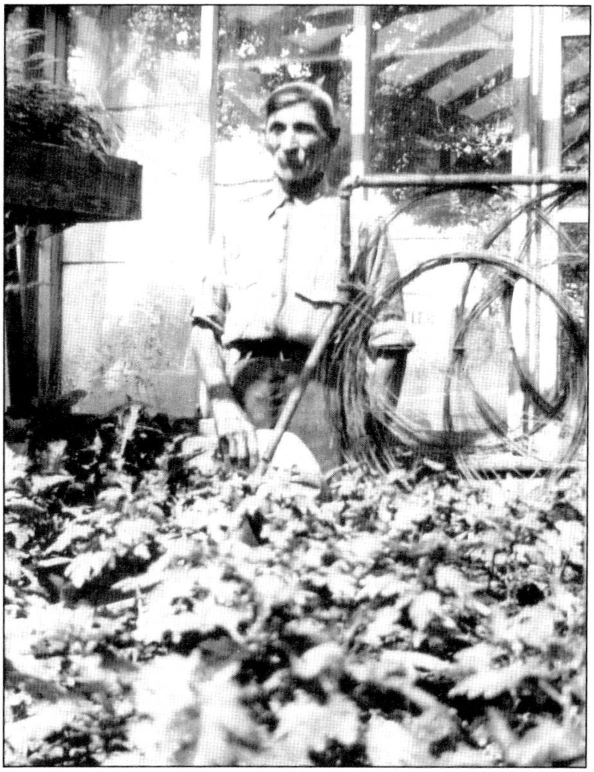

John Van Arsdale began the Glyndwr Floral Gardens in 1902 at the intersection of Center Ridge and Lear Nagle Roads. The Glyndwr Floral Garden flower truck delivered flowers to many residents in and around Ridgeville Township. Van Arsdale was well known in the area for growing pansies. The flower shop, now known as Hales Florist and Greenhouse, is owned by Jim Hales and is still located on the same site. At one time, a portion of the building that is now part of the sales floor was a garage. Hales Florist and Greenhouse has been in business since 1959. (Courtesy of Jim Hales.)

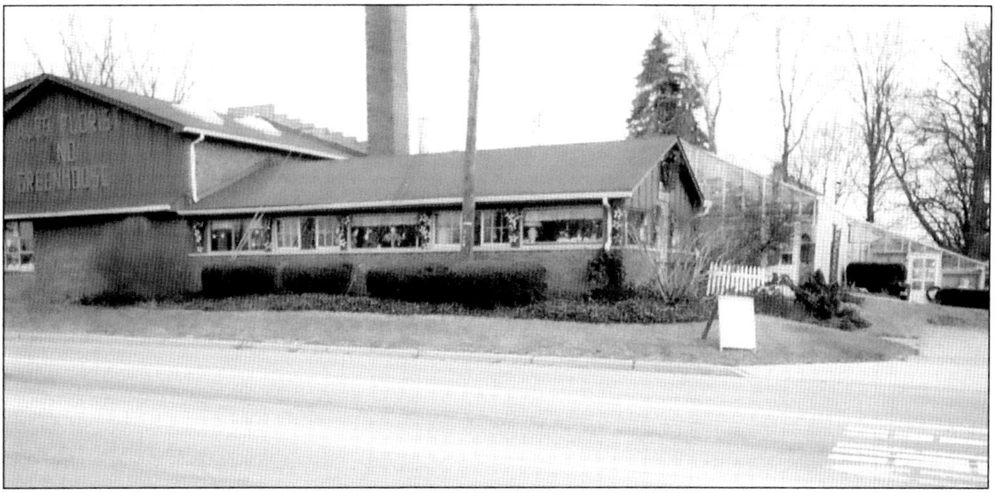

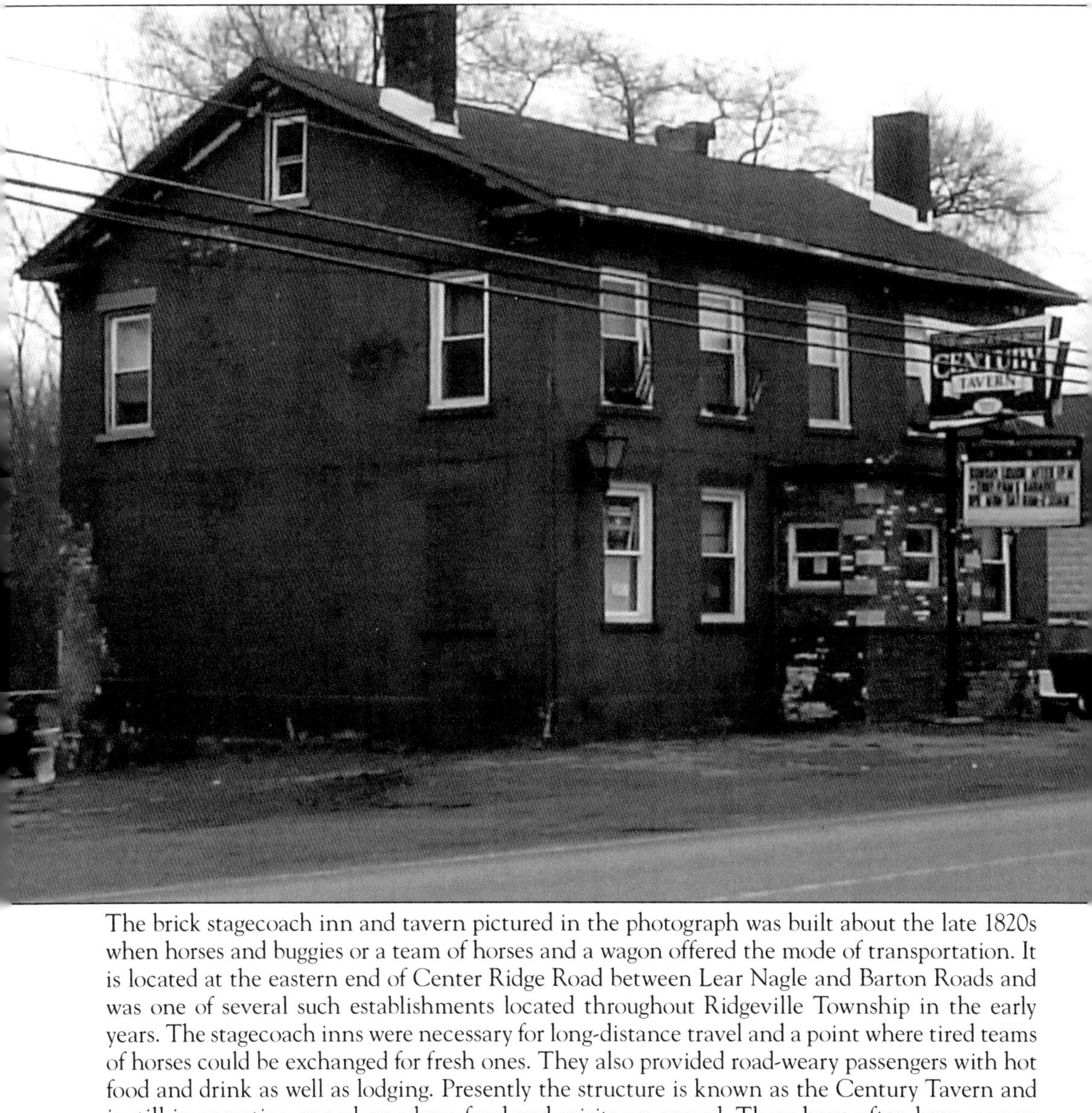

The brick stagecoach inn and tavern pictured in the photograph was built about the late 1820s when horses and buggies or a team of horses and a wagon offered the mode of transportation. It is located at the eastern end of Center Ridge Road between Lear Nagle and Barton Roads and was one of several such establishments located throughout Ridgeville Township in the early years. The stagecoach inns were necessary for long-distance travel and a point where tired teams of horses could be exchanged for fresh ones. They also provided road-weary passengers with hot food and drink as well as lodging. Presently the structure is known as the Century Tavern and is still in operation as a place where food and spirits are served. There have often been rumors that real spirits inhabit the building as well. In recent years, the former stagecoach inn also has been known as Bert's Tavern and Pat and Grace's. It is one of the oldest buildings still standing in North Ridgeville.

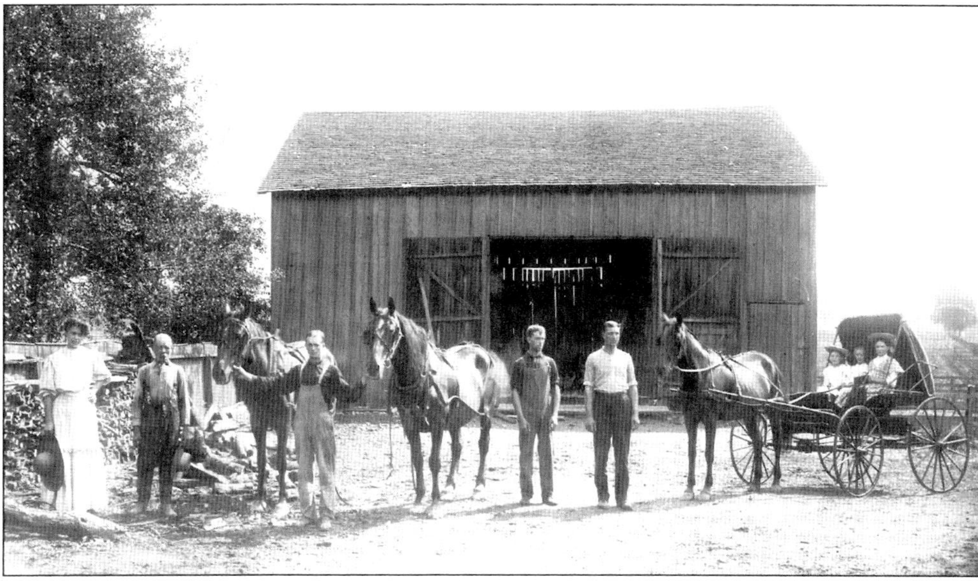

This photograph was taken on the Schneider farm located on Stoney Ridge Road, which runs north off Center Ridge Road. The farm was about a mile north of Center Ridge. From left to right are Catherine Schneider; her father, Joseph Schneider; and his sons, Leo, Joseph, and Mathias Schneider. Another son, Frank, is not pictured. The children in the buggy are unidentified. (Courtesy of Marian Schneider Taylor.)

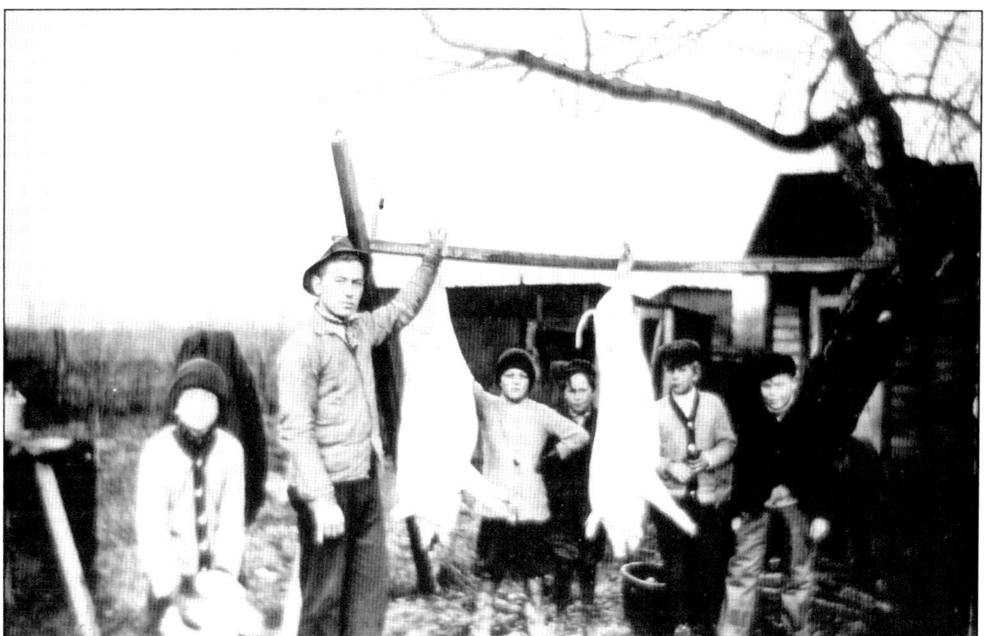

Since the days of the Civil War, pig slaughtering was for celebrations as well as church events and political rallies. This photograph, taken in the early 1900s, shows an area farmer who had just slaughtered pigs to sell at the market, to use for gatherings, or for his family's meals. This was a common way of butchering pigs at that time.

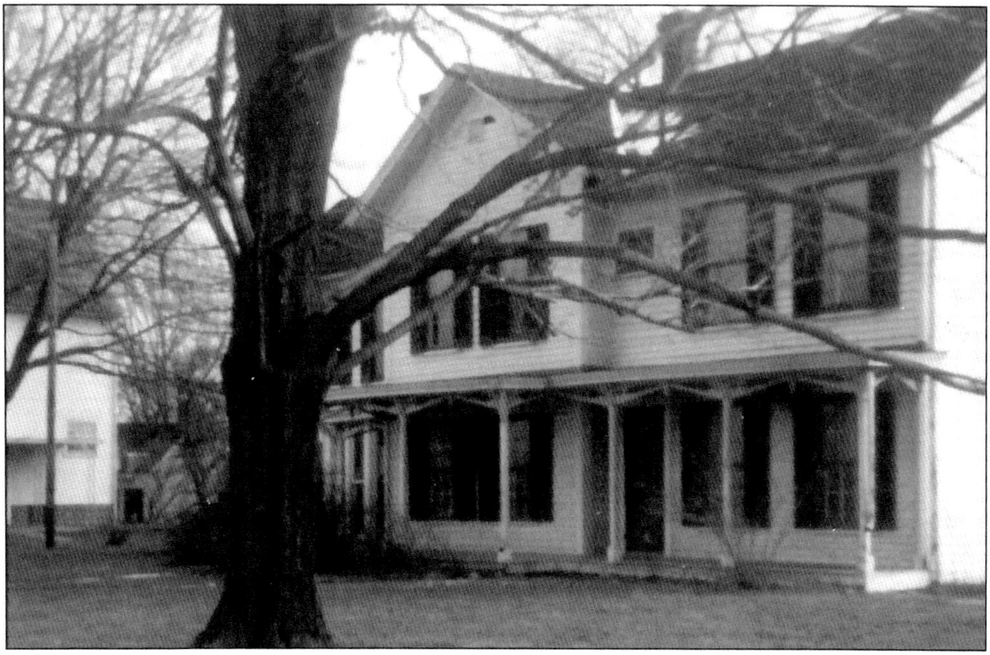

This house stood just east of the First Congregational United Church of Christ on Center Ridge Road and was built around 1857 by Alton Henry Mooers. Mooers operated the Ridgeville Chair Works, which stood to the rear and east of the home from about 1859 to 1910. Mooers' wife, Arlette Terrell, was the daughter of pioneer Wyllis Terrell Jr. After Mooers's death in 1909, the family of Dr. I. N. Oakes bought the house, and by 1920, it was operated as the Inn of the Four Chimneys or the Four Chimneys Inn, a sort of forerunner of the modern bed-and-breakfast. It was owned from the 1930s to the 1950s by the Lasch family but was torn down about 1970 to provide for expanded church parking.

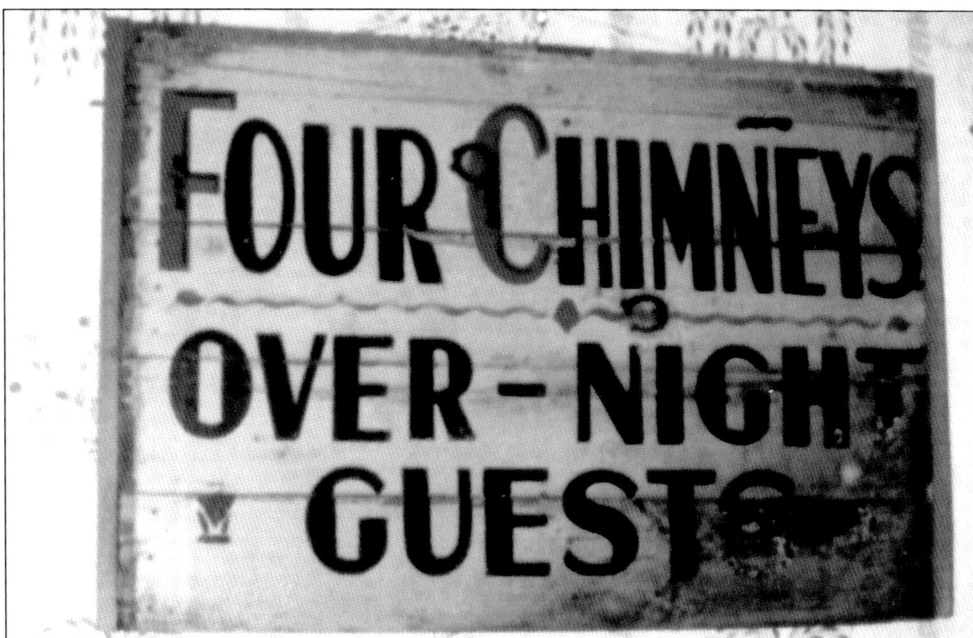

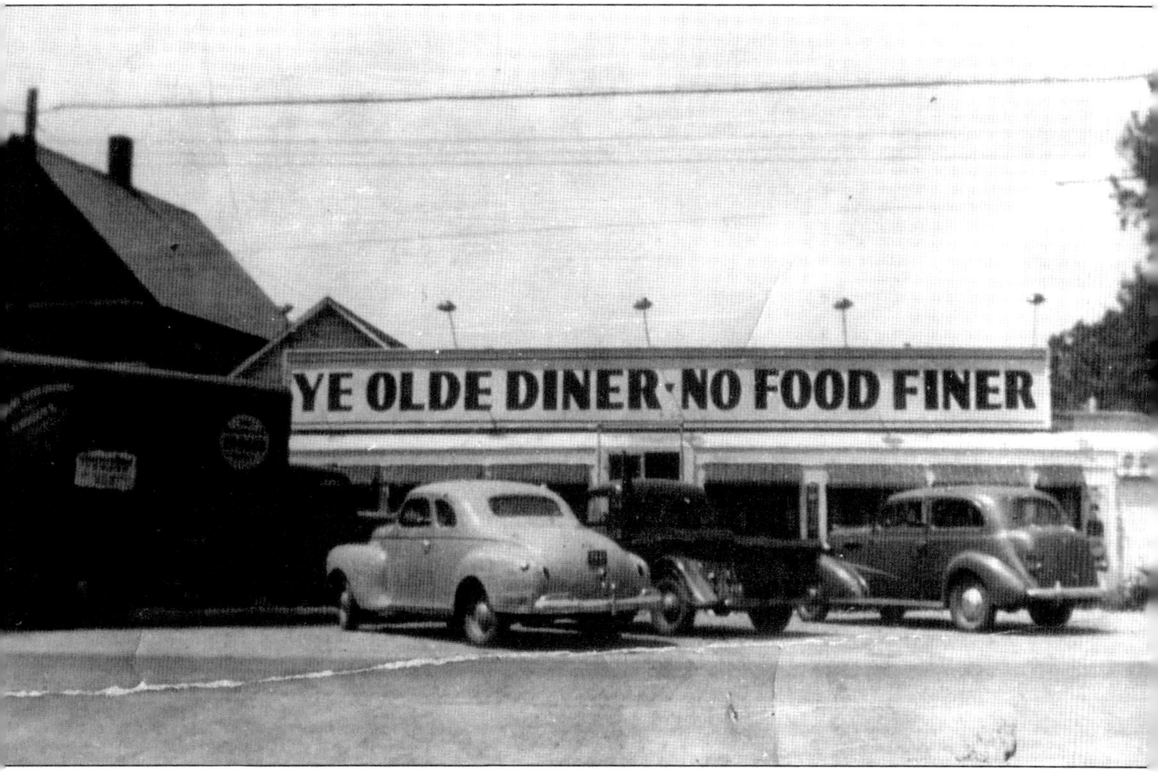

Following the abandonment of the Green Line electric interurban railway in 1931, Earl Burrer of Elyria bought parlor car No. 200, originally called the *Alvesta*, and used it on his West Ridge Road farm as a private residence for his sister. The interior was mahogany paneled, and the dome windows were colored Tiffany-style glass. In April 1936, John and Marie Johnson bought the trolley car and had it moved near the northwest corner of Ridgeville Center (Center Ridge and Avon Belden Roads), where they opened it as Ye Olde Diner, as seen in this 1940 photograph. After two years, the Johnsons built an addition that included a dance floor. The diner also served for some years as the Greyhound bus line ticket office. Marie retired and sold the diner in 1972. It was demolished in the spring of 1996 after being unoccupied for a number of years.

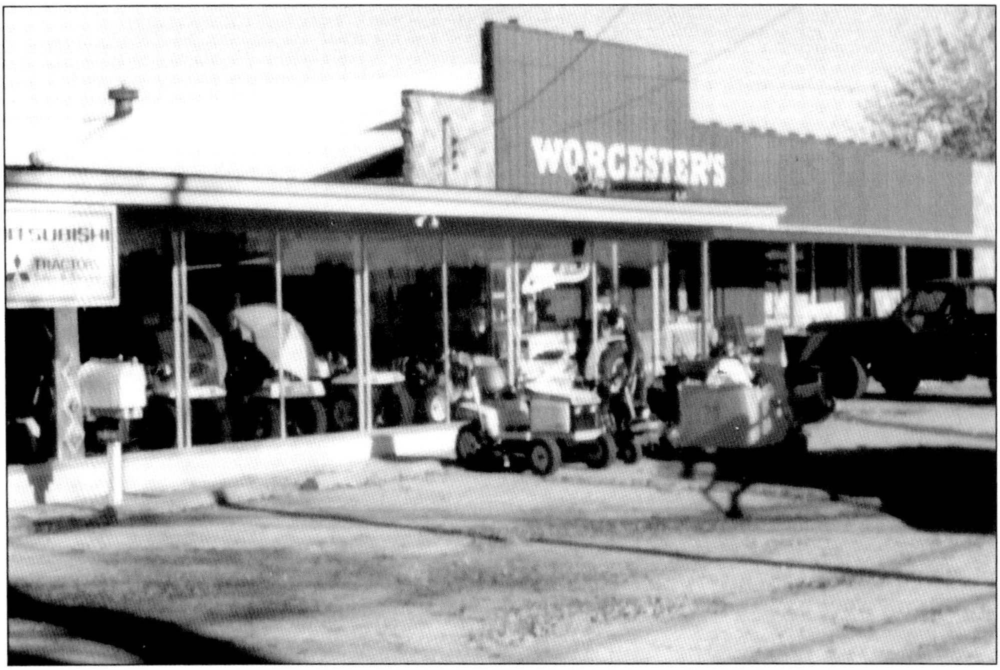

In 1927, John A. and Esther Worcester received a mother hen and 18 baby chicks as a gift from Esther's mother. They thought they could sell eggs along with vegetables from their gardening truck on Chestnut Ridge Road. The chicks led to hatching eggs and selling baby chicks. Soon they purchased an incubator and erected a brooder room. Later houses were built for breeding stock. The business was named Worcester Hatchery and Breeding Farms. In 1942, a fire nearly put them out of business; however, years before, they had purchased the Smith Standard Nursery on the northeast corner of Route 10 and Root Road at Fields Corners, so they erected a new building. By 1950, the family, which included two children, Eleanor and Delbert, had two businesses, Worcester Hatchery and Feed Store and Worcester Sales and Service. (Courtesy of the Worcester family.)

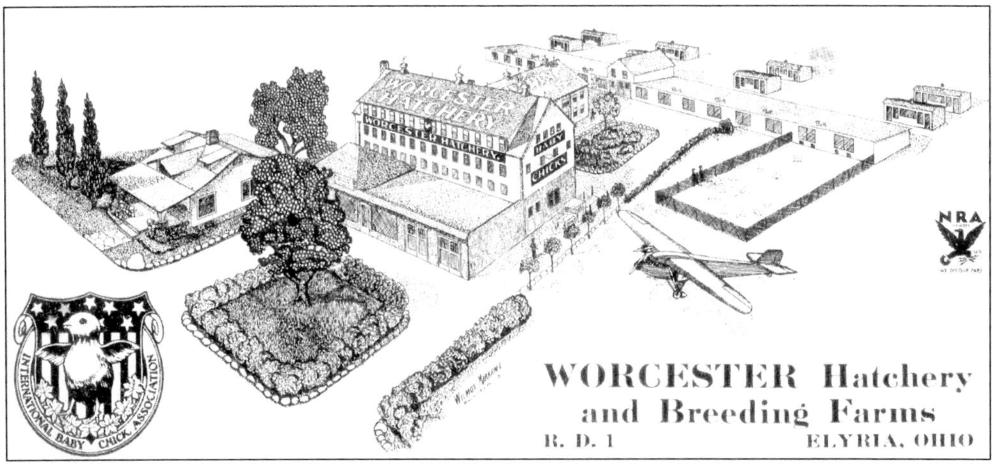

John A., the founder of Worcester's Hatchery and Feed Store and Worcester Sales and Service, enjoyed maintaining the family business, as he may have been doing when photographed standing on the roof of the building. His young son, Delbert, can be seen on the lower rung of the ladder. (Courtesy of the Worcester family.)

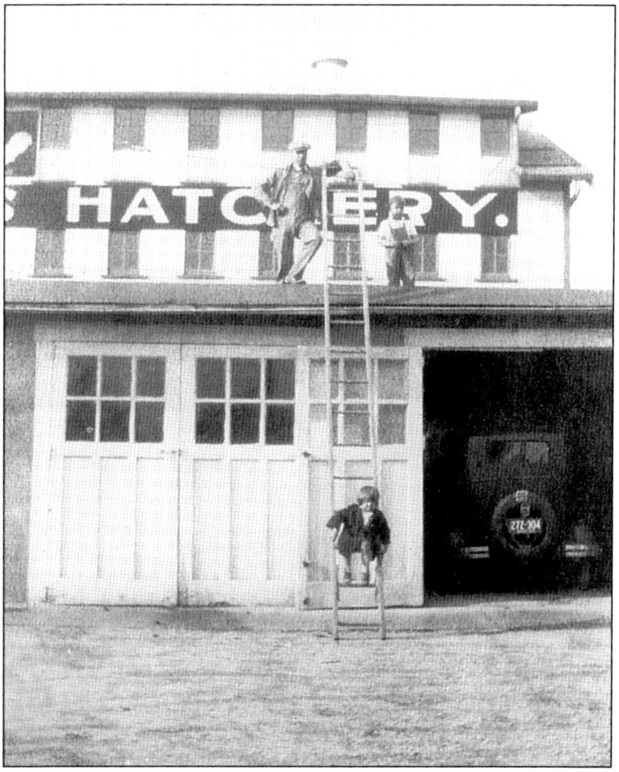

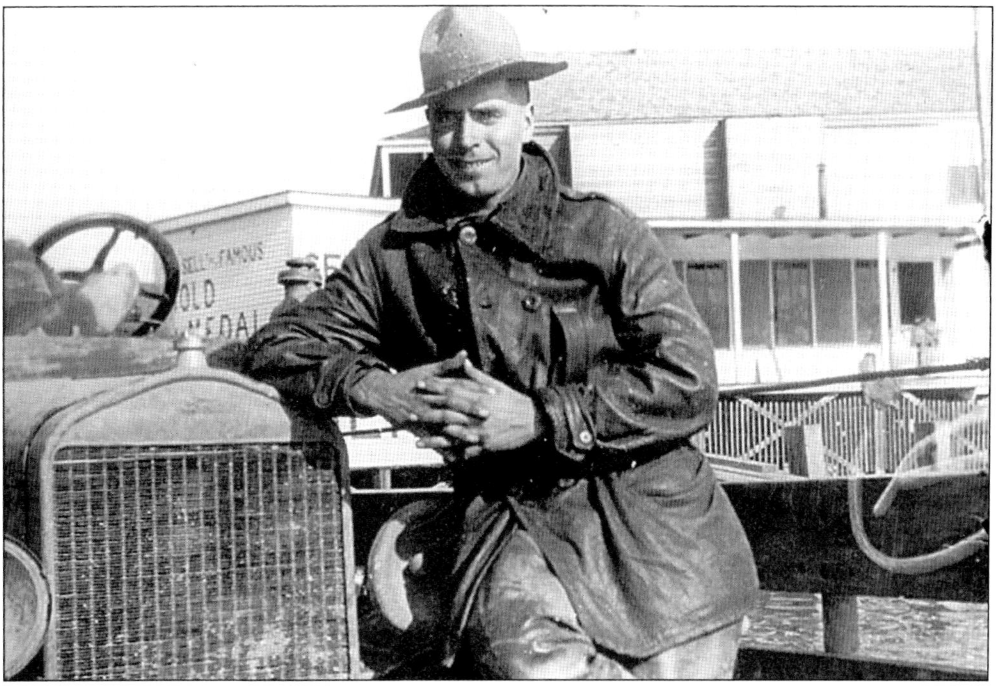

John A. was born in 1895 and enjoyed life as well as a number of hobbies. His interests included automobiles, and one of his favorite automobiles was the 1926 Buick he is shown with in this family photograph. (Courtesy of the Worcester family.)

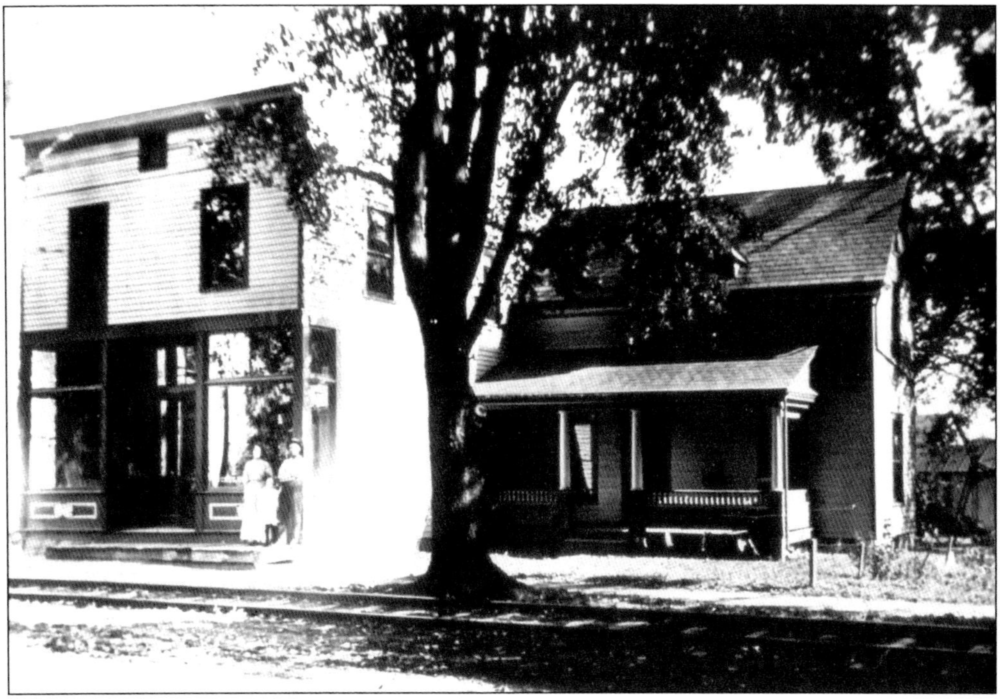

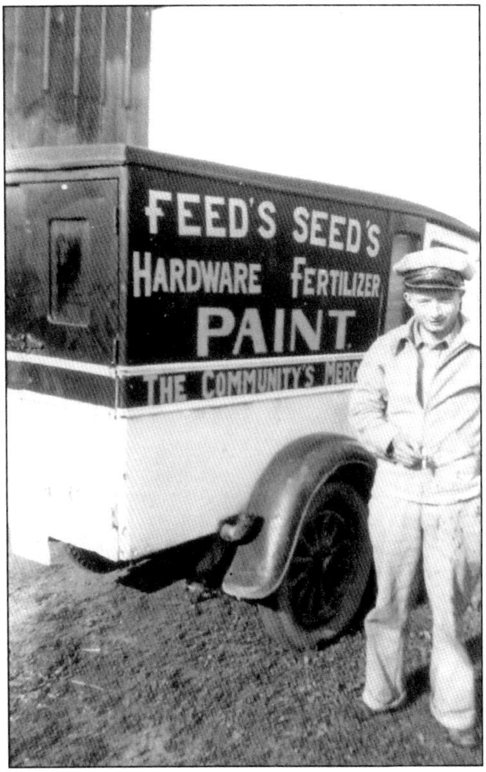

The building pictured on the left served as a store on Center Ridge Road just west of Avon Belden Road (Route 83) for more than 100 years. It was known by different names and owned by different men. It was first called Fisher's, later it became Loescher's General Store, and then it changed to Diederich's Grain and Feed Store. In 1936, Cleveland native Urban Buescher opened Buescher's Feed Store, later known as Buescher's True Value Hardware Store. Not long after this 1910 photograph was taken, the house to the right was purchased and incorporated into the store. Several other additions and improvements have been made to the structure since that time, and it is still a popular place to make hardware purchases. The Green Line interurban tracks, which ran along the south side of Center Ridge Road, can be seen in the foreground. Deliveries from Buescher's hardware store were made in a truck advertising some of the things sold at the store and bearing the motto, "the Community's Merchant." Sylvester Schneider is standing in front of the truck in this 1940s photograph. (Courtesy of Ken Buescher.)

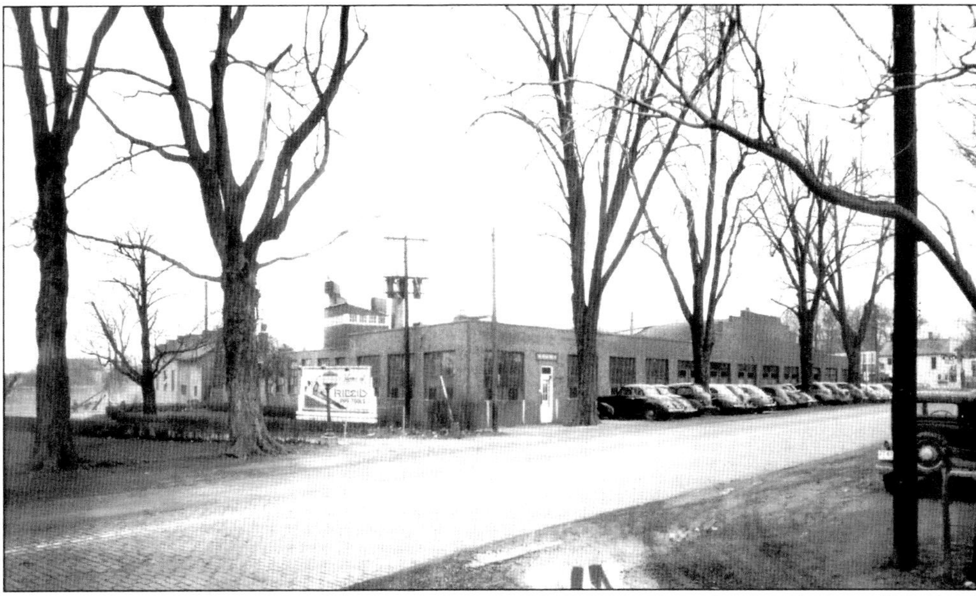

The Ridge Tool Company had its beginning in 1923 on Center Ridge Road west of the high school, which is now the middle school. The company remained in that location for 18 years until the operation relocated to the neighboring town of Elyria, where it has remained and expanded. Today RIGID tools are known worldwide, and the company's products include power tools, pipe and tubing, and air tools. (Courtesy of Ridge Tool Company.)

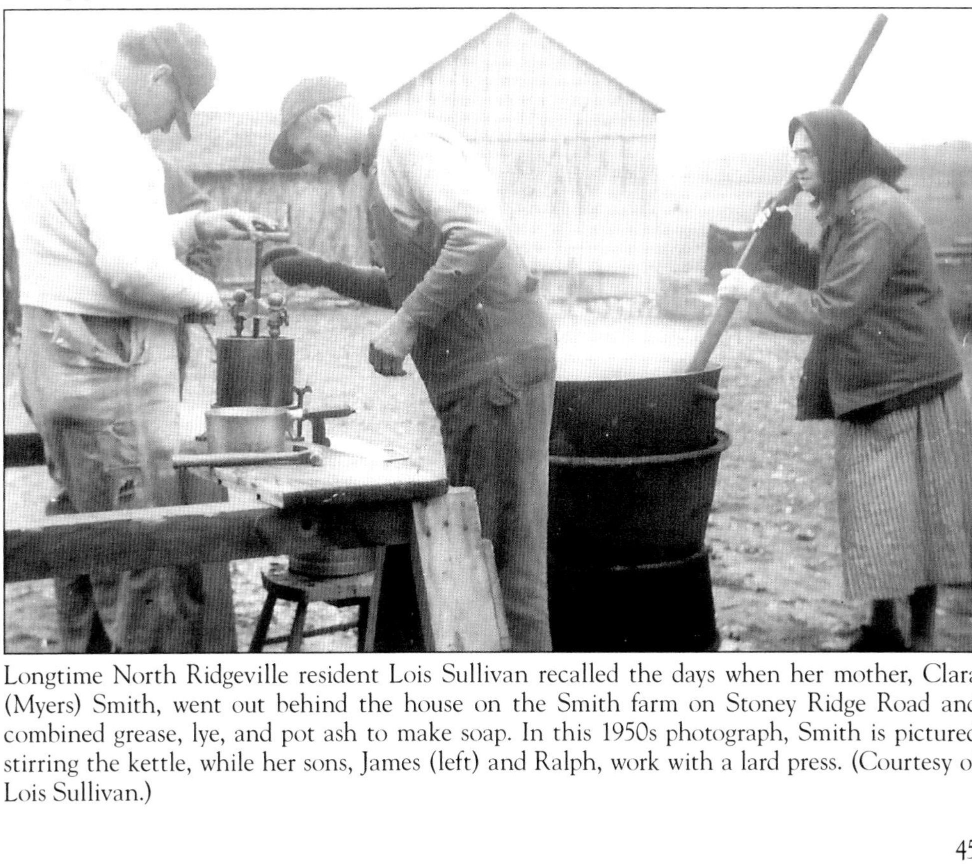

Longtime North Ridgeville resident Lois Sullivan recalled the days when her mother, Clara (Myers) Smith, went out behind the house on the Smith farm on Stoney Ridge Road and combined grease, lye, and pot ash to make soap. In this 1950s photograph, Smith is pictured stirring the kettle, while her sons, James (left) and Ralph, work with a lard press. (Courtesy of Lois Sullivan.)

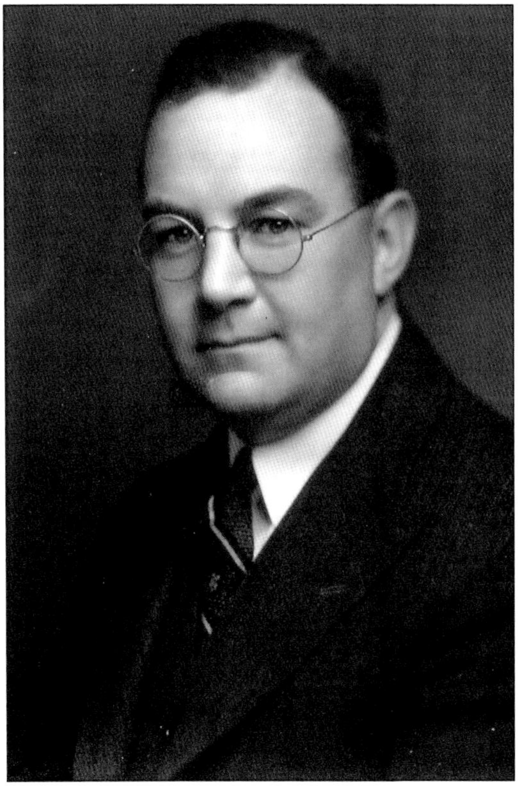

Reginald W. Beckett, born in 1897, founded the R. W. Beckett Corporation in 1937 in Elyria. Beckett was an entrepreneur, even as a child, when he earned money by using his wagon to haul soil for people's gardens. As an adult in the mid-1930s, he began working on oil burners from his home in Elyria and introduced the product at a trade show. It was a success, and eventually Beckett opened a plant, which despite difficult economic times in the United States, he was able to keep open. The war ended, and Beckett was able to return to producing oil burners. It was around 1952 that he opened the present facility in North Ridgeville, shown in the photograph below. Since that time, it has continued to expand and is now the largest manufacturer of residential oil burners in North America. (Courtesy of R. W. Beckett Corporation.)

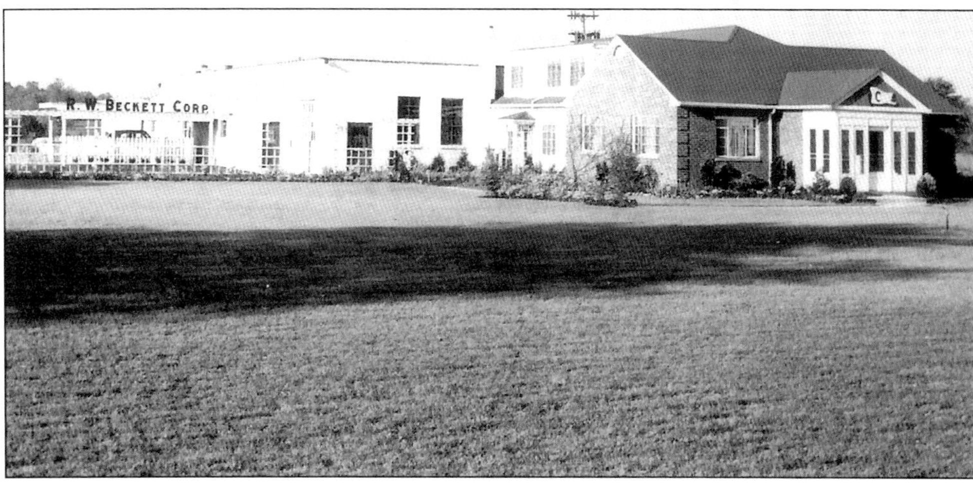

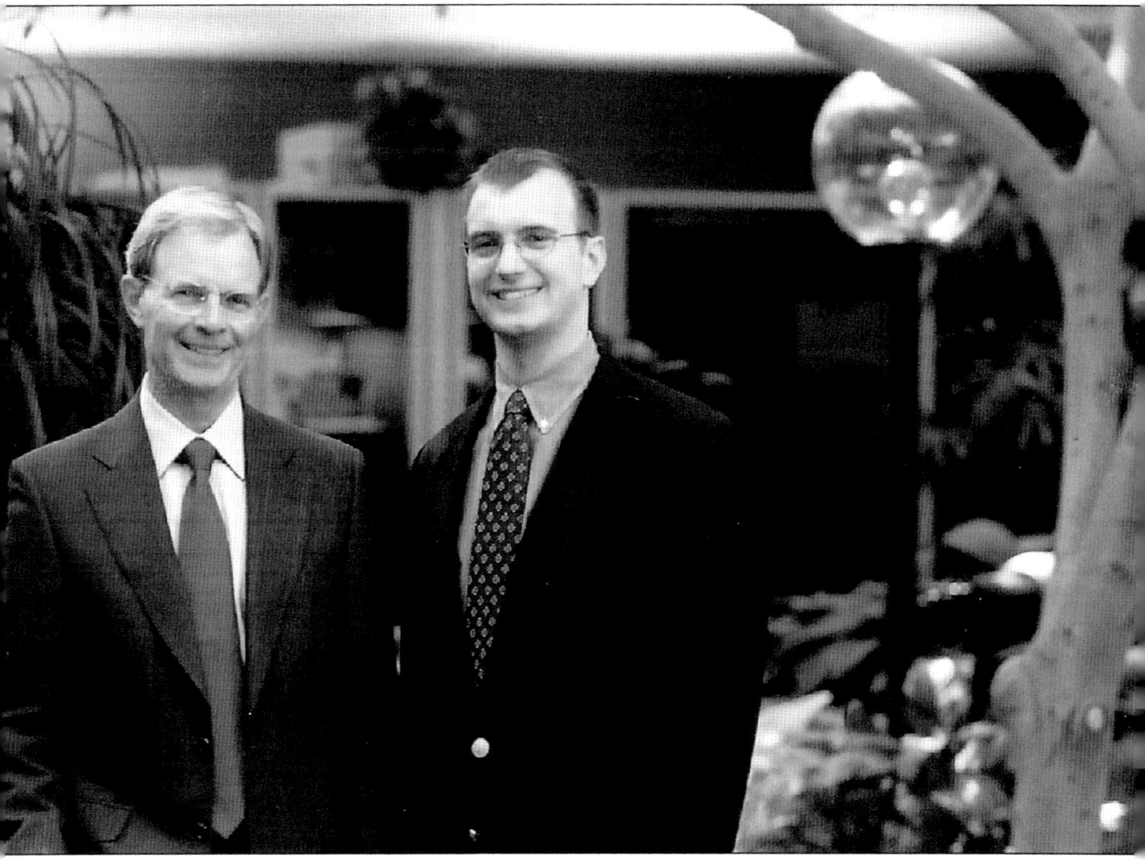

In 1963, Beckett invited his son John, a graduate of the Massachusetts Institute of Technology, to join him in the R. W. Beckett Corporation. The father and son worked together successfully for less than two years, when, in 1965, Reginald unexpectedly died of a heart attack. John had to decide whether or not to continue the business. Although he had offers from outsiders, the decision was made, and he continued to work in the family business. In 1997, John's oldest son, Kevin, became the third-generation Beckett to be part of the firm. John's second son, Jonathon, also joined the R. W. Beckett Corporation in 2000 as the firm's commercial division manager. John and Kevin are shown in this recent photograph. Although John continues to be active in the business, Kevin is the chief executive officer and president of the company. (Courtesy of R. W. Beckett Corporation.)

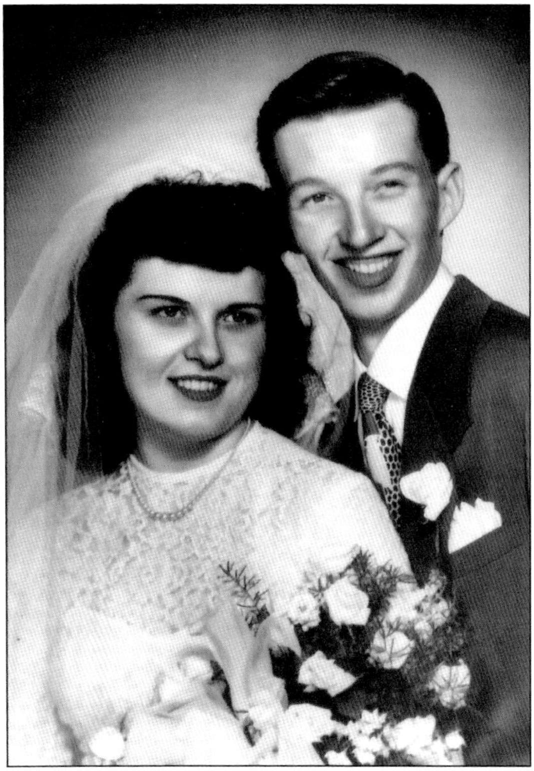

Don and Hazel Mould are pictured on their wedding day, July 3, 1951. In 1961, Don started Don Mould's Plantation in North Ridgeville as a Christmas tree farm. Forty years later, the family-run business, located on Lorain and Island Roads, has developed and expanded, as shown in the 1989 aerial photograph. It now offers a number of services, including plant outlet centers in North Ridgeville and in Amherst, a landscape division, which offers design and installation services, and more recently a construction enterprise was added. (Courtesy of the Mould family.)

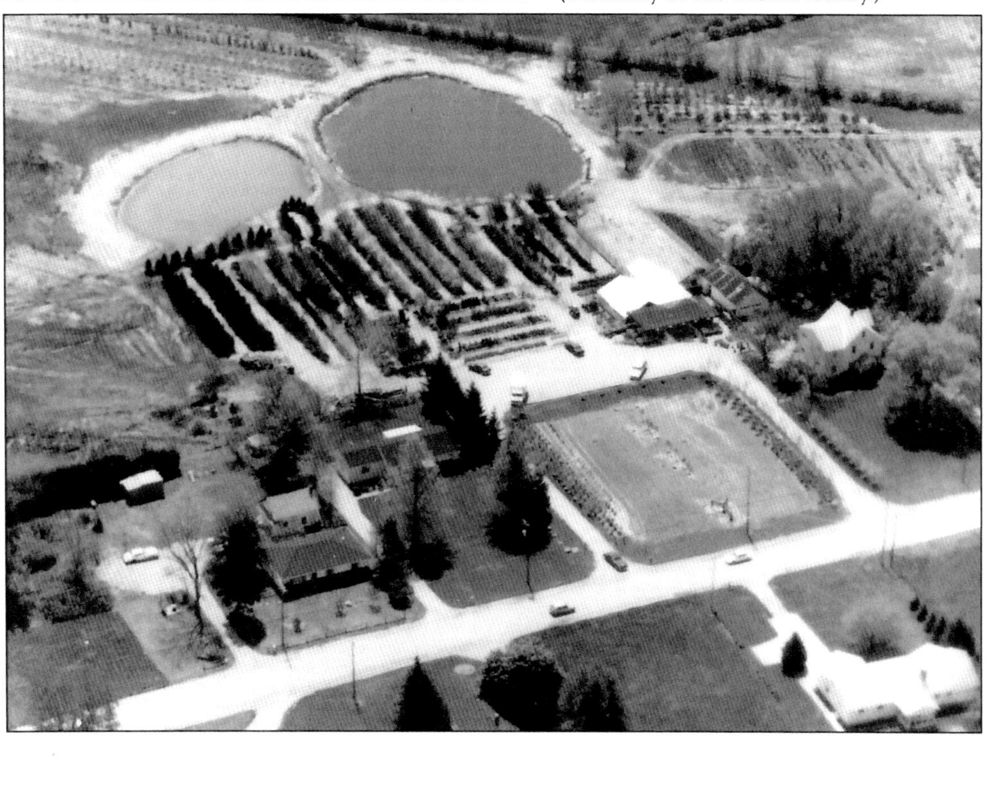

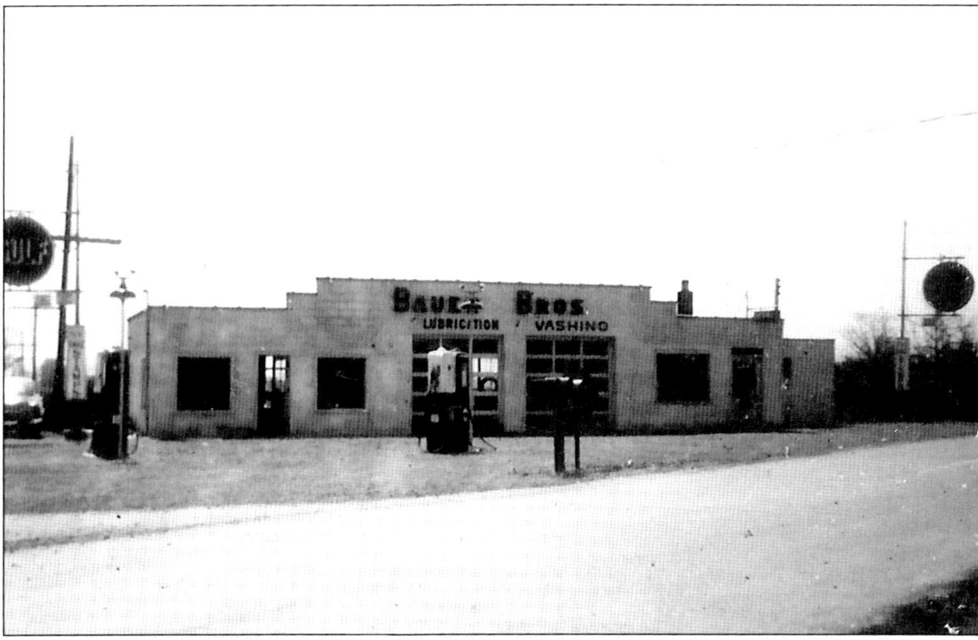

The Bauer Brothers Garage that stood at the intersection of Chestnut Ridge Road and Route 76 (now Route 83) was a familiar sight to motorists who traveled through that intersection. The business did everything from lubricating automobiles to washing them. The garage was sold in 1950, and the property is now the site of a dog grooming business. (Courtesy of Ron Bauer.)

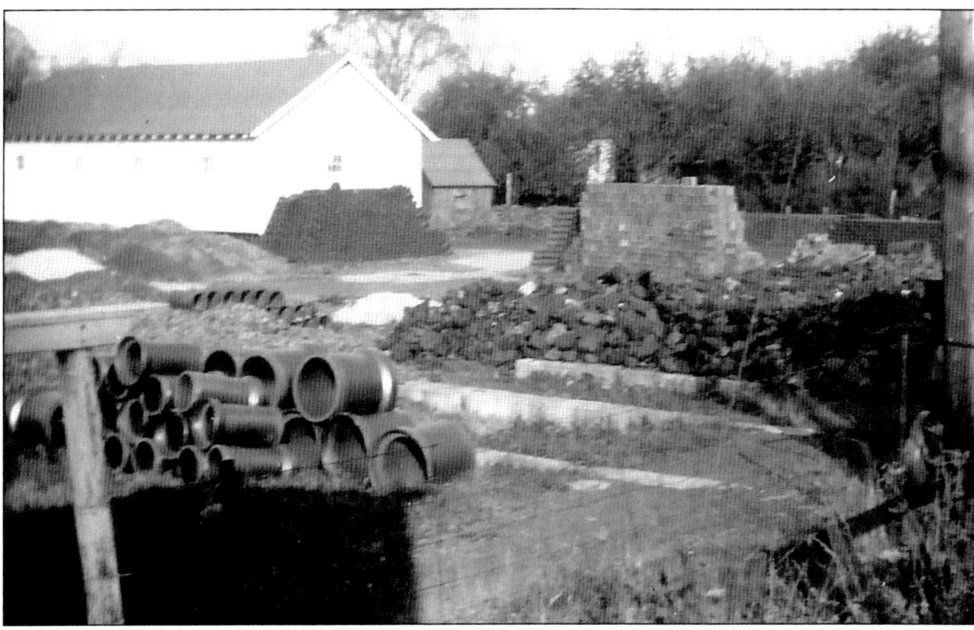

William Barnes owned and operated the Barnes Coal and Supply Company, which was located in what was known as Shawville near the railroad tracks. This view of the business is from where the tracks cut through town, looking down into the coal yard. William retired in 1963 after 60 years of operating the company with his son James. William also served two terms in the 1930s as a Ridgeville Township trustee. (Courtesy of Ron Bauer.)

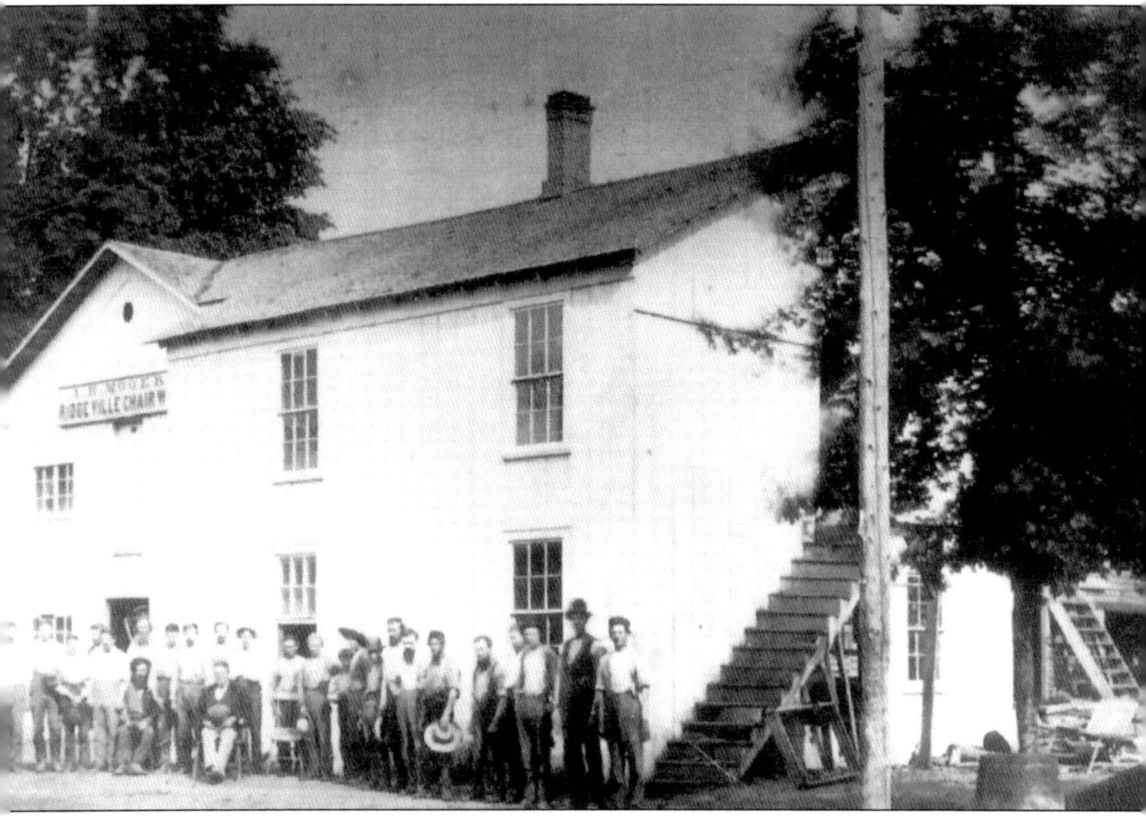

When Alton Henry "Hen" Mooers, born in 1830, started his chair factory, he started with just $7.50 and rented a room in a sawmill. With a few tools and a borrowed lathe, he began making chairs. The business, which was located on the south side of Center Ridge Road just east of the First Congregational United Church of Christ, grew until Mooers employed as many as 60 men at one time. By 1873, he had nearly 75 employees and was making not only wooden chairs but also settees and round-cornered bedsteads. Many of the chairs and beds can still be found in the community. The chair company was in business from 1853 to 1909, with a sales office in downtown Elyria. When it went out of business, Mooers sold the building for $100 to Harry Haven, who used the lumber to build a barn and part of his house in neighboring Eaton Township.

Three

Growing Up

In 1813, the adult males in the settlement approved the creation of Ridgeville Township, a designation that remained for 145 years. However, in 1829, due to persistent mail mix-ups with another Ridgeville that was located near Dayton, the postmaster general asked that the community in northern Ohio be called North Ridgeville. In 1958, due to increased population, the area was named the Village of North Ridgeville, and two years later in 1960, the village became a city. Once known as the Buffalo Trail because it started in Buffalo, New York, and extended to Detroit, Center Ridge Road became the city's main thoroughfare. In May 1959, a special election was held to select temporary officials for the new village who would serve from June 1, 1959, to January 1, 1960. Luke Loufman was elected mayor, along with a contingent of councilmen, a clerk, and a treasurer. Although North Ridgeville did not become a city until 1960, the people who lived there had the protection of the Ridgeville Township Volunteer Fire Department that began in 1931. In 1967, the first full-time firemen were sworn in. An organized police department began in 1958 when the first patrolman was hired.

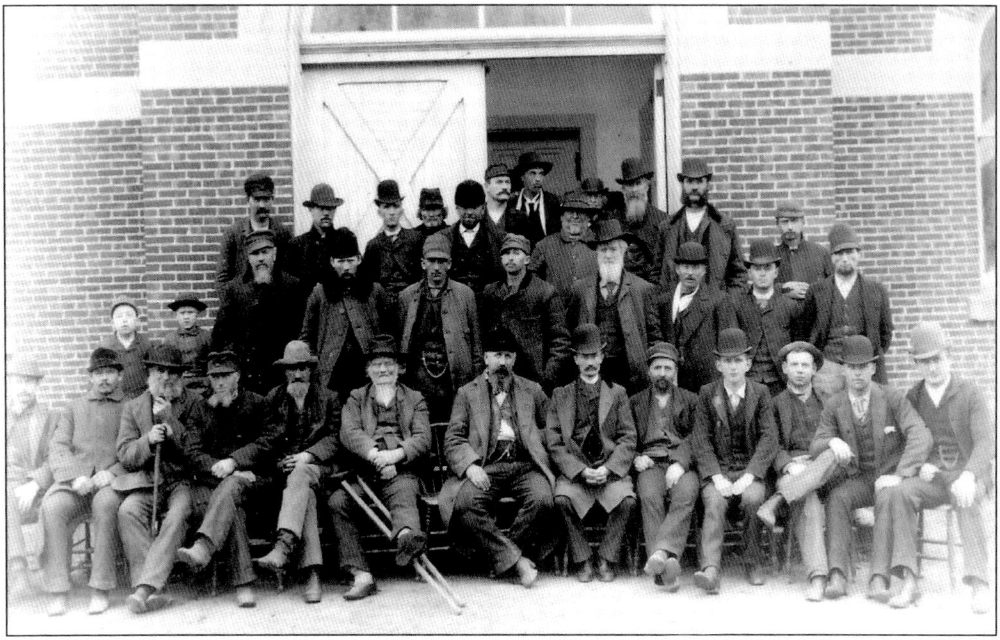

The unidentified Ridgeville Township men in this photograph from about 1885 are on the front steps of the new town hall on Center Ridge Road to hold a caucus to elect township officers. Officers usually consisted of three elected trustees, a township clerk, and justices of the peace. (Courtesy of the Lorain County Historical Society.)

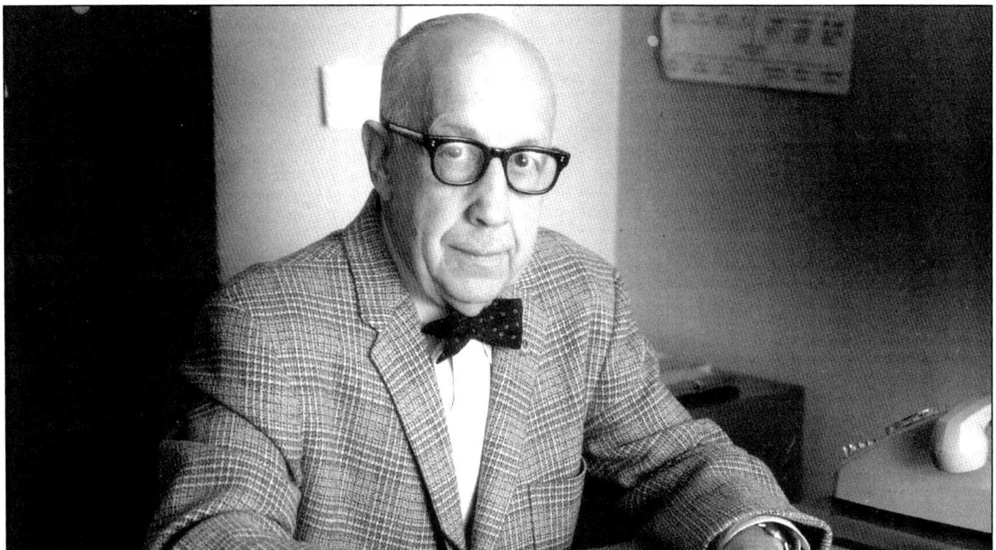

In 1958, Ridgeville Township was given approval to incorporate. The following year, a special election was held for the temporary officials of the new village. The following people served from June 1959 to January 1, 1960: Luke L. Loufman, mayor; C. Val Spicer, clerk; and Charlotte Lovell, treasurer. Loufman was the first and only mayor of the Village of North Ridgeville. When North Ridgeville became a city in 1960, he served as the city's first mayor until 1963. Loufman was instrumental in the formation of both the village and city governments. (Courtesy of Ron Bauer.)

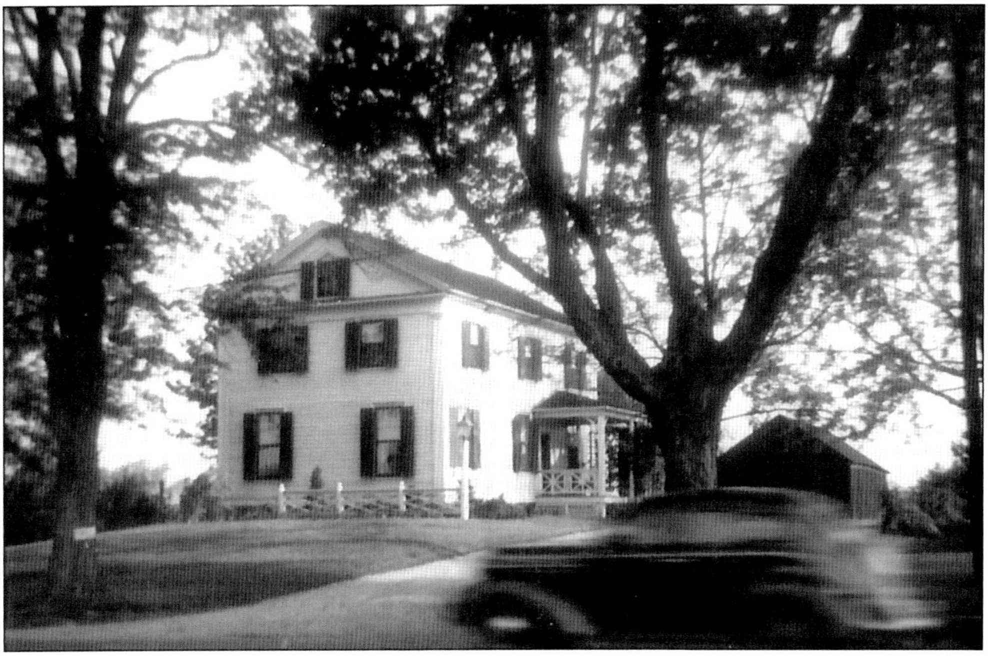

This stately home, located on the west end of Center Ridge Road, at one time belonged to Loufman, the first mayor of North Ridgeville. He and his family lived on the property. The house no longer exists and is currently the site of the Center Ridge Nursing Home. (Courtesy of Loyola Diederich.)

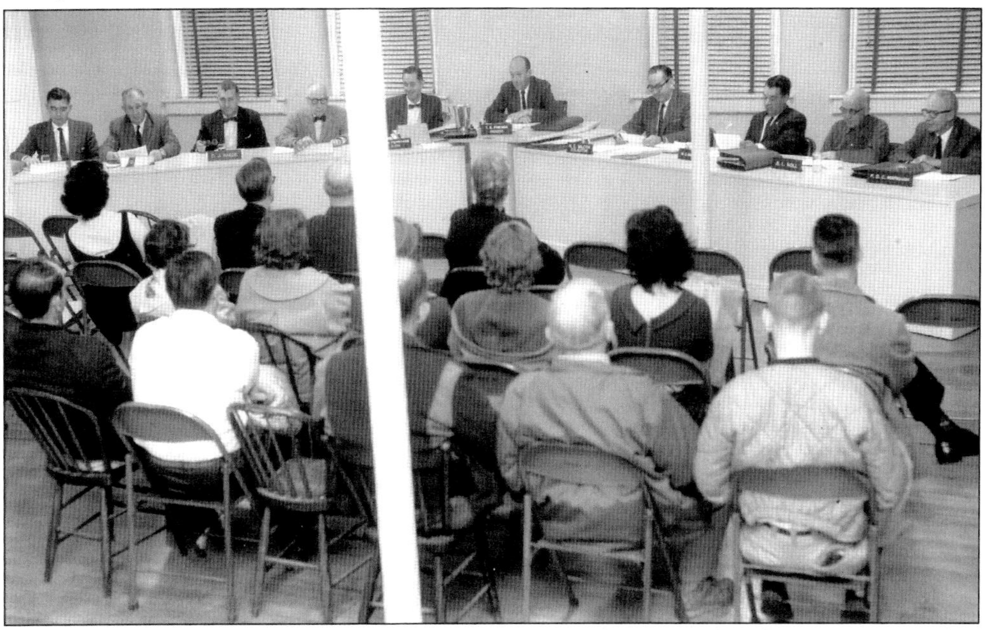

Loufman (fourth from left) is shown during a city council meeting that drew quite a crowd of residents. Pictured from left to right are Pete Pszenitski; Harold Sweet; David Gaede; Loufman; council clerk Cliff Perryman; Dr. Ted Finegan, council president; Hubbard Wilcox, solicitor; William Gardner; Bernard Noll; and Dr. Frederick DeWitt Clinton Markham. (Courtesy of Ron Bauer.)

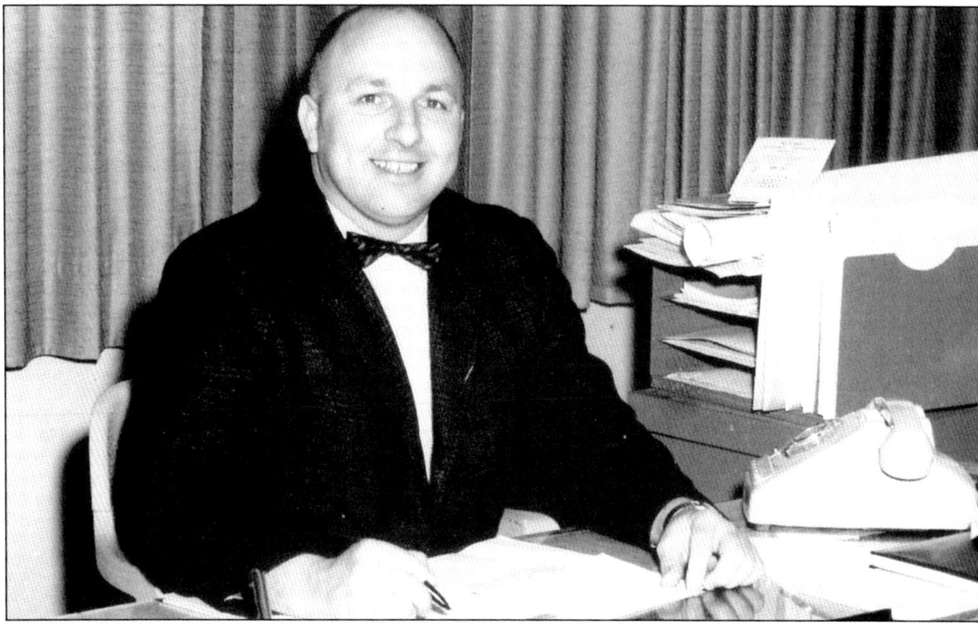

Paul G. Sweda was mayor of North Ridgeville from 1963 to 1965. The members of Sweda's council were Urban J. Buescher, councilman-at-large; Pete Pszenitski, councilman-at-large; M. B. Diederich, councilman-at-large; Ralph Smith, Ward 1 councilman; Kenneth Alten, Ward 2 councilman; Bernard Noll, Ward 3 councilman; and Ward 4 councilman Harold D. Sweet. John E. Vessalo was clerk of the council, and Harold "Red" McVeigh was street superintendent.

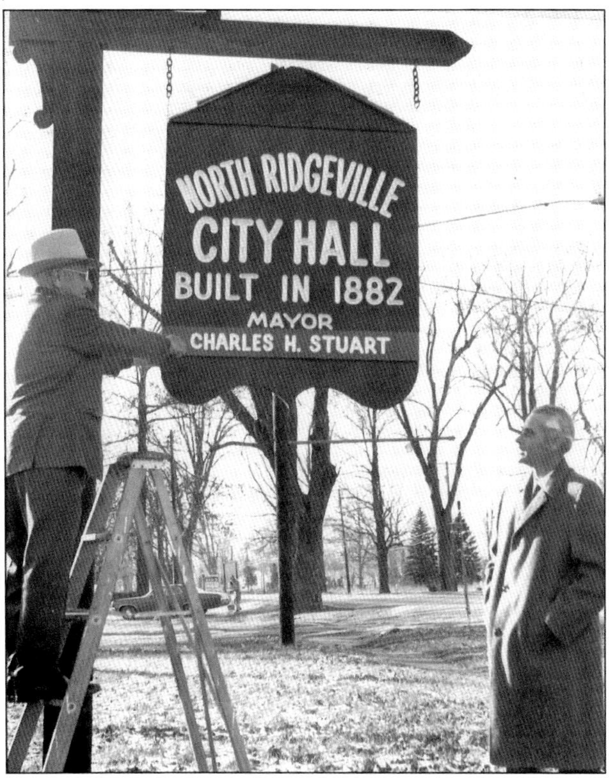

Charles H. Stuart admires his nameplate as it is hoisted up on the North Ridgeville sign at the entrance to the city after he won the election for mayor and was sworn in as the city's top administrator. Stuart served three consecutive terms as mayor between 1972 and 1977.

Dick Noll served the City of North Ridgeville for four two-year terms as mayor. His first two terms were from 1965 to 1969. In this 1979 photograph, Noll had just been sworn in for the first of his last two consecutive terms, which began in 1979 and lasted until 1983. Judge Robert Corts officiated at the ceremony. From left to right are Corts; Noll; his wife, Janyce Noll; Gayle Manning, and her husband, Jeffery Manning, who was the North Ridgeville city law director. (Courtesy of Dick Noll.)

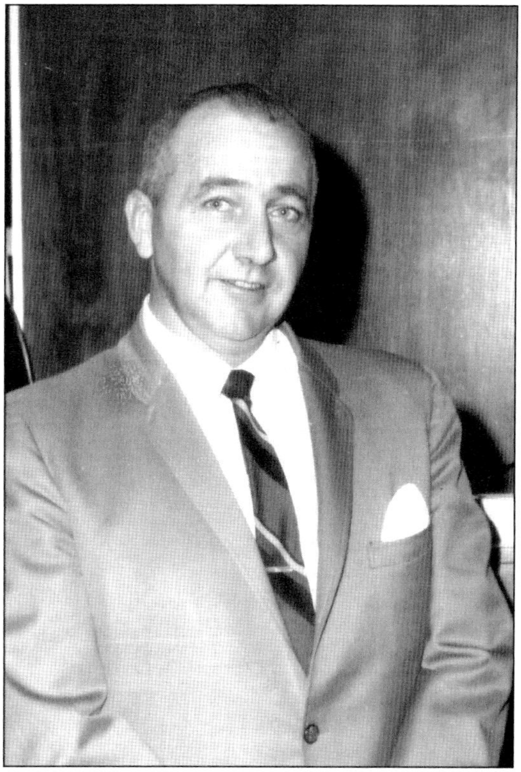

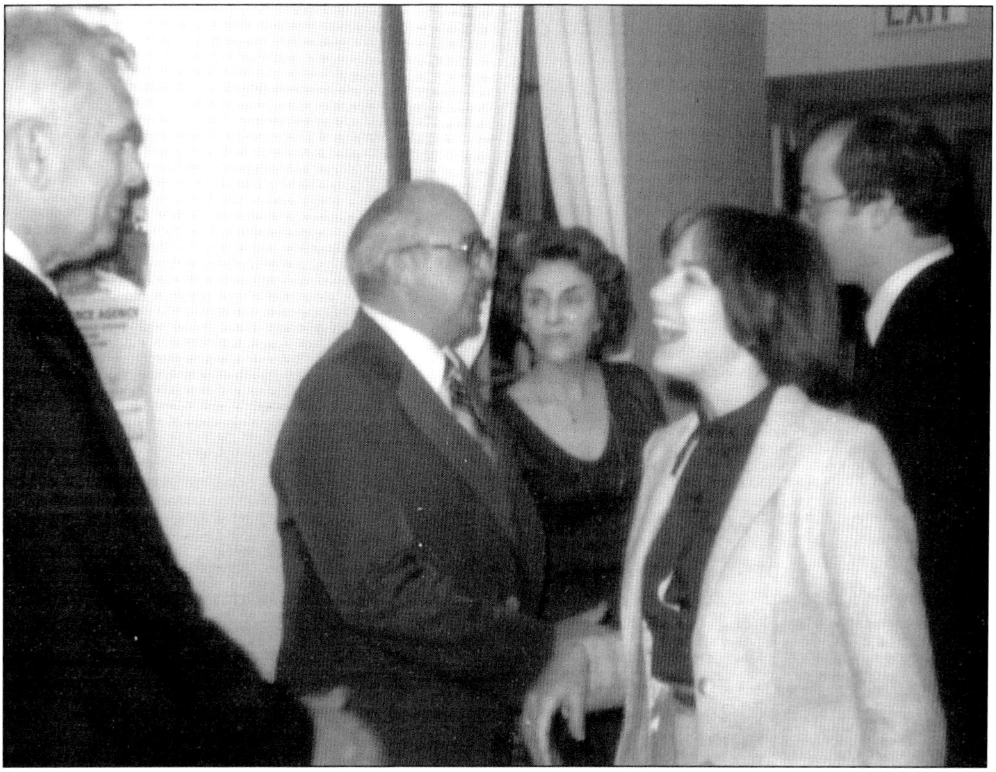

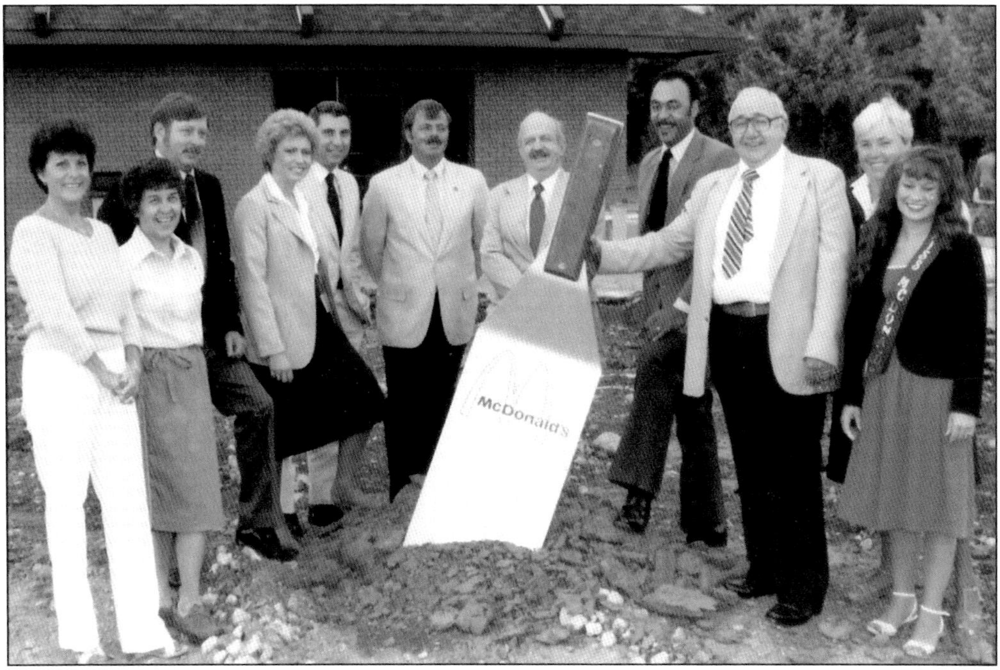

Mayor Dick Noll and his administrative staff gather for the groundbreaking of the playland addition to the new McDonald's restaurant in August 1982. The fast-food restaurant was first opened in 1962 in the former Ridgeville Shopping Center on Center Ridge Road and was replaced by a new building in 1976. The North Ridgeville McDonald's was one of the first in the area to construct a play area for children. The last building, which was vacant for a number of years, was razed recently in preparation for a new shopping strip. A new McDonald's was constructed on Lorain Road several years ago. (Courtesy of Dick Noll.)

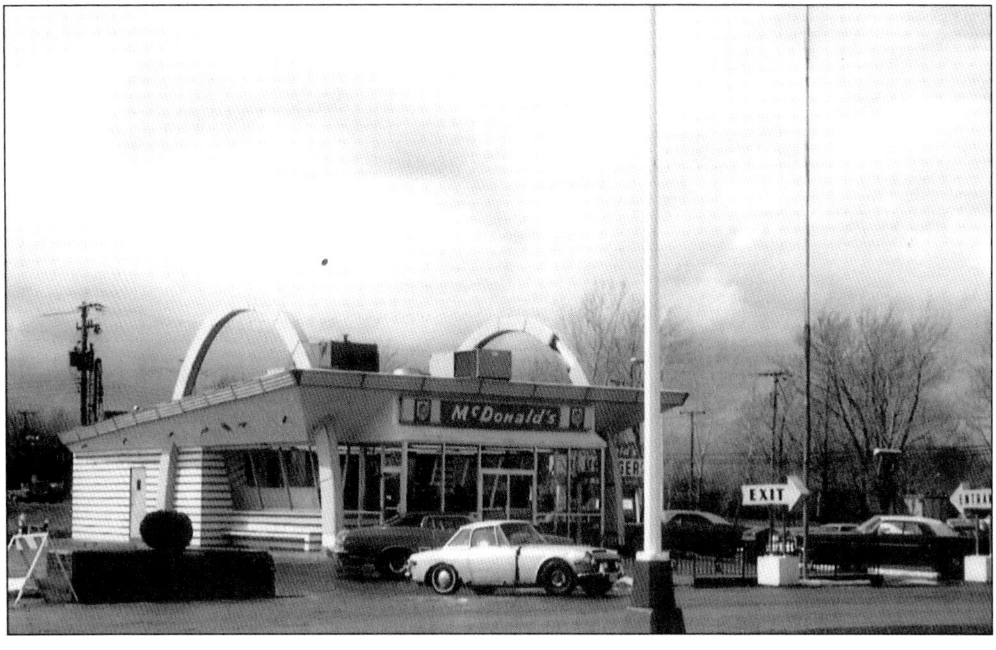

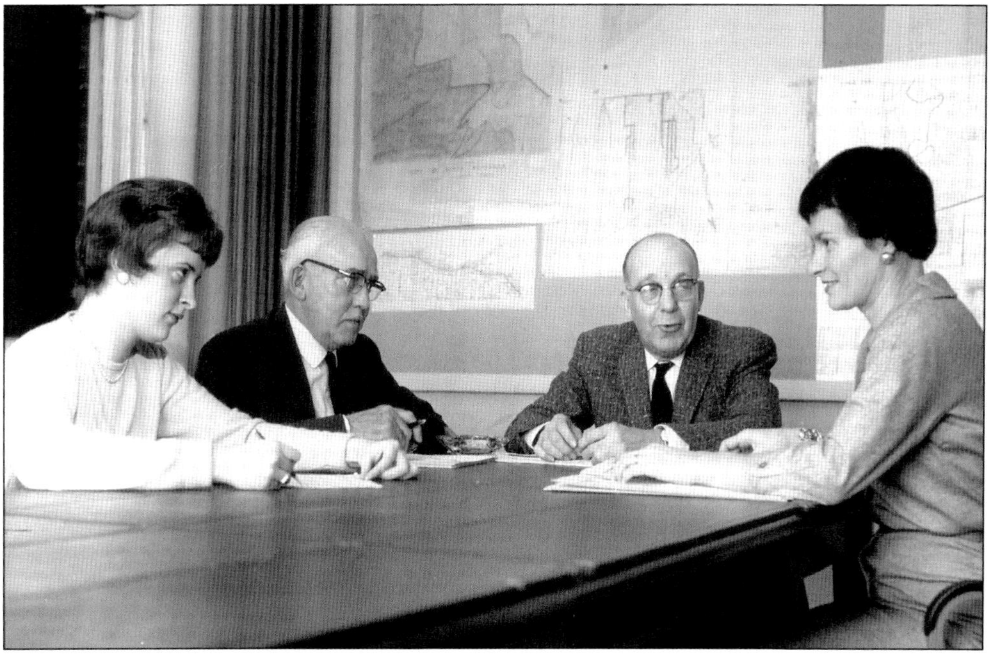

Members of North Ridgeville's civil service commission sit at a table during a meeting in the early 1960s to discuss upcoming business issues, probably including some dates for testing prospective police and firemen. From left to right are Carol Baldauf Hamm, Arthur Myers, Albert Underwood, and Rita Urig. (Courtesy of Ron Bauer.)

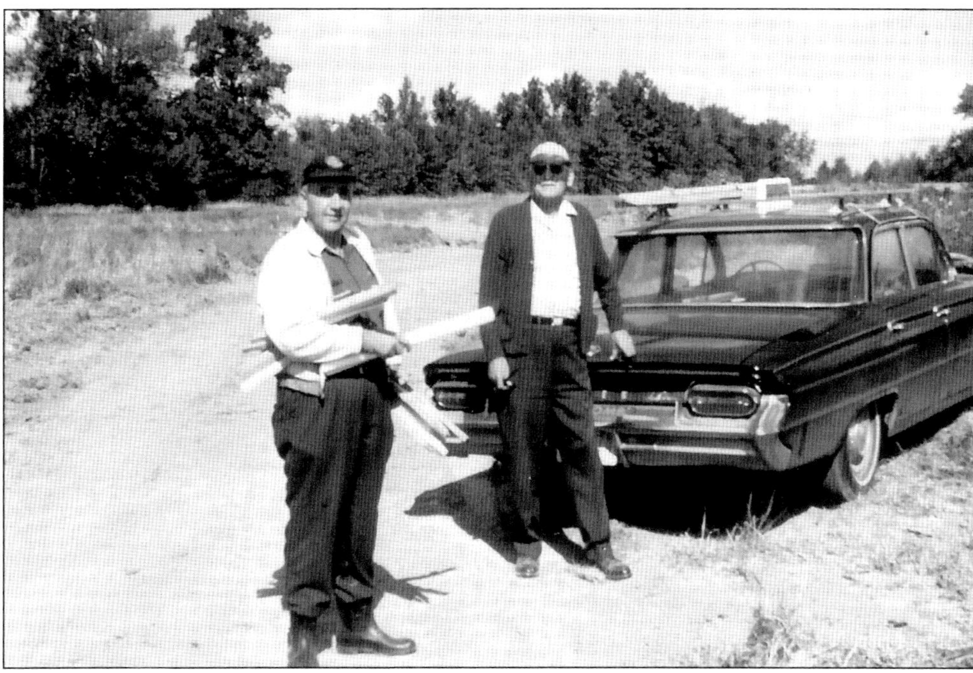

In this 1966 photograph, Noll, holding blueprints, and city engineer Harvey Holcomb are discussing plans for a new park for the city. Before becoming the city engineer for North Ridgeville, Holcomb had served as engineer for Lorain County. (Courtesy of Dick Noll.)

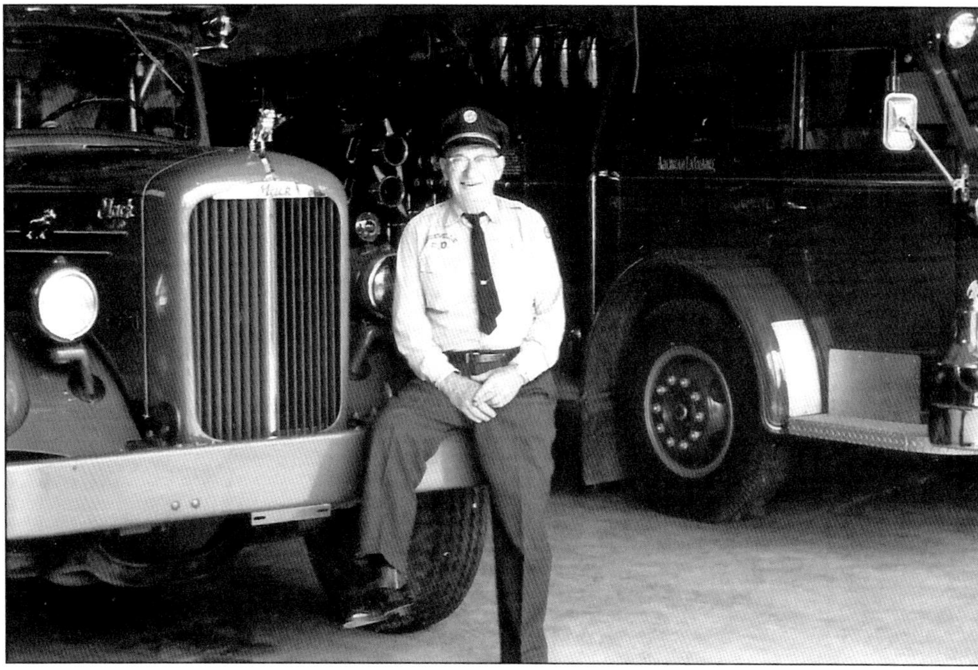

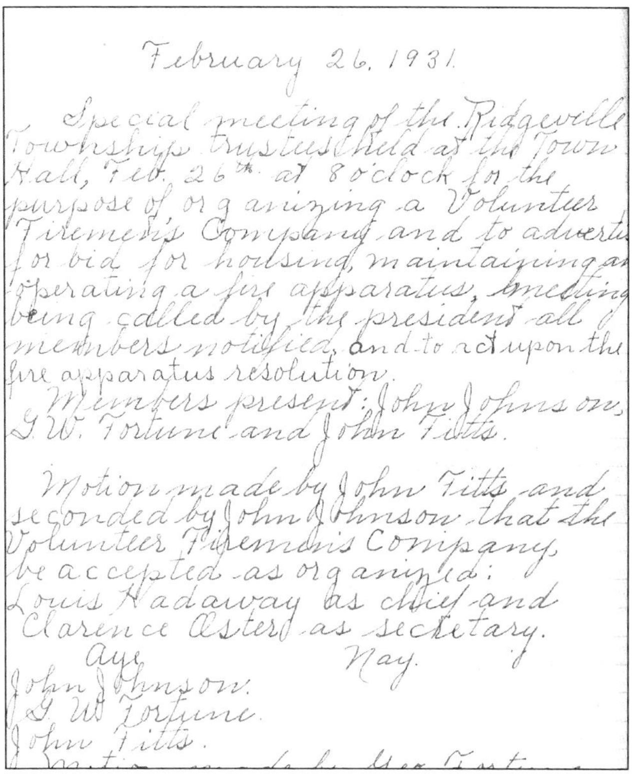

February 26, 1931.

Special meeting of the Ridgeville Townships trustees held at the Town Hall, Feb. 26th at 8 o'clock for the purpose of organizing a Volunteer Firemen's Company and to advertise for bid for housing, maintaining and operating a fire apparatus, meeting being called by the president all members notified, and to act upon the fire apparatus resolution.

Members present: John Johnson, G. W. Fortune and John Fitts.

Motion made by John Fitts and seconded by John Johnson that the Volunteer Firemen's Company be accepted as organized: Louis Hadaway as chief and Clarence Oster as secretary.

Aye Nay

John Johnson.

G. W. Fortune.

John Fitts.

Motion made by Geo Fortune

The Ridgeville Fire Department was organized on February 26, 1931, by action of Ridgeville Township trustees John Johnson, G. W. Fortune, and John Fitts, in a special meeting on recommendation of the Ridgeville Grange. The original department consisted of 25 volunteers, a new 1931 Buffalo fire truck, and a small-frame garage building that housed the truck and equipment. Louis Hadaway served on the department beginning 1931, and in the mid-1950s, he became the township's first fire chief. Pictured is a copy of a portion of the minutes of the meeting, which led to the Ridgeville Fire Department. (Courtesy of the North Ridgeville Fire Museum.)

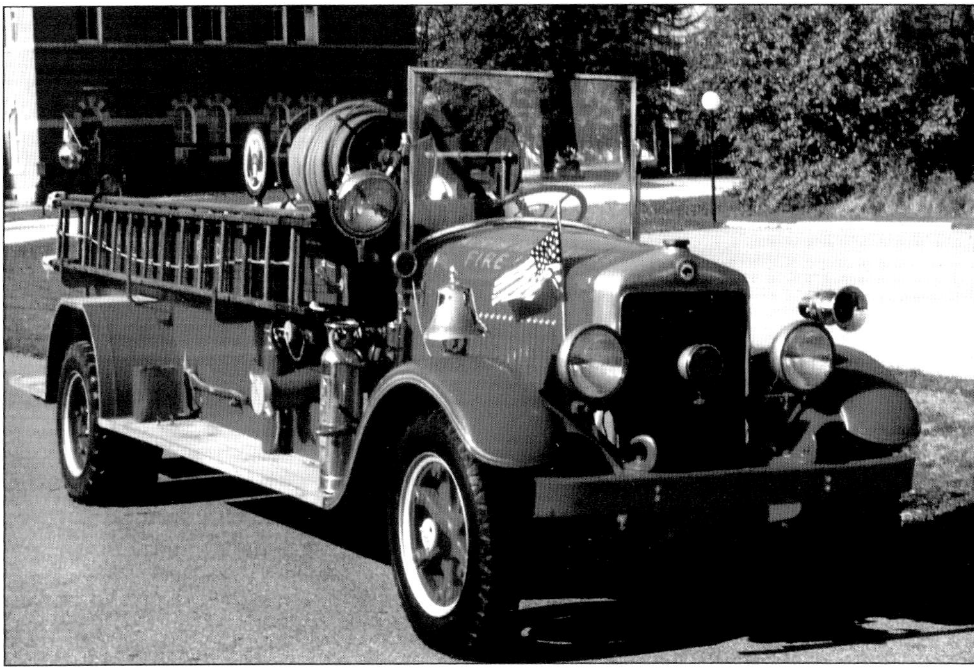

In August 1931, the Ridgeville Township trustees purchased this 500-gallon Hale pumper mounted on a two-and-a-half-ton fire truck chassis from the Buffalo Fire Appliance Corporation of Buffalo, New York. In the years since its retirement from active duty, "Old Buffalo" has been used extensively in community parades and celebrations. (Courtesy of the North Ridgeville Fire Museum.)

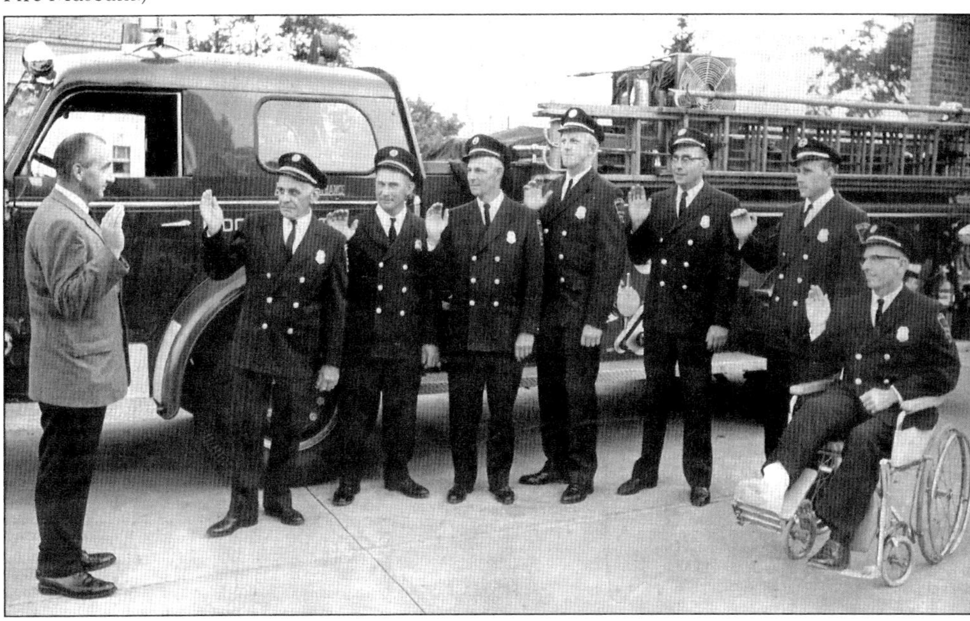

August 11, 1967, was a special day for North Ridgeville, as Mayor Dick Noll swore in the first full-time members of the North Ridgeville Fire Department. From left to right are Noll, Ralph Steinmetz, Eugene Diederich, Robert Dreger, Fred Dorow, Robert Gilder, James Barnes, and Albert Krueger. (Courtesy of the North Ridgeville Fire Museum.)

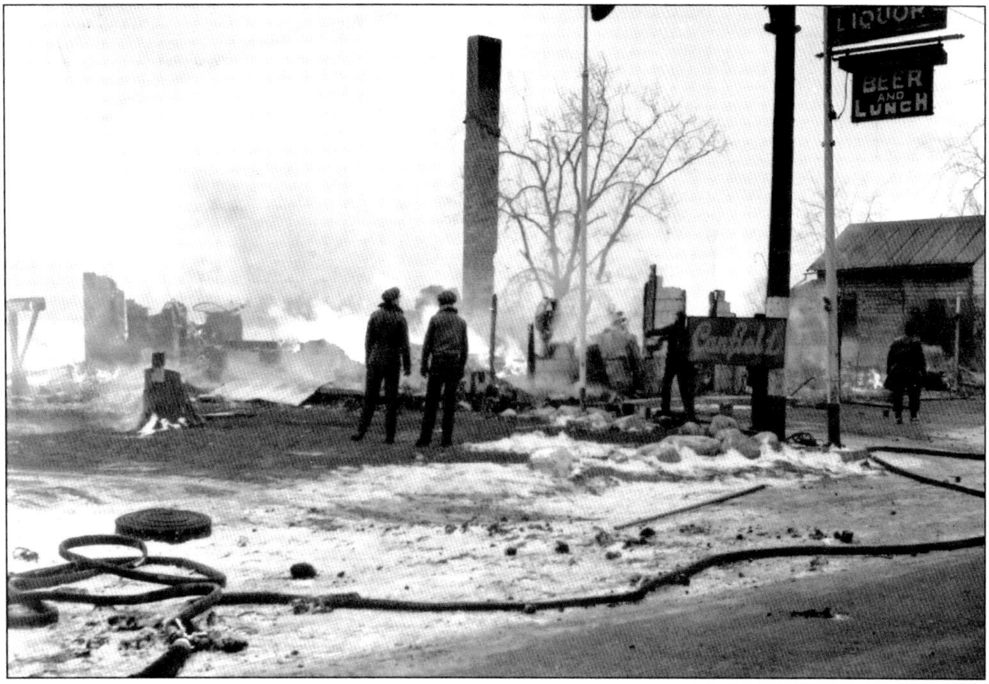

A fully involved blaze on Lorain Road brought out not only members of the North Ridgeville Volunteer Fire Department but also a number of nearby residents in this 1930s photograph. The fire occurred just west of Root Road at the Fields Tavern and the building next to it. The tavern was located across the road from where Automotive Equipment is presently. (Courtesy of the North Ridgeville Fire Museum.)

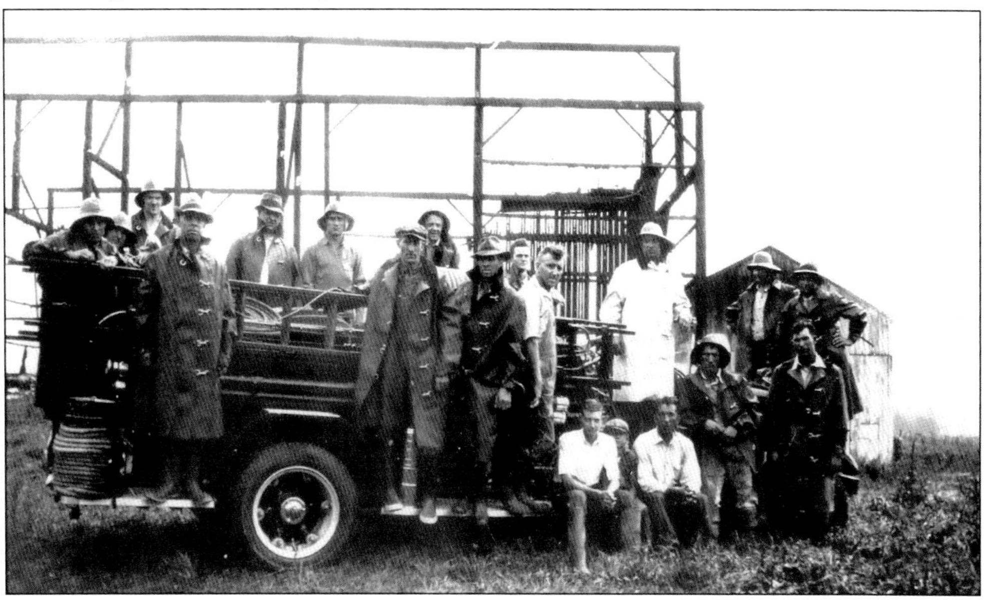

Members of Ridgeville Township's volunteer fire department are pictured as they returned from a barn fire in the early 1930s. The barn referred to in this photograph is unidentified; however, barn fires were common during the township's early days. None of the men pictured were identified. (Courtesy of the North Ridgeville Fire Museum.)

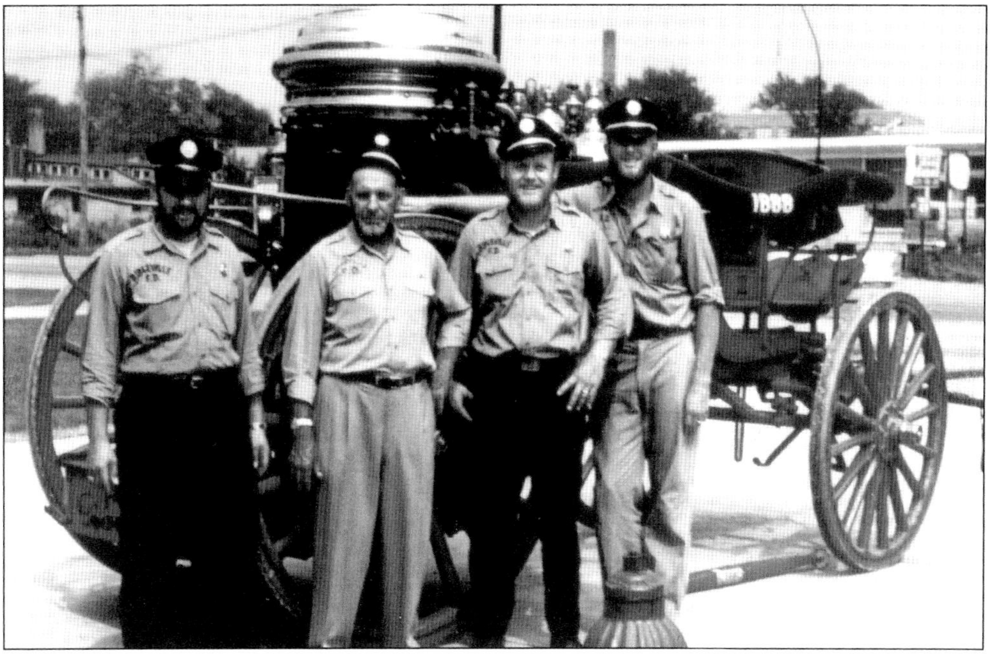

Four members of the North Ridgeville Volunteer Fire Department pose in front of an old horse-drawn steam engine in 1960. From left to right are John Campana, Ralph Steinmetz, Richard Capell, and Fred Dorow. All four of the men are wearing beards they were growing in preparation for the city's sesquicentennial celebration. (Courtesy of the North Ridgeville Fire Museum.)

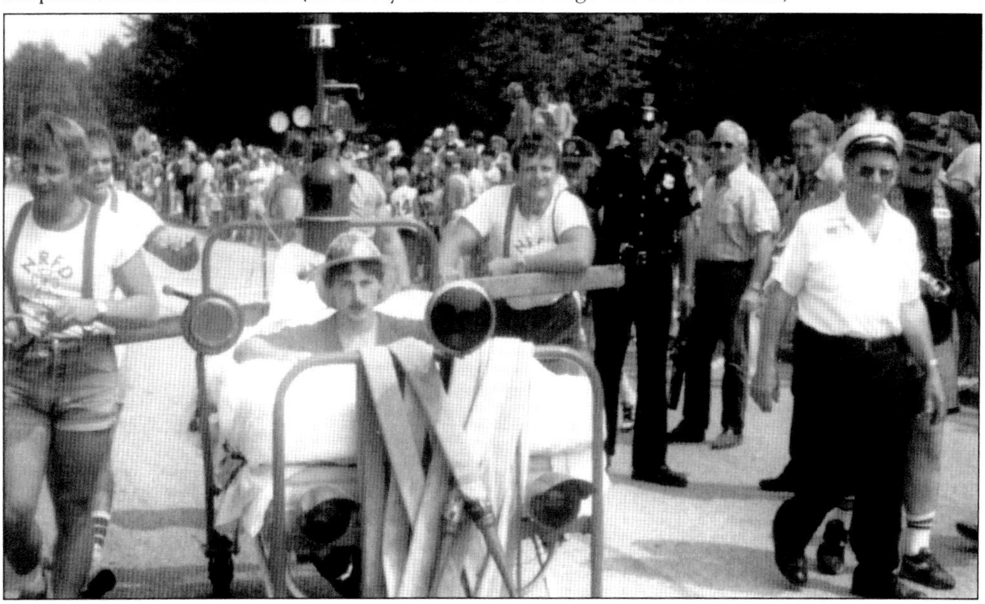

In the mid-1980s, some members of the North Ridgeville Fire Department participated in the bed race in conjunction with the community's Corn Festival. From left to right are Robert Kleinholz, Gary Bacher, Scott Bement (in the bed), Gene Kleinholz, and Chief Eugene Diederich. In the back, North Ridgeville patrolman Richard Stiles can be seen handling traffic detail, and Tom Schultz of the North Ridgeville Police Department and Michael Patterson of the fire department watch the event. (Courtesy of the North Ridgeville Fire Museum.)

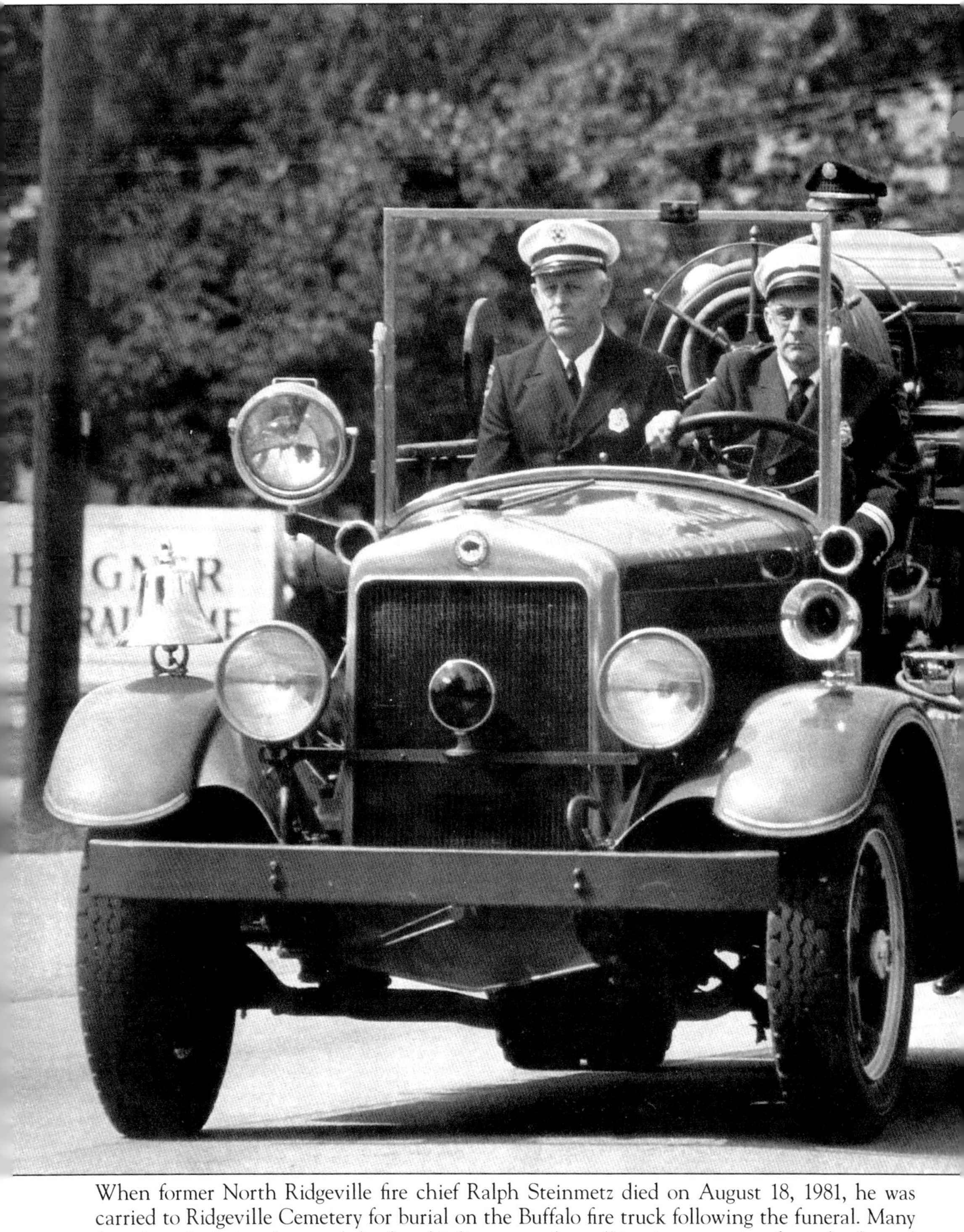

When former North Ridgeville fire chief Ralph Steinmetz died on August 18, 1981, he was carried to Ridgeville Cemetery for burial on the Buffalo fire truck following the funeral. Many friends and relatives honored the fire chief's memory by walking in procession from the funeral home to the cemetery. Born in Lakewood, Steinmetz served as a Ridgeville fireman for 40 years and was instrumental in buying the Buffalo fire truck in 1931, the year he and 22 other men

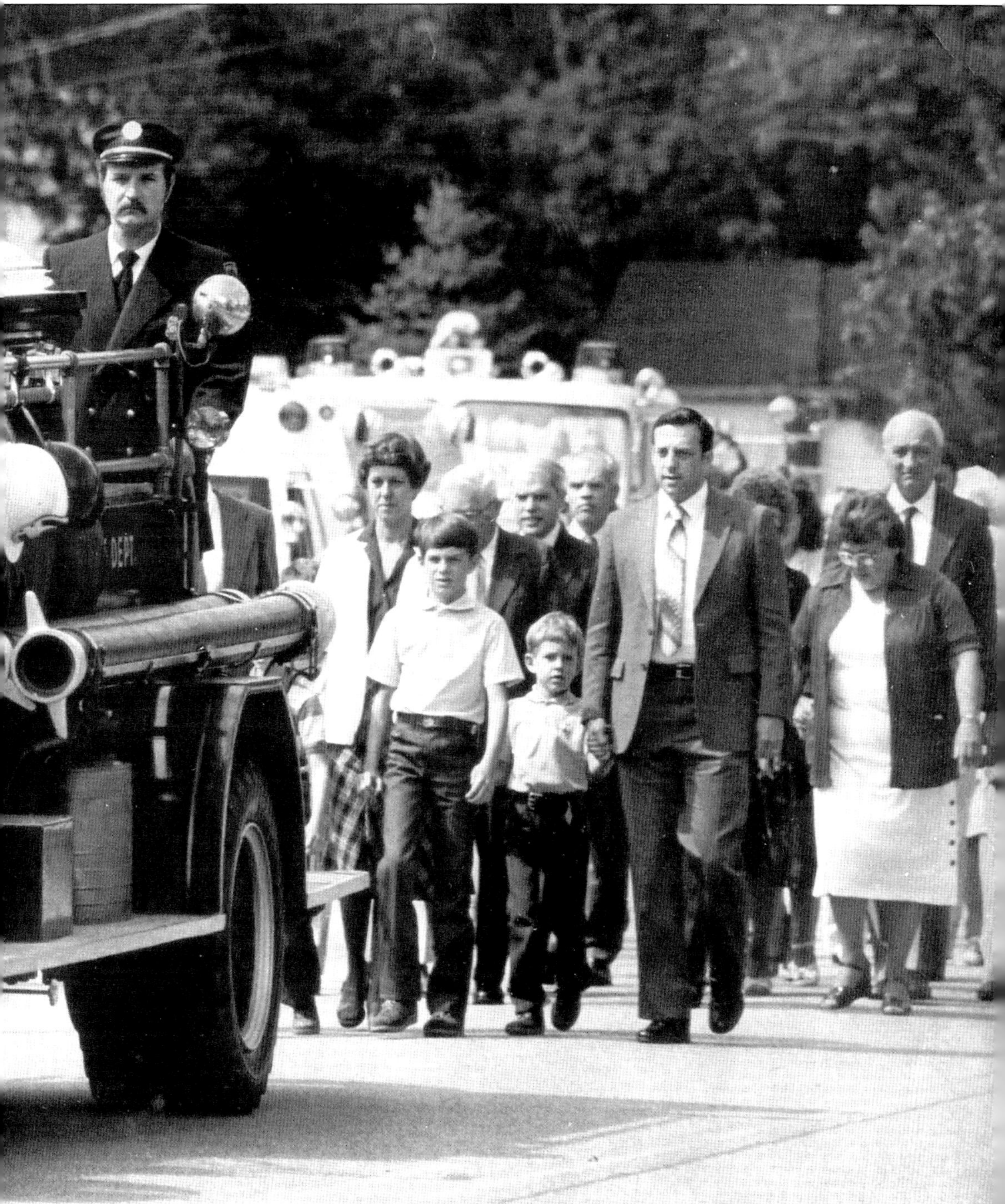

organized the Ridgeville Fire Department. Steinmetz served as fire chief from 1957 to 1971, becoming the department's first full-time chief in 1967. Capt. Eugene Diederich is driving the Buffalo, and seated at his right is then chief Robert Dreger. Firefighter Andy Wagner stands in the rear of the truck. (Courtesy of the North Ridgeville Fire Museum.)

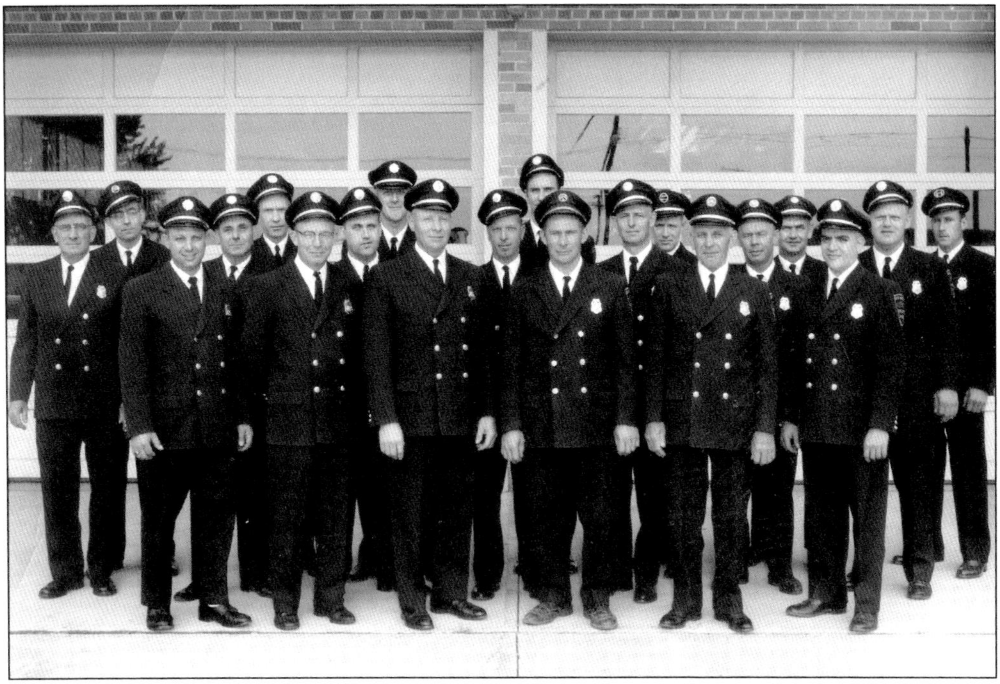

Members of the North Ridgeville Volunteer Fire Department celebrate the department's 25th anniversary. From left to right are (first row) John Campana, Herbert Hales, Joseph Guggenbiller, Assistant Chief Gene Diederich, Chief Ralph Steinmetz, and James Hershey; (second row) James Diederich, Donald Hadaway, Richard Laubenthal, Alfred Krueger, Robert Dreger, Frank Bober, and Richard Capel; (third row) Lt. Robert Gilder, Martin Thibo, Fred Dorow, Robert Impicini, Lt. Robert Taylor, James Smith, and Capt. James Barnes. (Courtesy of the North Ridgeville Fire Museum.)

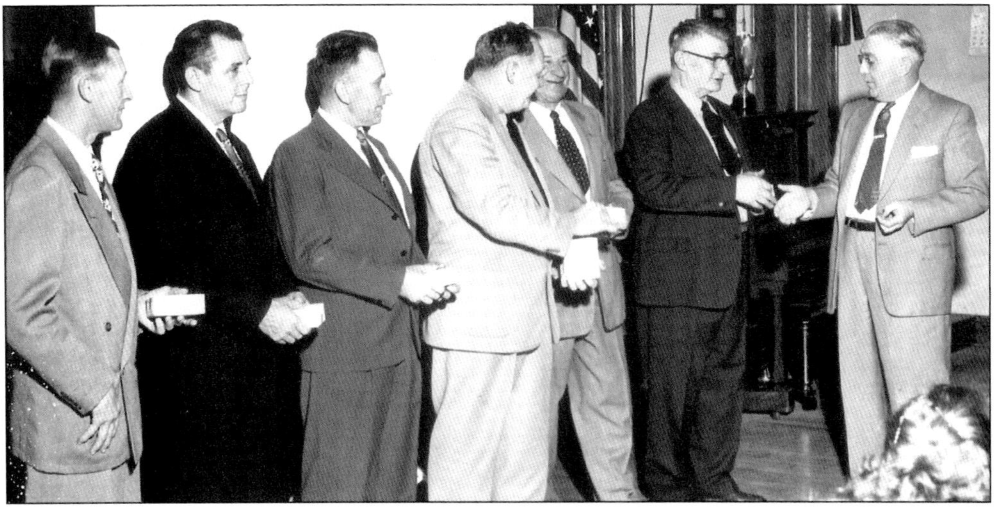

North Ridgeville police chief Emory Hershey presented watches to six members of the Ridgeville Volunteer Fire Department for 25 years of service during the silver jubilee dinner in the Grange hall in 1956. From left to right are Malcolm VanWormer, Don Hadaway, Ralph Steinmetz, Capt. Albert M. Diederich, Assistant Chief Carl Lehman, Chief Louis Hadaway, and Hershey. (Courtesy of the North Ridgeville Fire Museum.)

Ridgeville Township did not have an organized police department until 1958. The first patrolman, Thomas P. Richards, was a lifelong resident of the community. The department did not own a vehicle, and both Hershey and Richards used their private cars while on duty. A citizens committee was formed, and on January 13, 1961, the committee presented the police department with a fully equipped 1961 Chevrolet police cruiser, paid for through donations from residents. From left to right, Mayor Luke Loufman presents keys to the new automobile to Hershey, as William Gardner (center) looks on. Following the presentation of the keys, residents gathered in front of the Old Town Hall to examine the vehicle. (Courtesy of Ron Bauer and the North Ridgeville Police Department.)

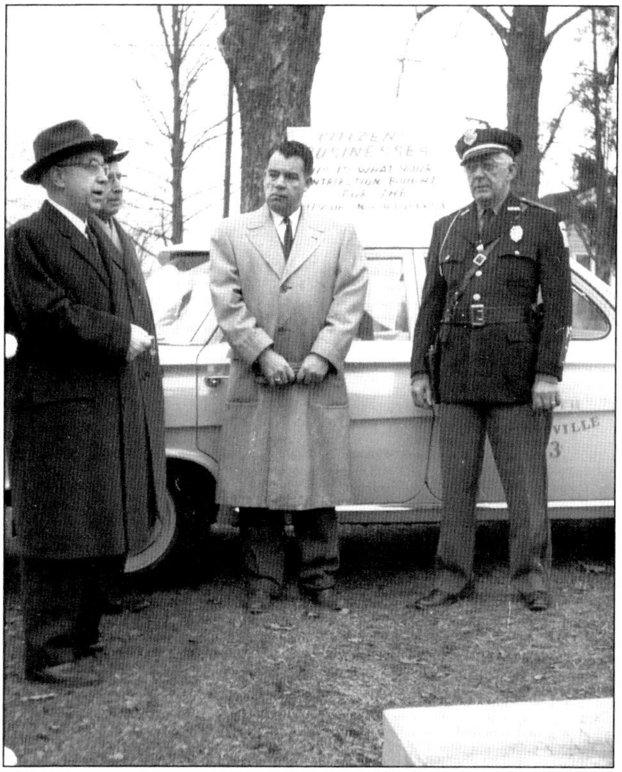

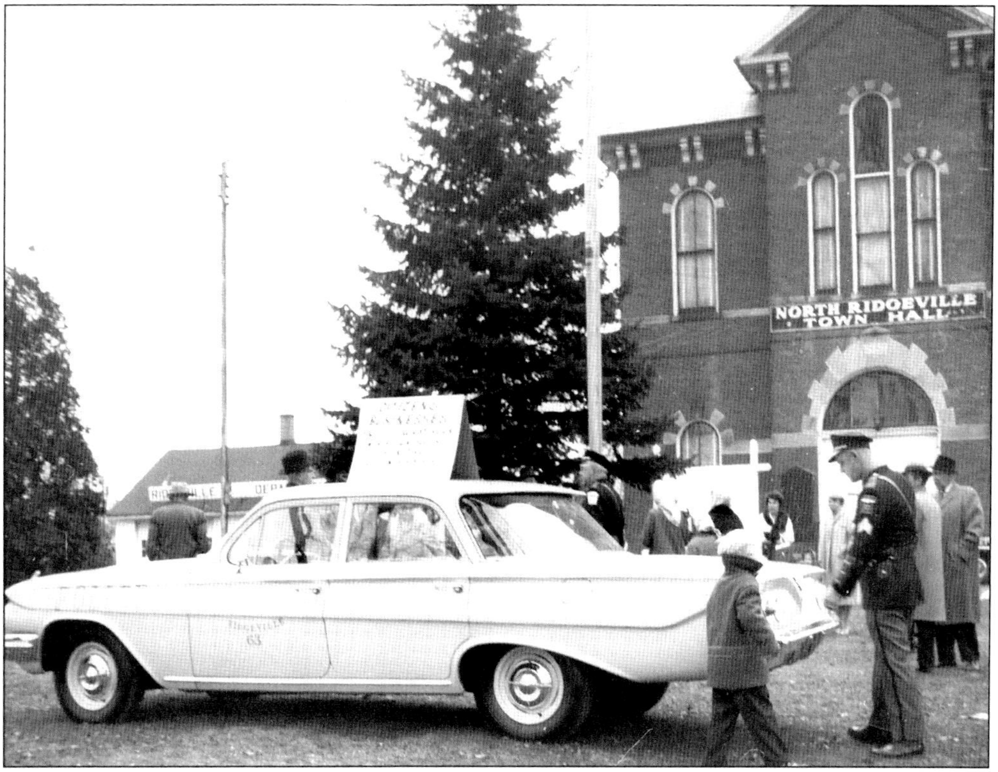

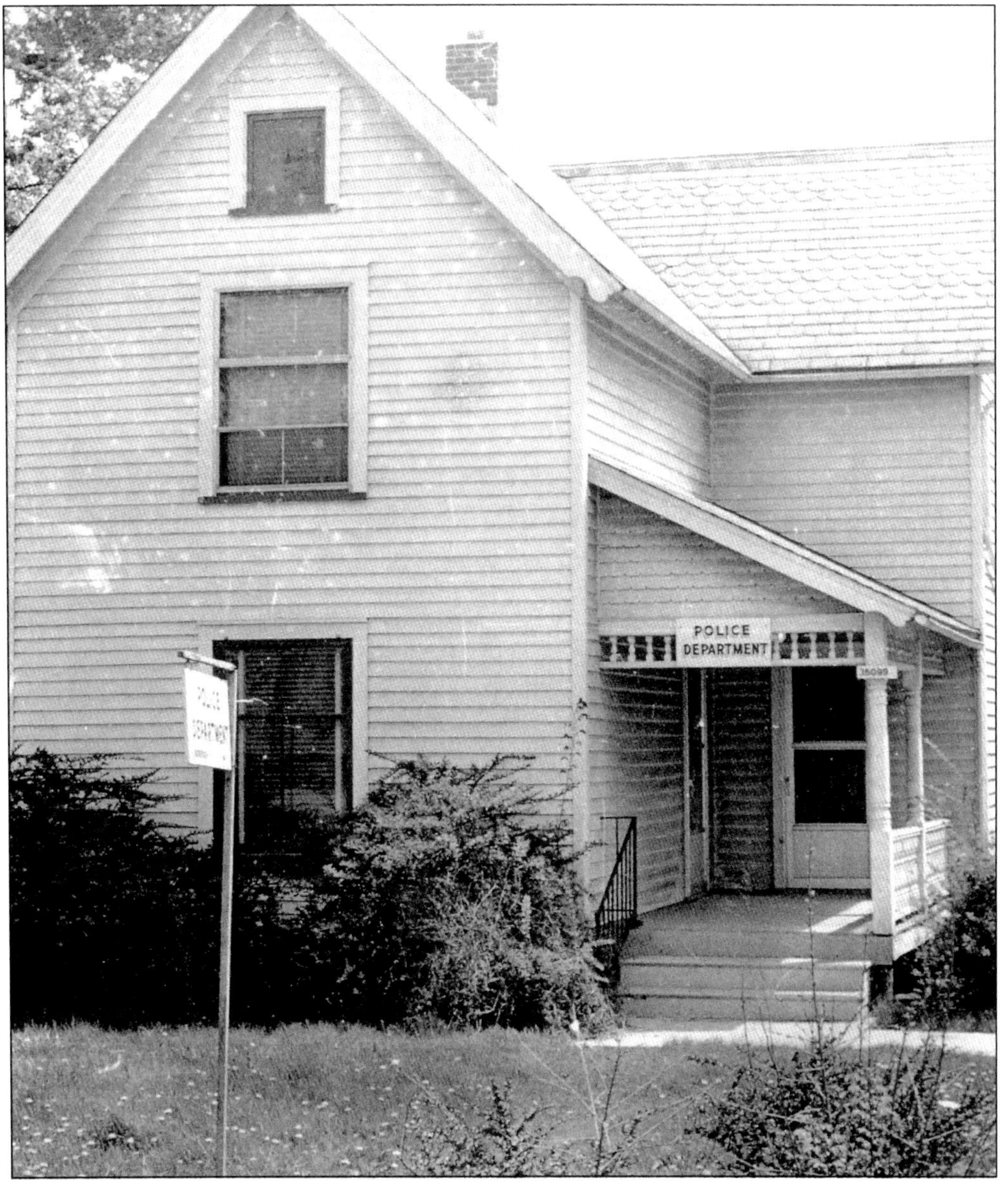

The two-story frame house, known as the Stacey House, stood between Ridgeville's Old Town Hall and what is now Buescher's True Value Hardware Store on the south side of Center Ridge Road. It was used from about 1968 to 1975 as the North Ridgeville Police Station, and it was torn down about 1976. It was the former home of Howard G. and Mabel Stacey, who arrived in Ridgeville about 1920. Howard raised and sold Rhode Island Red chickens in Noble, located east of Cleveland. He was also the justice of the peace in Ridgeville. Mabel served on the Ridgeville School Board as a civil defense worker. Their daughter Florence Stacey Steele was among Ridgeville High School's first graduating class in 1926. (Courtesy of the North Ridgeville Police Department.)

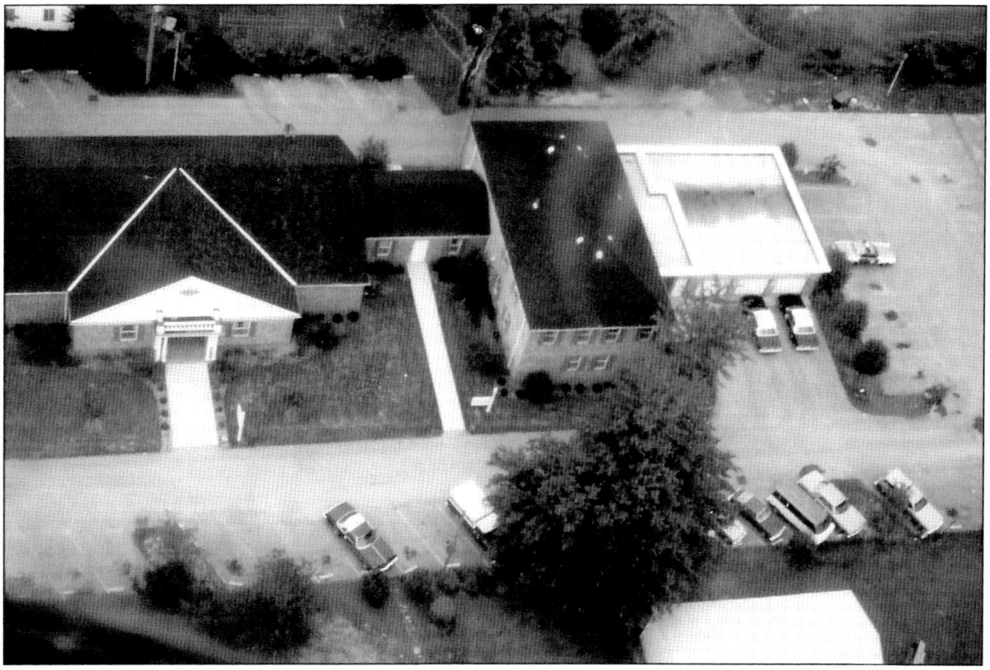

The North Ridgeville Police no longer use an old house as their headquarters. Today the North Ridgeville Police Station is located at the east end of the North Ridgeville City Hall complex on Avon Belden Road, as shown in the aerial photograph above. It is a two-story structure with administrative offices on the second floor, along with a training room. The dispatcher's office is on the first floor, and the public can access one by means of a telephone. The sally port and jail cells are also located on the first floor adjacent to the dispatch and clerical offices. The photograph below is a close-up view of the police station and is a definite contrast to the former days. (Courtesy of the North Ridgeville Police Department.)

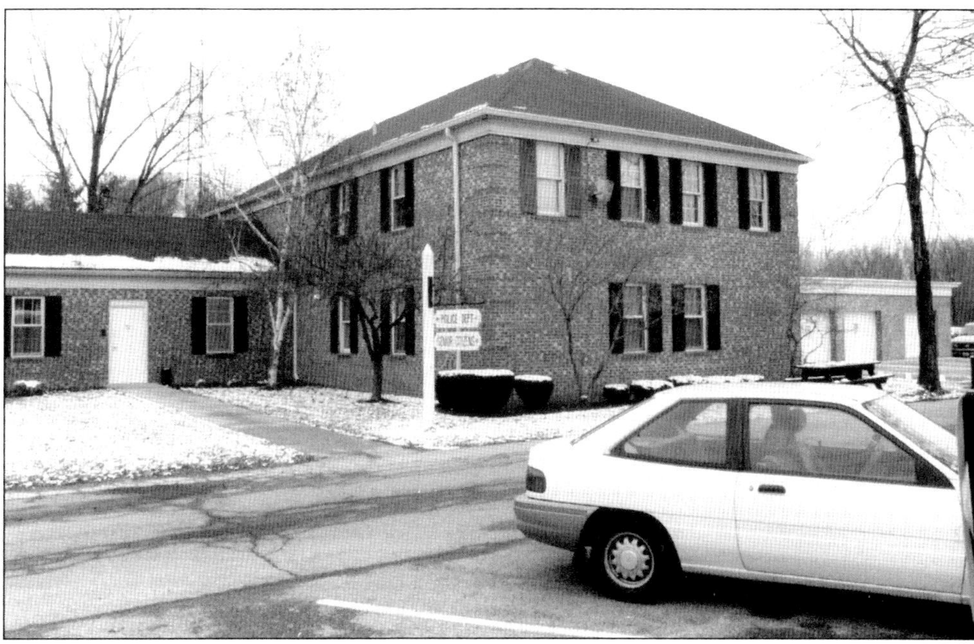

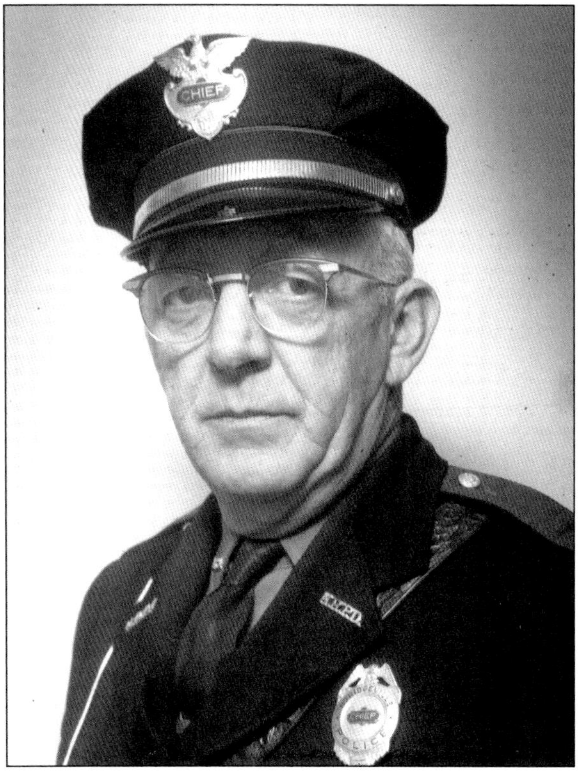

Emory Hershey, born in 1910, was the first chief of police when North Ridgeville became a city in 1960. He was employed for 37 years at the Ridge Tool Company in North Ridgeville and Elyria, and he was a Ridgeville volunteer fireman for 17 years. In 1945, he began serving 15 years as constable for Ridgeville Township and the Village of North Ridgeville. After becoming police chief, he continued serving part-time until 1966. Hershey and his wife, Ethel, had three children and belonged to the First Congregational United Church of Christ. Hershey died in 1988 at the age of 78. (Courtesy of the North Ridgeville Fire Museum.)

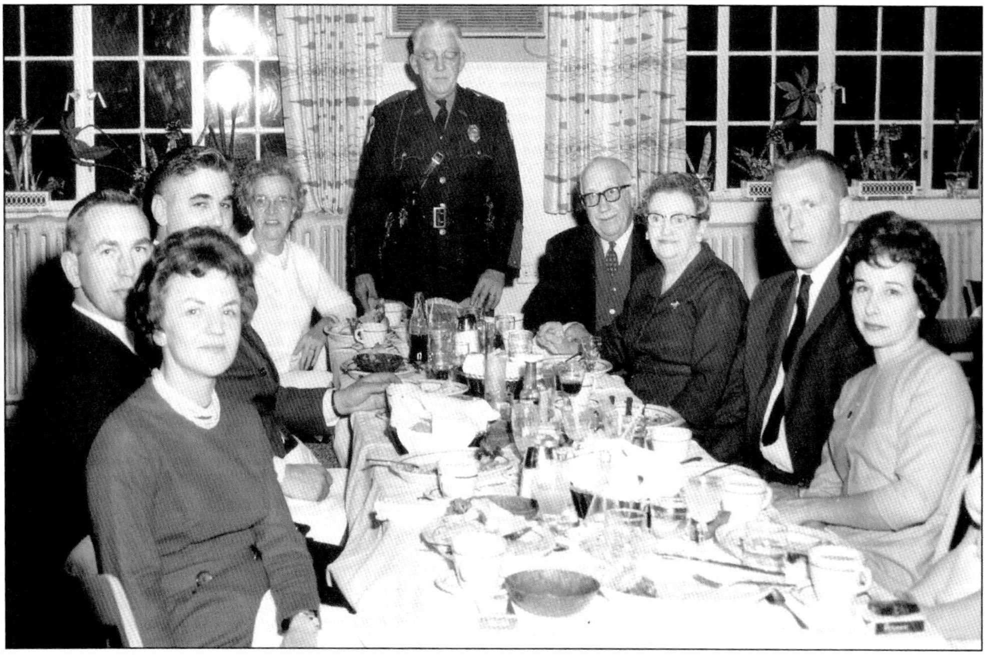

Hershey addresses a group of city officials and their wives during a dinner at Eddy's Chalet in the 1960s. Pictured from left to right are Jean and Harvey Jarvis, Steve Yonkof, Ethel Hershey, Hershey, Mayor Luke Loufman, Lena Loufman, Jerry Hansen, and Val Hansen. (Courtesy of Ron Bauer.)

Sgt. Thomas Richards was called to Big Town Super Mart to investigate a burglary on March 7, 1961. Empty boxes that contained watches and radios can be seen behind the counter. Richards was hired as the city's first patrolman in 1959 and became a sergeant in 1960 and captain in 1965. He was promoted to chief on January 1, 1966, and held the position until June 2, 1970. (Courtesy of Ron Bauer.)

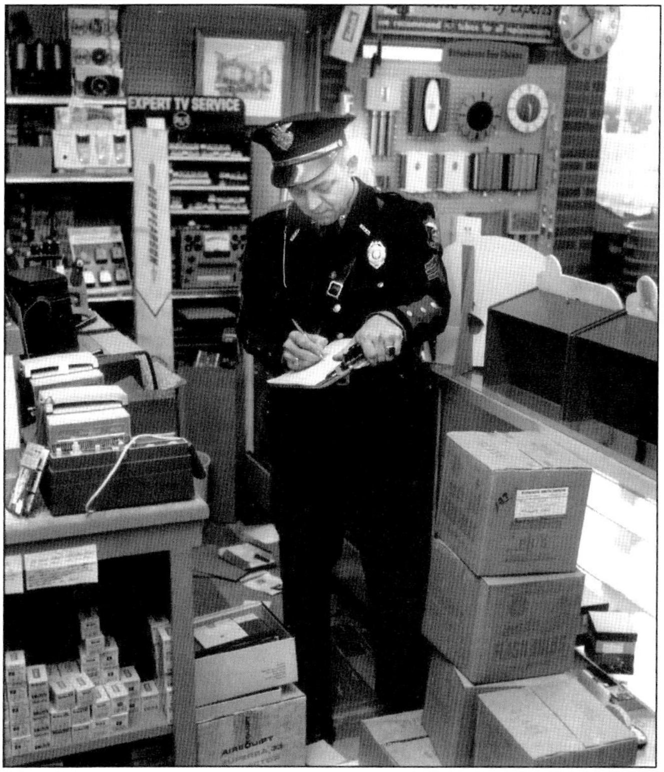

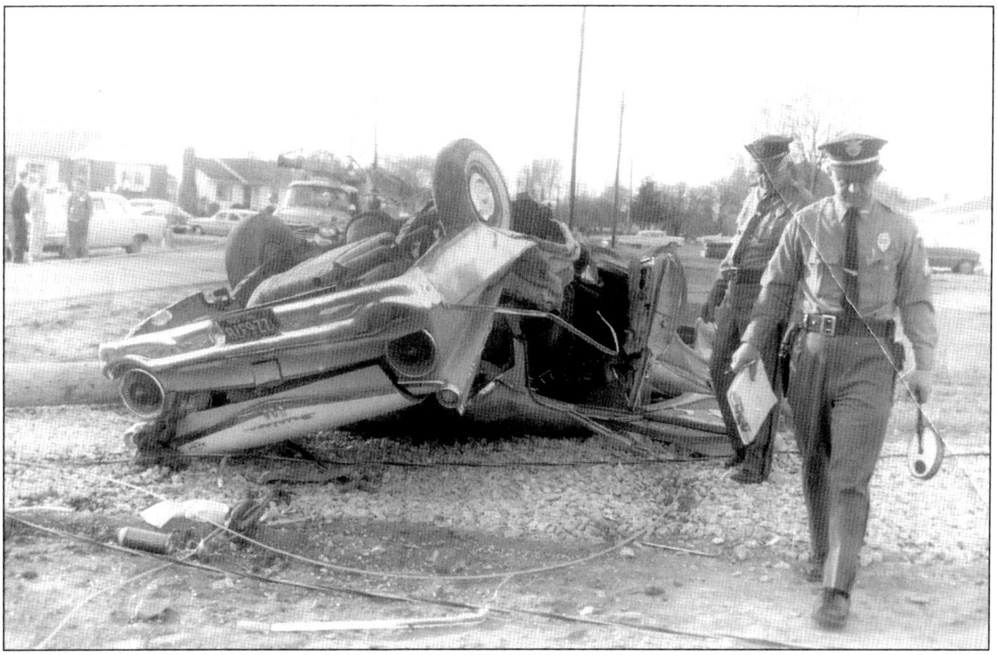

Hershey and Richards investigate an accident on April 25, 1963, when an out-of-control car broke a utility pole on Root Road. Ambulance driver Maynard Hintz was electrocuted by contact with high-voltage wires while on duty serving the city of North Ridgeville. A plaque in his honor hangs in the North Ridgeville Fire Museum. (Courtesy of the North Ridgeville Fire Museum.)

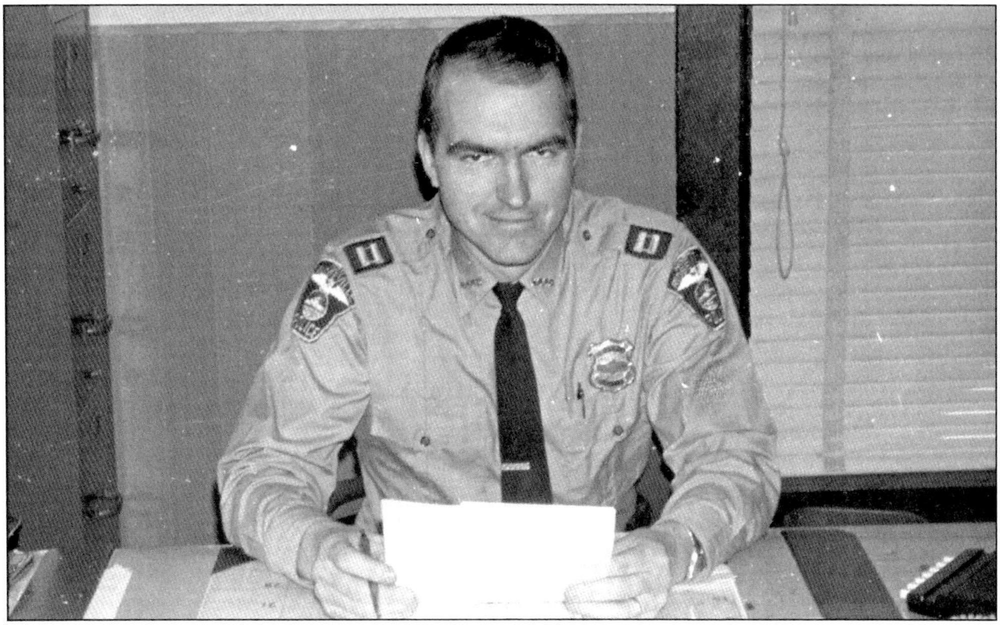

In this late-1960s photograph, Thomas Sigsworth was a captain with the North Ridgeville Police Department. In 1970, he was named acting police chief when Thomas P. Richards resigned the position. Sigsworth was sworn in as chief on September 22, 1970, and served until 1987 when Richard Kreps succeeded him. Sigsworth joined the force in 1964 but served on the auxiliary force from 1960 to 1964. (Courtesy of the North Ridgeville Police Department.)

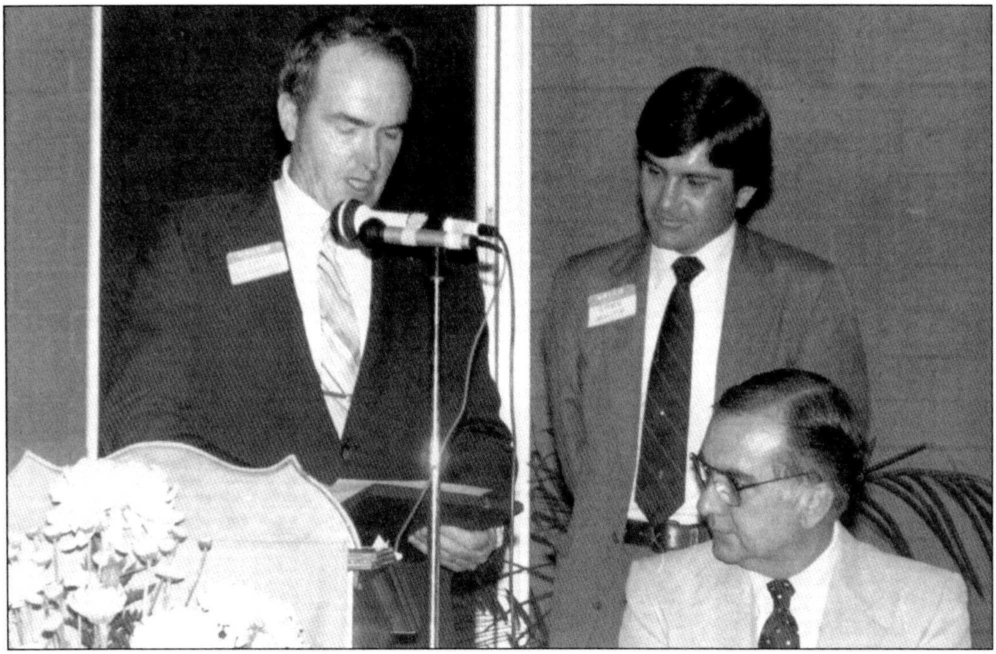

Sigsworth presents a plaque of appreciation to Gregory White in this 1970s photograph. At the time, White was the Lorain County prosecutor, a position he held for 22 years. In 1995, White was honored as the outstanding prosecutor of the year. The other man is unidentified. (Courtesy of the North Ridgeville Police Department.)

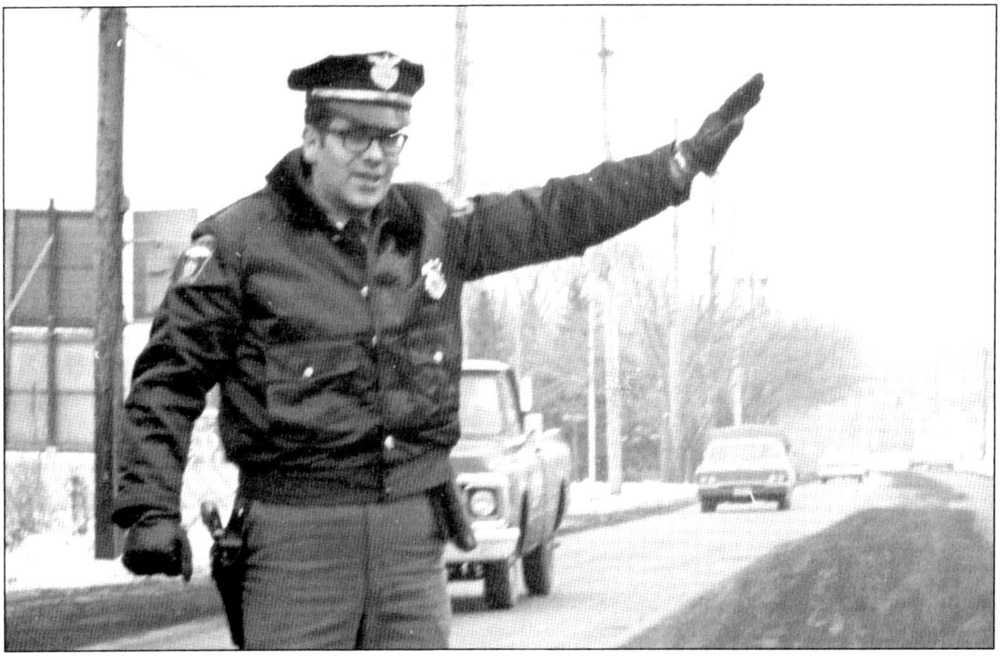

North Ridgeville Police patrolman Andy Grega directs traffic on Center Ridge Road in 1969. The police often had traffic detail at that location in front of St. Peter Parish, particularly during times when church services concluded and many automobiles exited the church parking lot. (Courtesy of the North Ridgeville Police Department.)

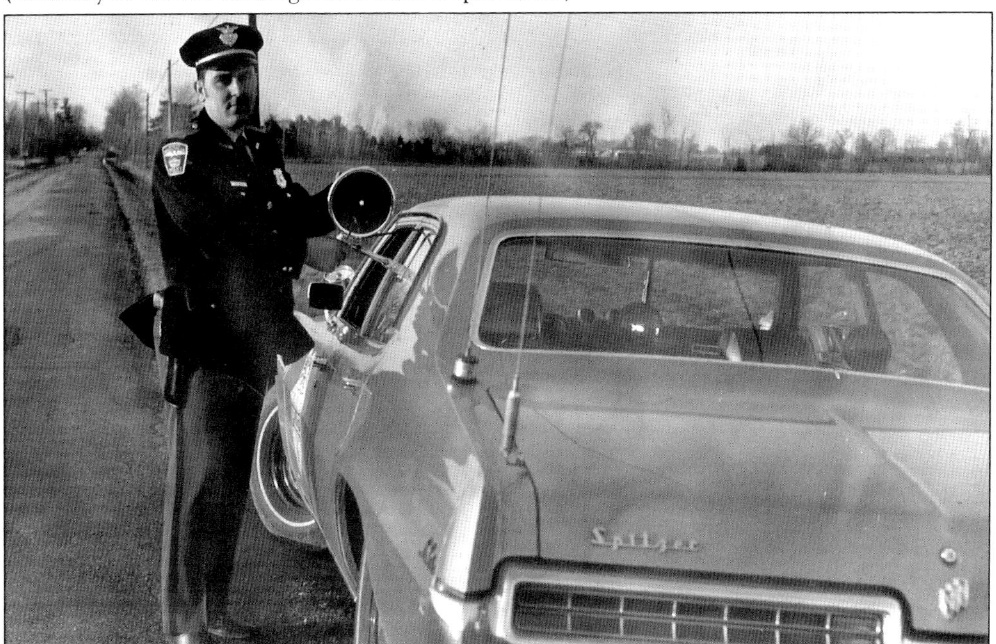

As the North Ridgeville Police Department grew, the city purchased additional equipment to aid the officers in their jobs. Officer George Binzer shows a new radar unit that was designed to help investigate situations that arose while North Ridgeville police officers were on the job. (Courtesy of the North Ridgeville Police Department.)

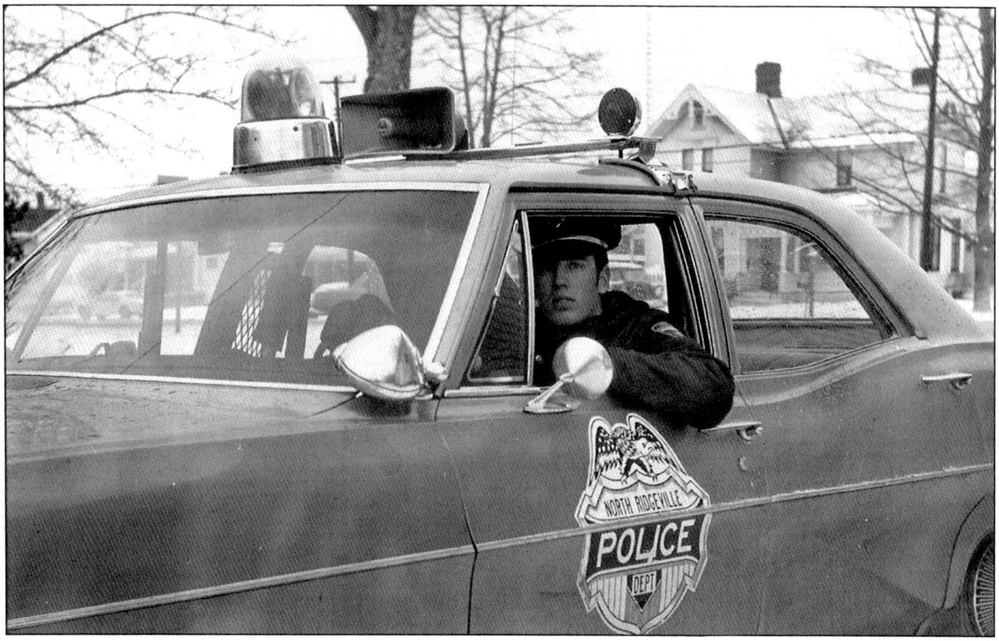

In his early days on the police department, Ron Bauer spent time patrolling the streets of North Ridgeville during his workday in order to help keep residents safe. In this photograph, the young patrolman is seen in one of the department's 1967 cruisers. Bauer was a member of the police department for 33 years and the chief of police from 1989 to 2001. (Courtesy of the North Ridgeville Police Department.)

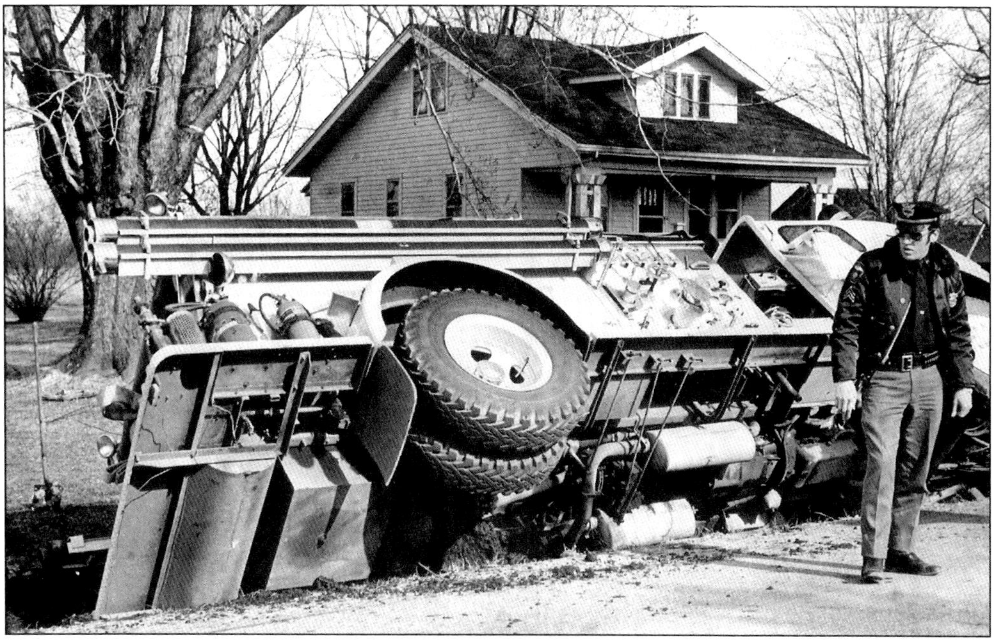

Bauer investigates an accident on Root Road in the 1970s, where a fire truck was turned over into a ditch. Members of the North Ridgeville Fire Department were putting a fire hydrant into the truck when the load apparently shifted, causing the mishap. There were no injuries. (Courtesy of the North Ridgeville Fire Museum.)

Four

Reading and Writing

Despite the hardships the pioneers from Waterbury, Connecticut, endured as they traveled to the Western Reserve, they realized the need for their children's education, and in 1812, they built a schoolhouse from logs. It was a simple construction with simple seats; however, there were no desks. The building burned down three years later, and the community divided into two school districts, one at the east end of town and the other at the west end. A schoolhouse was built in the center of town, and eventually the town had 10 school districts, although there were not enough buildings for each district. The first teacher was Lydia Terrell, who began teaching in the summer of 1814; however, she died before she was able to finish the term. The District No. 3 school was established on the south side of Center Ridge Road between Race and Case Roads. Most of the early schools were log cabins, which later were replaced by brick schoolhouses; however, the Snow Road schoolhouse was a frame building constructed on what is now called Jaycox Road. In 1880, the school was moved farther north on Snow Road and to the opposite side of the street. The one-room schoolhouse now belongs to the North Ridgeville Historical Society. It has been renovated and is open to the public at scheduled times during the spring and summer.

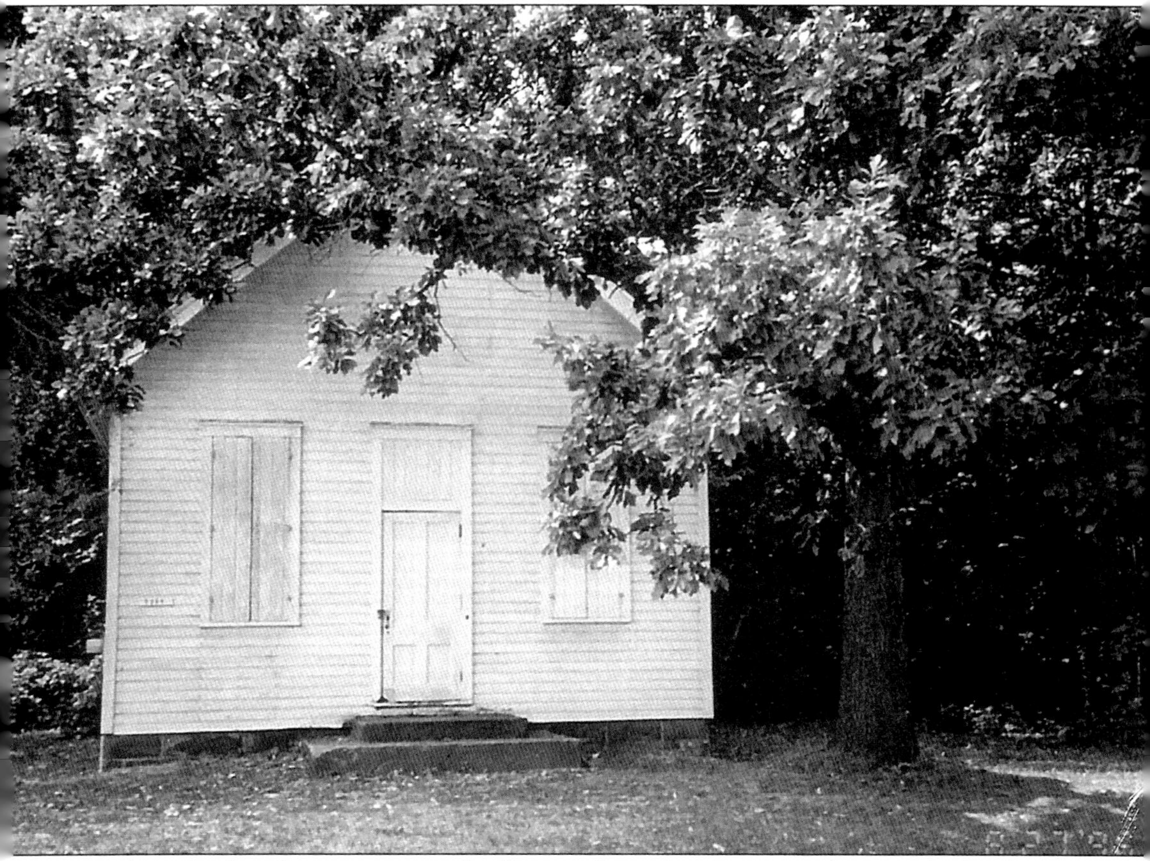

The 1859 white frame one-room schoolhouse is located on Jaycox Road just south of Mills Road, the dividing line between North Ridgeville and Avon. The school was once known as the Snow Road School (the former name of Jaycox Road), and for 65 years, it served as the Ridgeville Township Joint Sub-District No. 9 school. Around 1880, the school was moved from the east side of the road to the west side. Children attended the school from 1859 to 1924, when most of the 10 district schools were abandoned. The school was donated to the North Ridgeville Historical Society in 1988 by the Sullivan family.

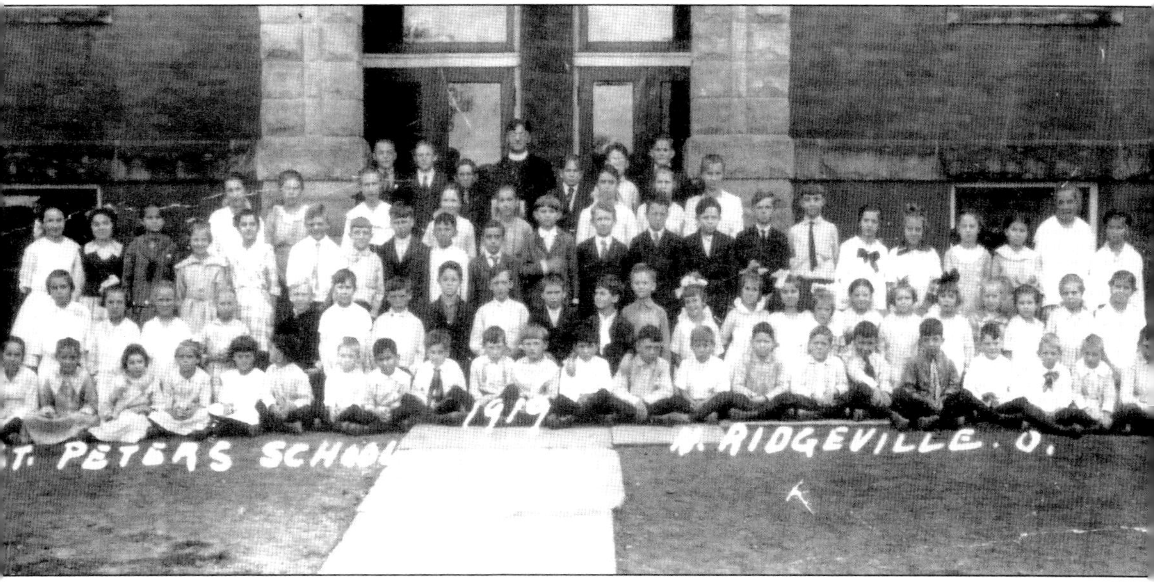

St. Peter School students are pictured in this 1919 photograph. From left to right are (first row) Juliana Diederich, Bertha Gerhart, Geraldine Juchem, Gertrude Snyder, Eleanor Kalter, unidentified, Harold Laubenthal, Leonard Diederich, Leroy Horwedel, Ralph Maringer, Wilbur Kalter, H. Loescher, Arnold Schuster, Irvin Zacharias, Oswald Alflen, Fred Snider, Roderich Gehring, Bernard Gilgenbach, Al Rothgery, ? Thome, Sylvester Scheider, and Walter Maringer; (second row) Rosella Snyder, unidentified, Josephine Fisher, Alta Fisher, ? Gibbons, Art Gerhart, Harold Diederich, Joe Alflen, Adelbert Schuster, Frank Weishirt, Robert Yunklas, Otto Laubenthal, Mildred Yunklas, unidentified, ? Meecha, unidentified, ? Juchem, unidentified, Luella Gilgenbach, Helen Gilbert, Coletta Diederich, Loretta Snyder, and Laurice Diederich; (third row) ? Slauf, ? Alflen, ? Justin, ? Kalter, Rosemary Snyder, ? Maringer, ? Gilgenbach, unidentified, Albert Horwedel, Ray Meecha, Julius Schneider, Marvin Gehring, Owen Laubenthal, Herbert Meyers, Elmer ?, Coletta ?, ? Zacharias, Rose Rothgery, Martin Diederich, Laura Maringer, and Genevieve ?; (fourth row) Verena Diederich, Pearl Maringer, Aurelia Pitts, ? Kalter, ? Snyder, ? Barnes, ? Beslick, and Hilda Myers; (fifth row) Ed Blaser, Al Smith, Ed Krejic, the Reverend Joseph Trapp, ? Waldecker, ? Rothgery, and Al Waldecker.

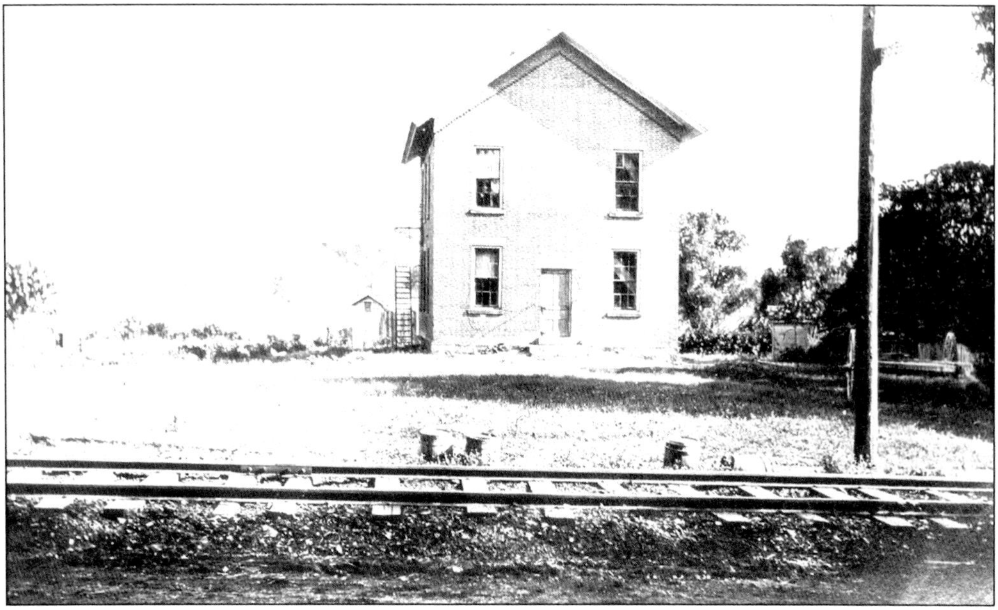

The two-room brick school was built in 1869 on the south side of Center Ridge Road east of Avon Belden Road, then called Center or Station Road. It was one of the successors to the first log school, which stood across the street from 1812 until it burned in 1817. District No. 1 school was one of 10 district schools that taught first through eighth grades in Ridgeville Township during the 1923 to 1924 school year.

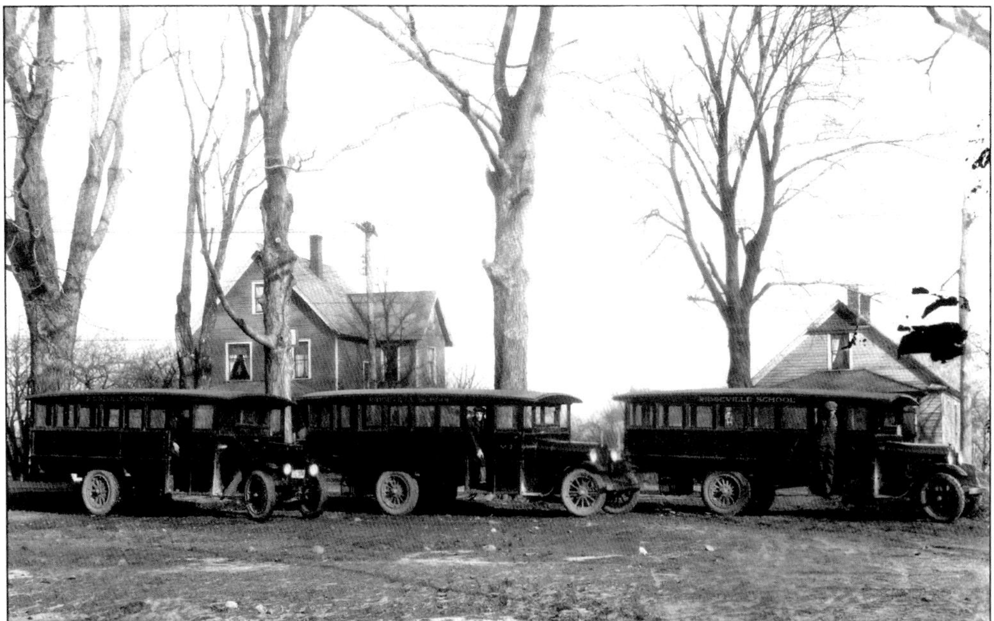

These vehicles were Ridgeville Township's entire fleet of school buses and parked along Center Ridge Road in front of the new high school, now the middle school, in the mid-1920s. Two of the three drivers pictured are Asa Taft and Malcolm Van Wormer. Prior to 1924, the closest high school was in the neighboring city of Elyria.

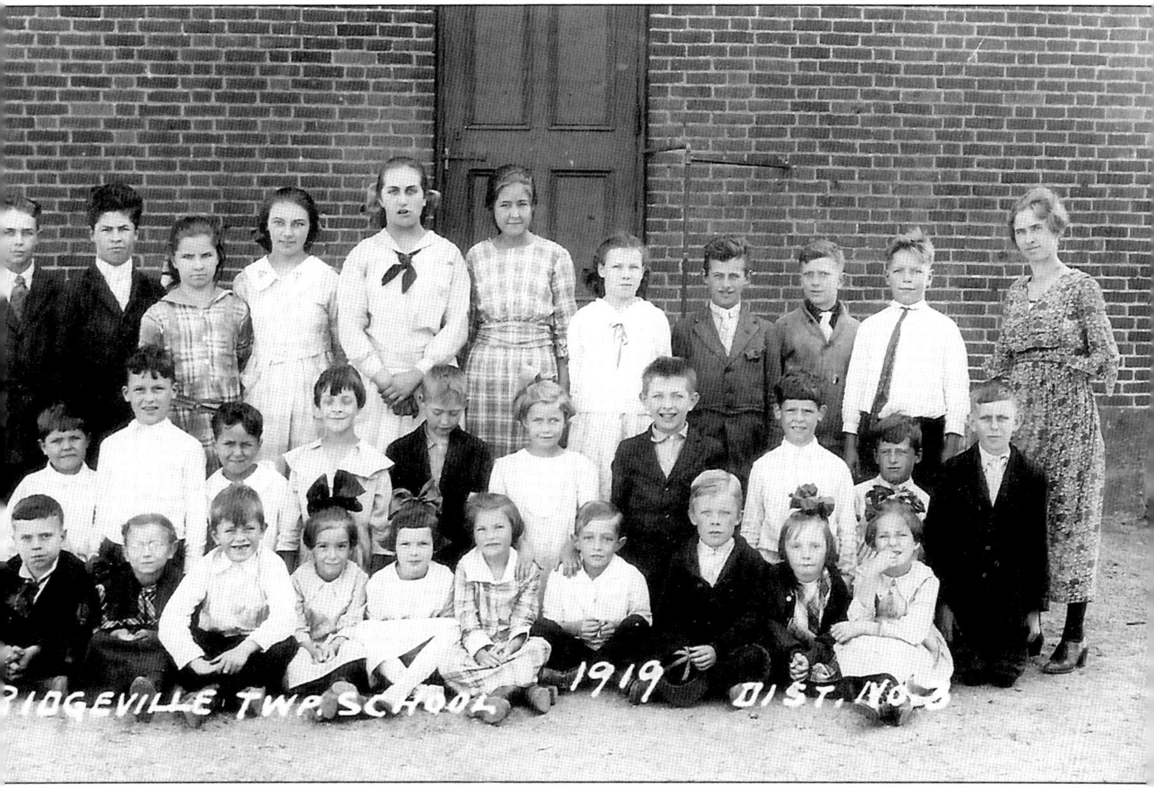

These 30 students, along with their teacher, Celia Myers, were photographed in 1919 in front of the District No. 3 one-room school on the south side of Center Ridge Road between Race Road and the present site of the R. W. Beckett Corporation. The building, known as the West End School, was built in 1868 on land purchased from Bradford Race for $30. It was one of the 10 district schools that once taught first through eighth grades in Ridgeville Township. It is now used as a private home. From left to right are (first row) unidentified, Elwood Thomas, unidentified, Barbara Kirsch (Finegan), Virginia Schmittgen, Lillian Hadaway, unidentified, James Ely, Mary Ely (Lyons), and unidentified; (second row) unidentified, Willard Schmittgen, Walter Diederich, Ethel Jamison (Hershey), unidentified, Rose Marshall, Melvin Haag, Richard Schmittgen, Harry Salisbury, and unidentified; (third row) Milton Taft, Walter Freeman, Thelma Freeman, Ivy Hadaway, Lucille Diederich, unidentified, Nellie Taft, John Salisbury, unidentified, unidentified, and Myers.

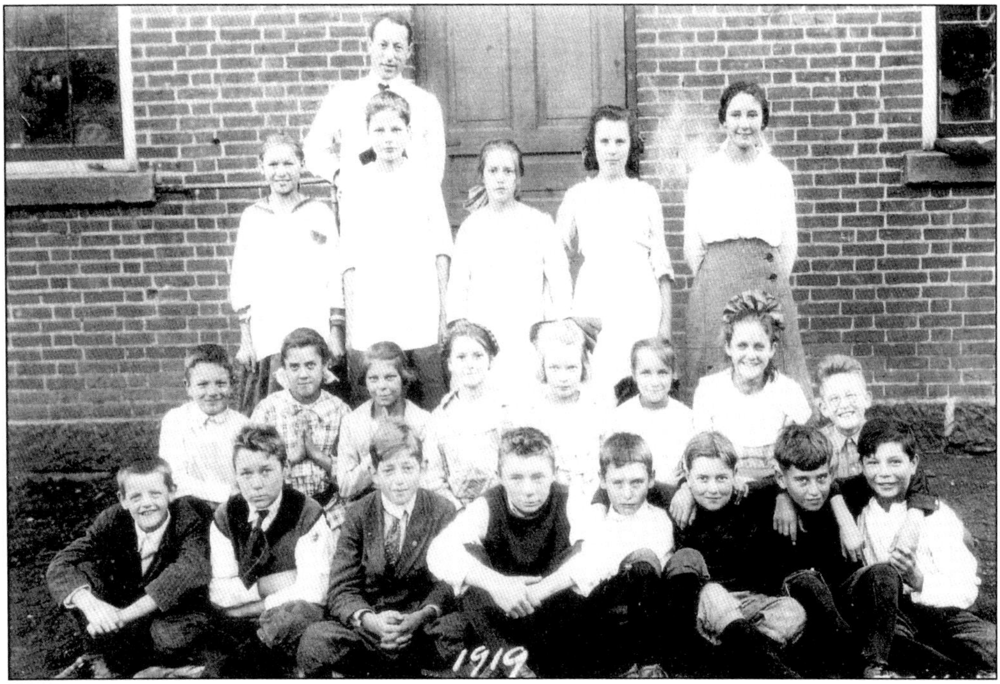

The unidentified boys and girls in this 1919 photograph were from the fifth and sixth grades in the Center Ridge District No. 1 school, which can be seen in the background. The two-story brick school was located about where the parking lot behind St. Peter's Parish is now.

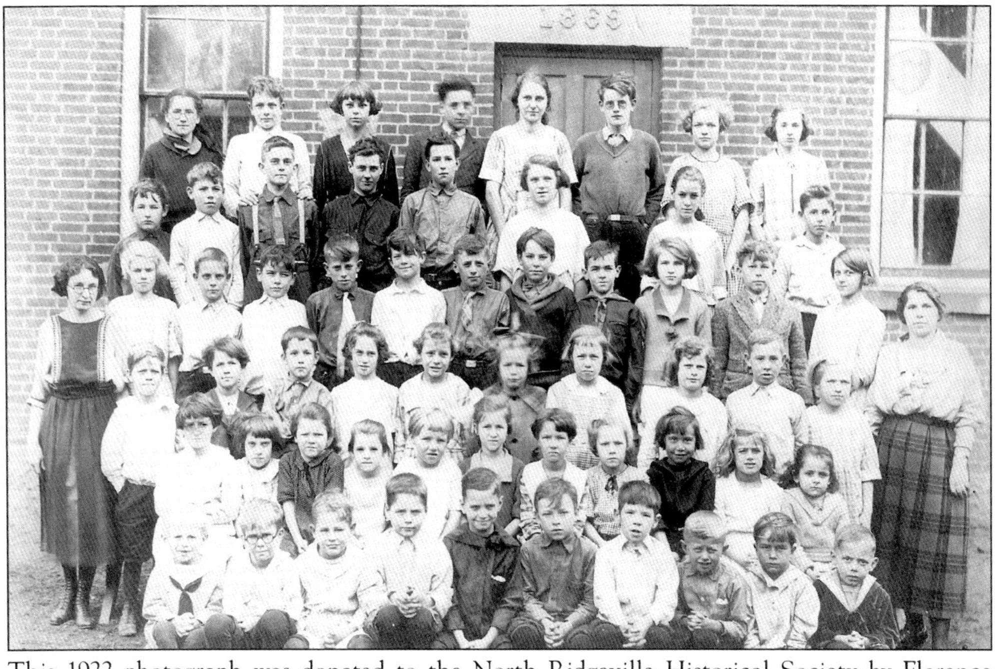

This 1922 photograph was donated to the North Ridgeville Historical Society by Florence Stacey Steele. These students were in the eighth grade at the District No. 1 school, which was located near the center of town. The date 1869 can be seen above the doorway. Steele is second from the right in the sixth row. The others are unidentified.

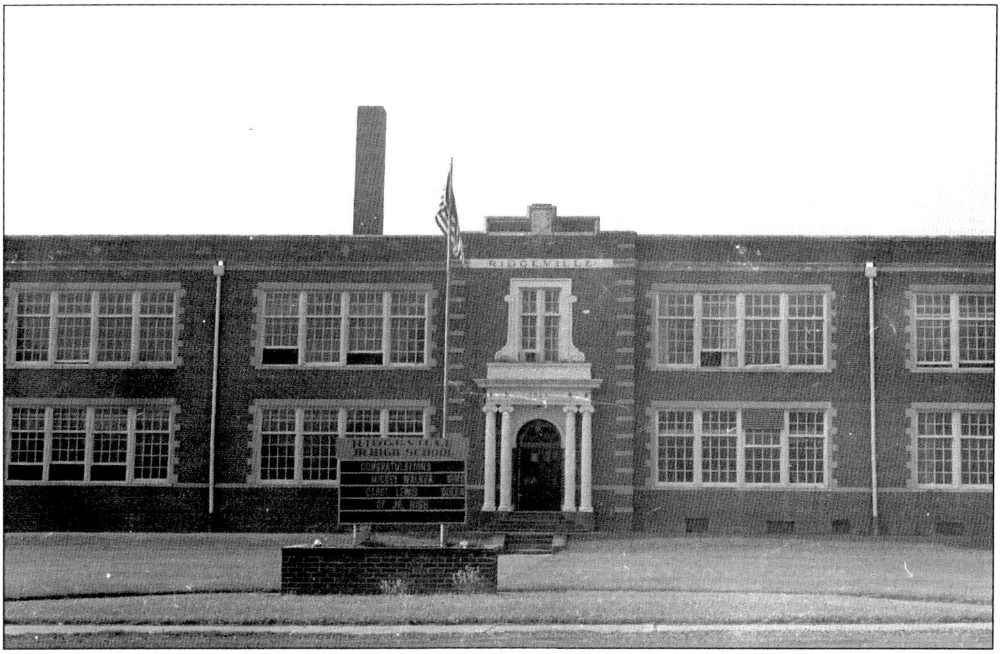

Ridgeville High School on Center Ridge Road was built in 1923 and 1924 and housed all 12 grades. It opened in the fall of 1924 with the first class of seniors graduating on May 25, 1926, in the high school auditorium. Frank A. Redmond was the superintendent at the time, and the school board members, whose first names are mostly unknown, were Hadaway, president; Knowles, clerk; Roth; Sweet; Mathias Myers; and Diederick. The building was expanded in 1928, 1952, and in 1969. In 1970, a brickwork mosaic depicting the *Apollo XI* moon landing was added to the front of the school. The building is presently used as a middle school. The Ridgeville High School class of 1926 held its 25th reunion on June 4, 1951.

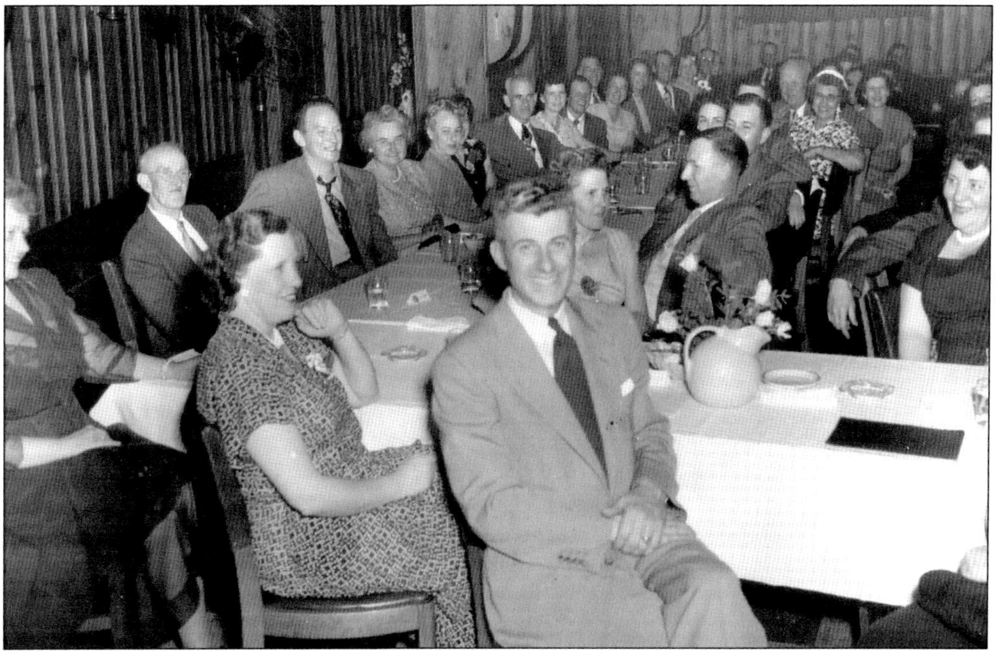

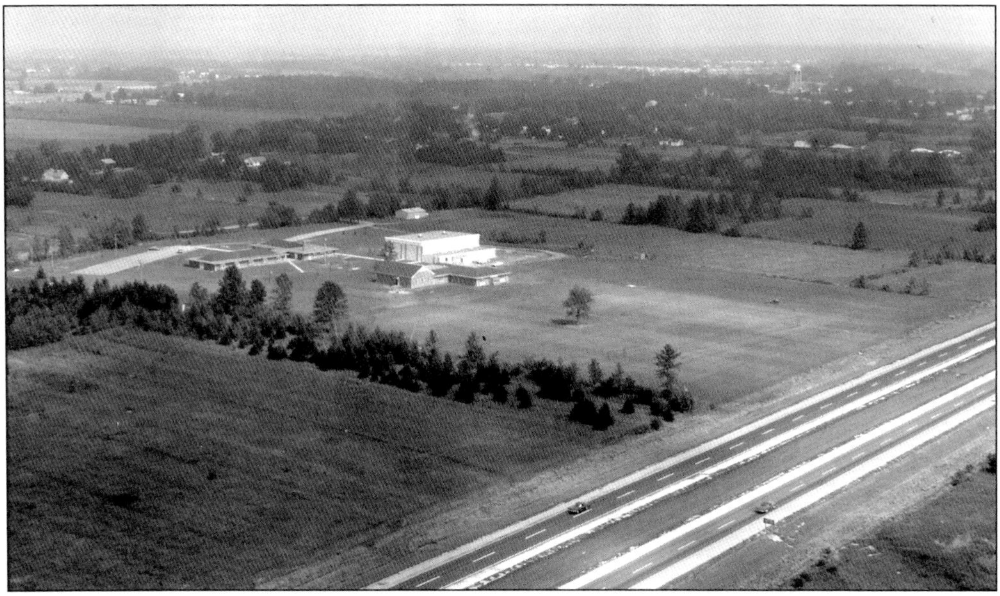

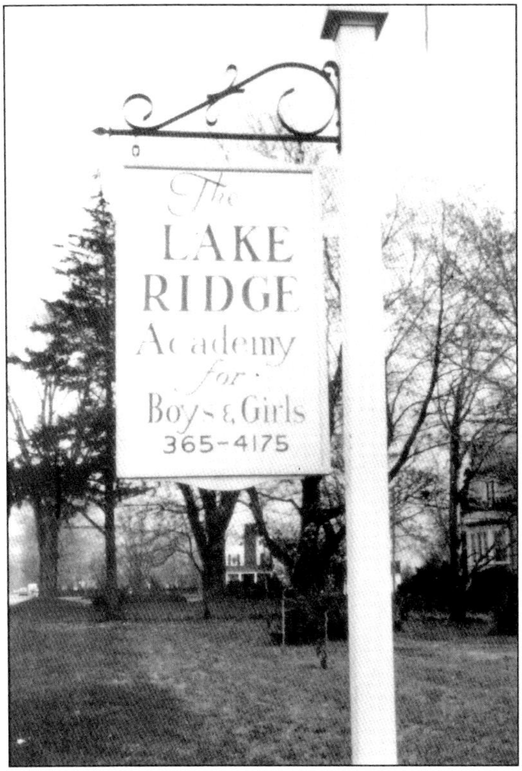

This is an aerial view of Lake Ridge Academy, which is situated off Center Ridge Road. The academy was founded in 1963 at LaPorte. The first year's classes were held at the LaPorte Methodist Church. It is the only independent school on the west side of the Greater Cleveland area. It started with an initial 25 acres followed by an additional 19. The campus presently is on a total of 88 acres. The first headmaster was Wilfred J. Hemmer. The academy opened the lower school building in 1965 followed by the upper school and gymnasium. It continued to develop and grow and now has a middle school, offices, a fine arts building, and the Bettcher Convocation Center. (Courtesy of Lake Ridge Academy.)

Five

Getting from Here to There

When the settlers from Waterbury, Connecticut, made their way to Ohio, they did so with the help of horses. Some of the original 17 pioneers rode on the backs of the animals across the terrain, and others harnessed their horses to wooden wagons in hopes that the creatures would be able make it to their new home. For quite some time, horses continued to be the means of transportation, whether ridden or tethered to carts or carriages, while teams of oxen were used to carry heavier loads. For short trips to visit friends or relatives, walking was often a method of choice. For longer journeys, there were stagecoach lines with inns along the way, offering food and a place to rest. In the mid-1800s, a small community of German, English, and Irish settlers developed near the railroad tracks on Avon Belden Road and became known as Shawville. In 1895, the Cleveland, Berea and Elyria Street Railroad offered rides from Cleveland to Elyria. The railroad, known as the Green Line interurban, developed an even faster ride with the advent of the electric cars. Coming from Cleveland, the cars traveled along Lorain Road until just about a quarter mile west of Barton Road and then curved to the north until eventually reaching Center Ridge Road, where the tracks followed the south side and into Elyria.

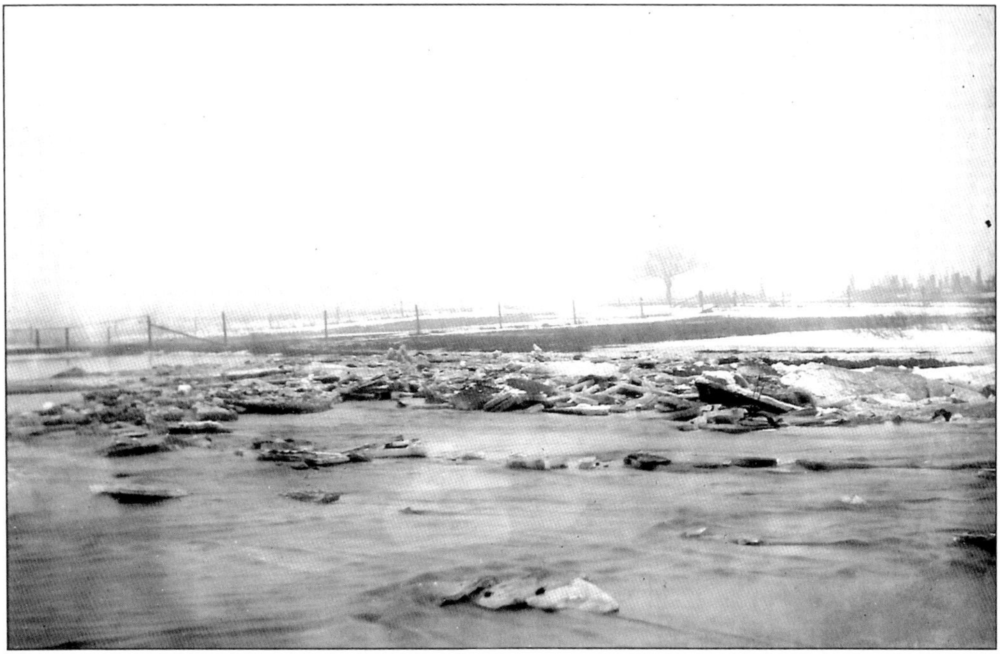

In the winter, the snowdrifts sometimes were so high that it was difficult to walk or ride. But in the spring and summer, it often rained so hard that the creeks in North Ridgeville swelled and sometimes overflowed their banks. This 1913 photograph shows the heavy flooding that caused the bridge at St. Peter Cemetery to collapse.

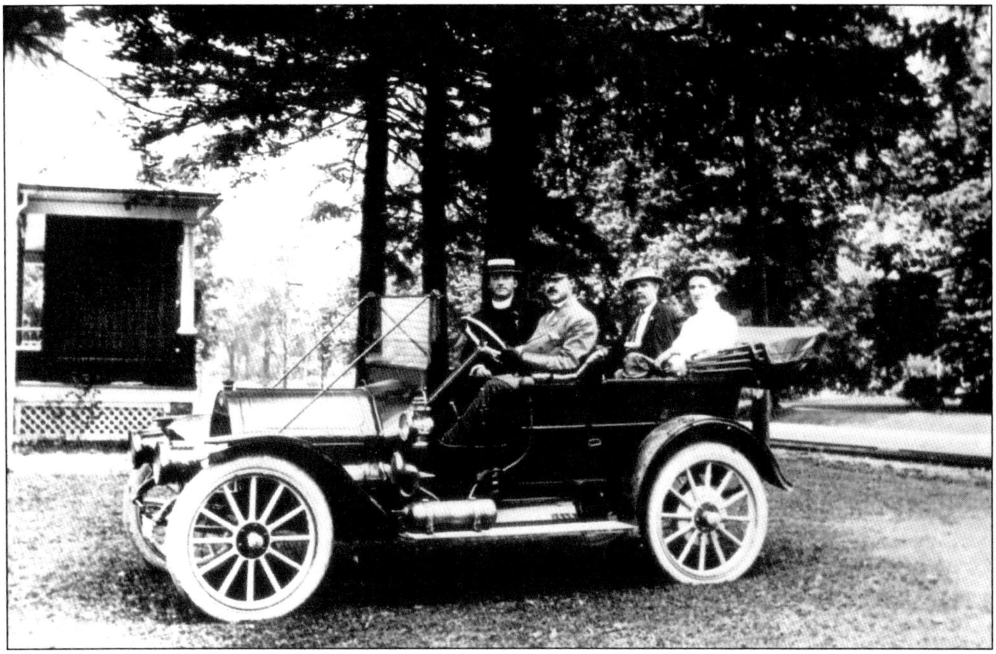

The Reverend Joseph Trapp, pastor of St. Peter Parish, and some unidentified friends go for a ride in an automobile in the early 1900s. It must have been a very warm day in the summer because, as is seen in the photograph, they chose to enjoy their ride around the town with the top down.

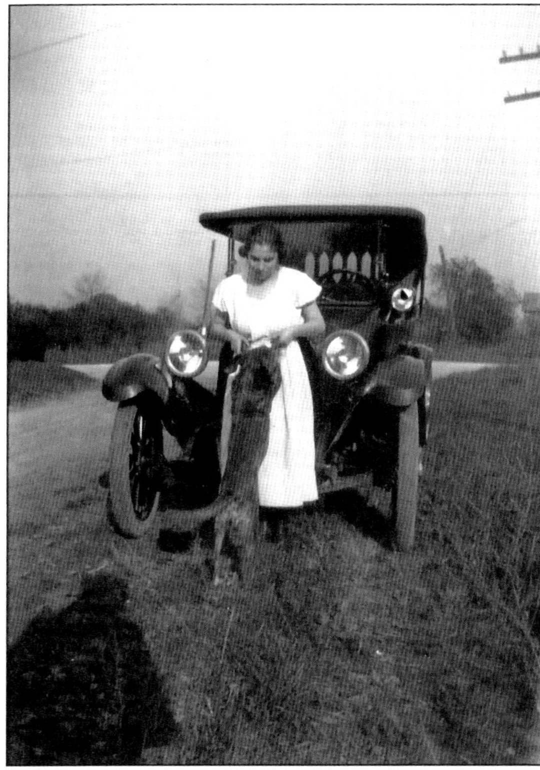

Mildred Worcester, at about age 16, is shown playing with a dog in front of her brother's sporty touring automobile around 1917. She is pictured in front of the home of her parents, John and Minnie Worcester, near the intersection of Chestnut Ridge and Root Roads, which were both dirt roads at the time. At one time, their house was owned by the Dicksons, and the area near the Root Road railroad crossing was known as Dickson's Crossing. Mildred later married Glenn Stranahan. She died in 1961. (Courtesy of Jeff Sigsworth.)

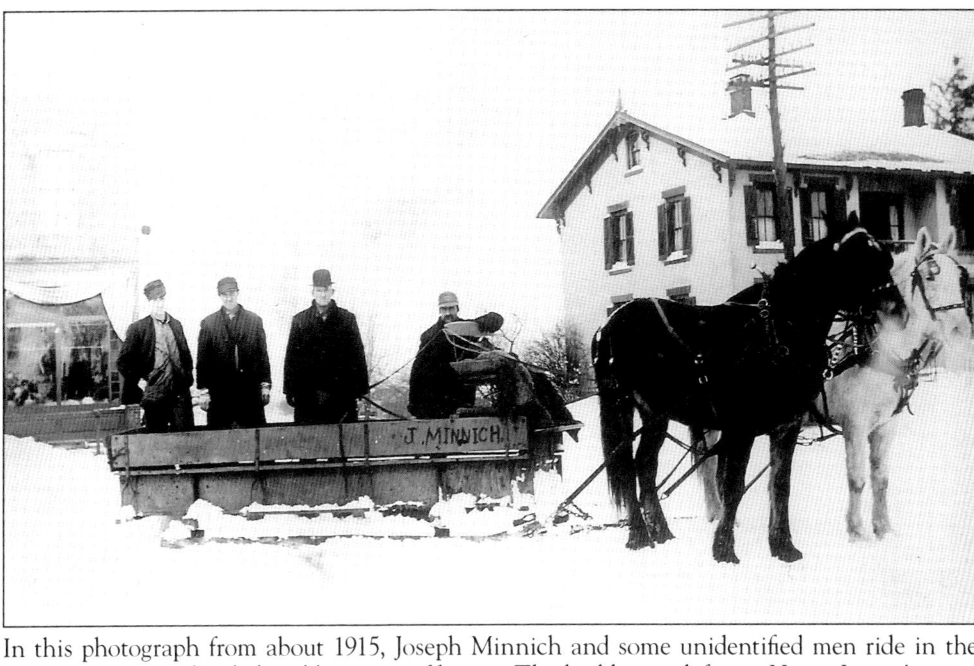

In this photograph from about 1915, Joseph Minnich and some unidentified men ride in the snow with Minnich's sled and his team of horses. The building at left was Henry Luster's store, built in 1889. The upstairs was used by the Maccabees Lodge. The building on the right was built around 1830 as a stagecoach inn. It was first called Farmer's Inn and then Humphrey's Tavern. After 1946, it was known as Brown's Jewelry and Towner's Drugstore.

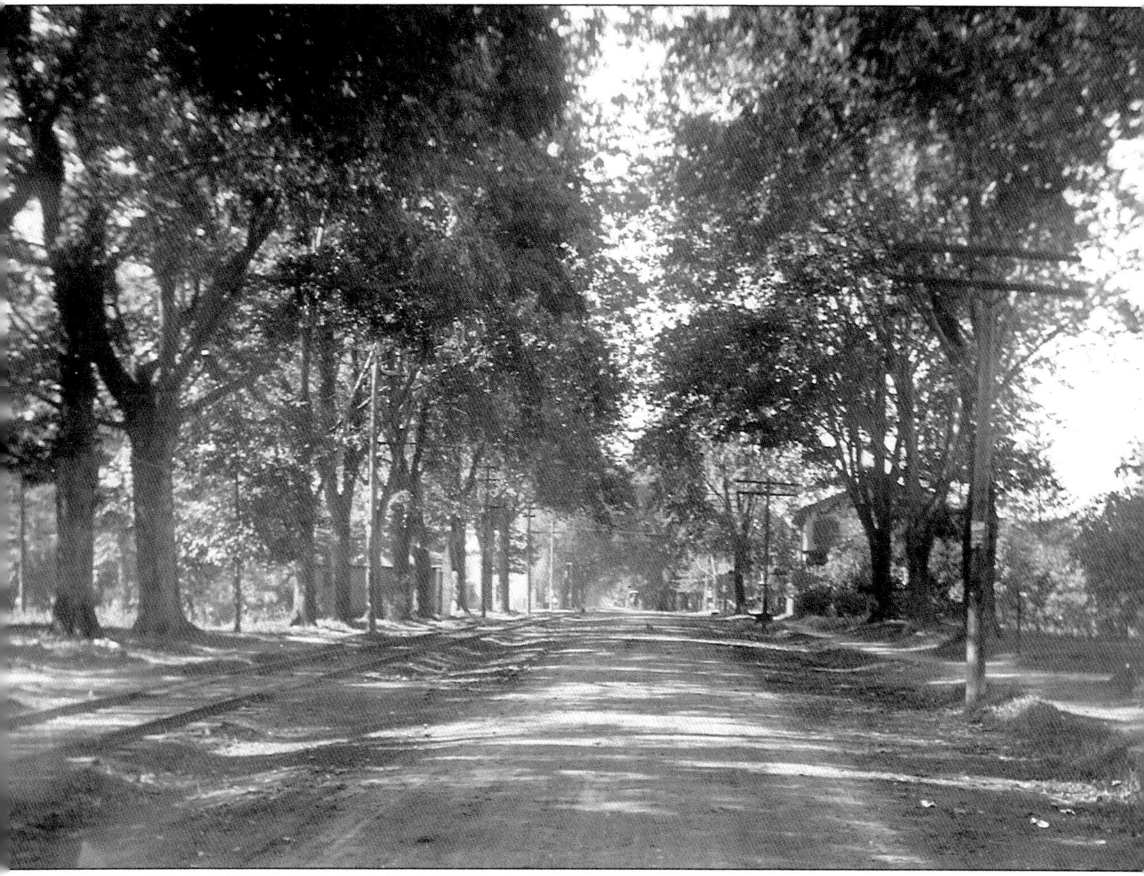

In pioneer days, Center Ridge Road was a stagecoach route and part of the Buffalo Trail, which extended west from Buffalo, New York, to Detroit. Later it extended east to Boston and west to San Francisco and was designated as Route 20. Ridgeville Township's first settlers planted many maple seedlings along both sides of Center Ridge Road in 1821. The trees eventually grew large enough to form a canopy of branches covering much of the road's length. For many years, families from the Elyria and Cleveland area took their Sunday drives to Ridgeville Township to enjoy the impressive sight. This photograph, taken in the 1920s looking west, shows the Green Line tracks on the south side of the road. The white two-story building at the far left is now occupied by Buescher's True Value Hardware Store.

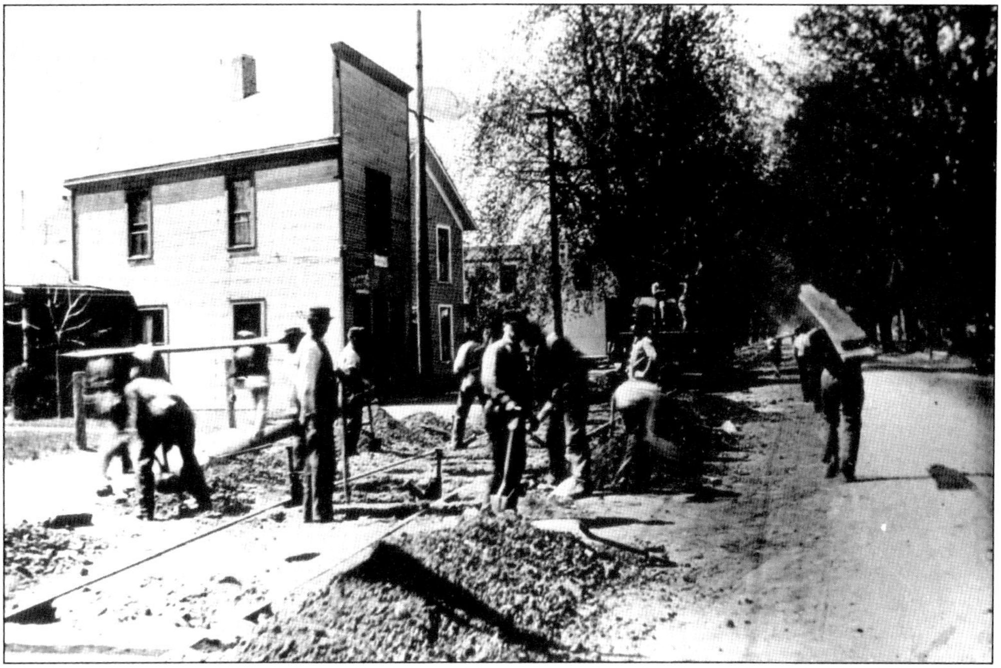

A track crew stops its work to pose on the Green Line interurban track that ran along Center Ridge Road in North Ridgeville around 1910. In the background, the Luster General Store can be seen. The Maccabee Lodge hall was located in the upstairs of the building, which is where members held their meetings.

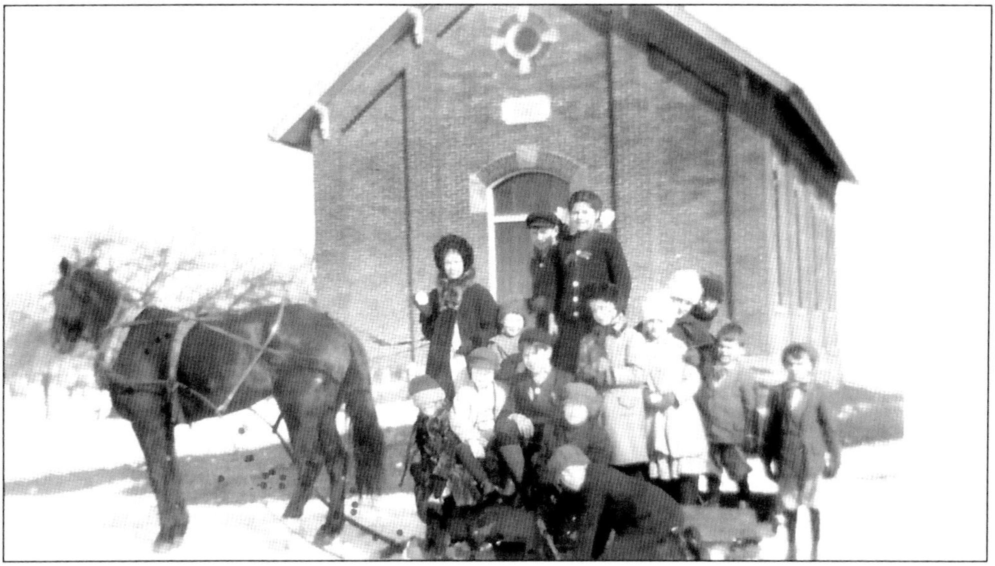

A group of unidentified youngsters enjoys riding on a horse-drawn sled in this early 1900s photograph. There is a school in the background, but it is unknown if the children were being taken to school in this fashion or just enjoying a winter ride. People very often used horses and sleighs as a method of traveling to their destinations at that time.

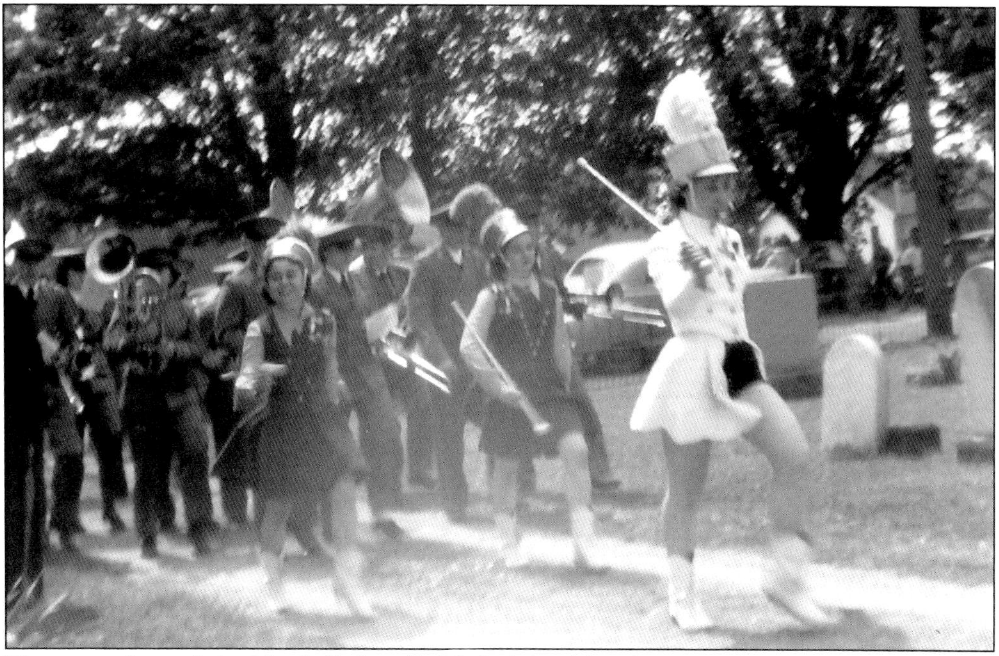

These members of the North Ridgeville High School band seem to have no trouble getting where they were going. In this 1950s photograph, the band is parading through the cemetery as part of the Memorial Day observance. The tradition of a Memorial Day parade and visits to the cemeteries continue today.

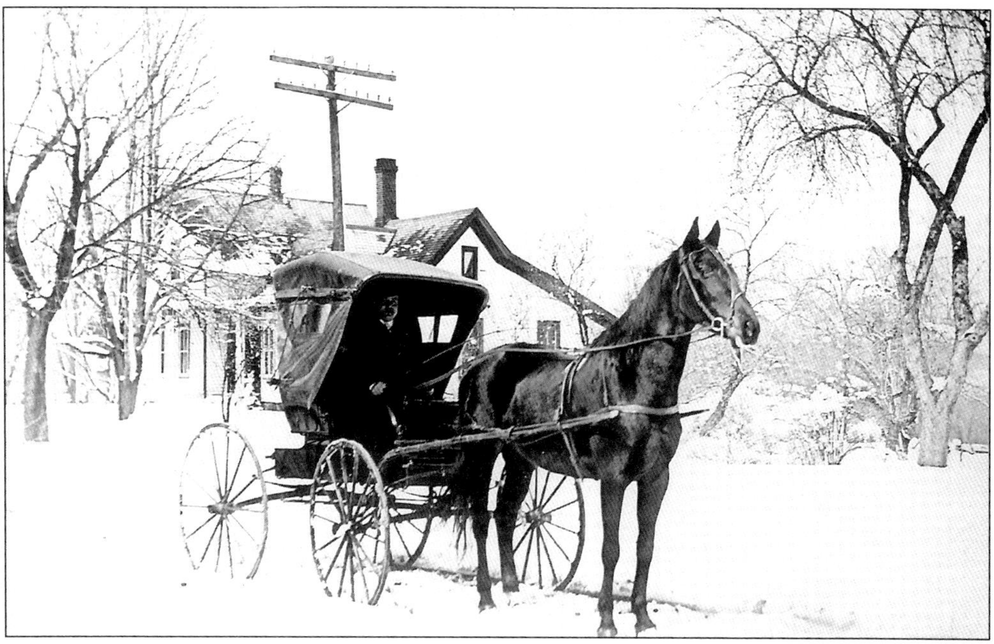

In Ridgeville's early days, it was not uncommon to see some residents traveling in horse-drawn carriages, which provided an easier way to get through the snow-covered paths; however, even the horses found it a bit difficult at times when the snow was very deep. This horse-drawn carriage is transporting riders along Center Ridge Road.

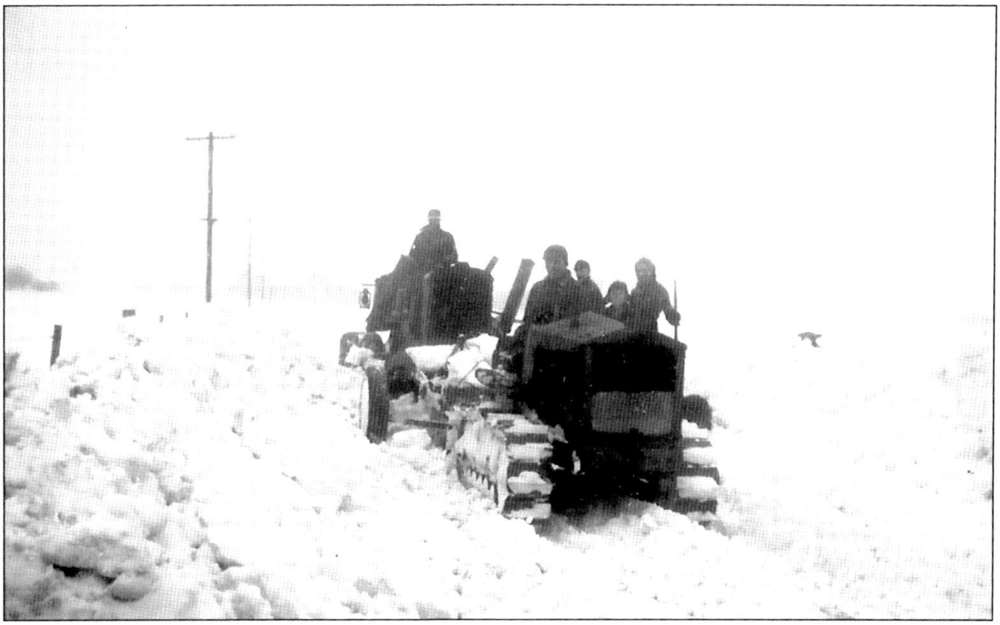

In 1945, Elmer Gilgenbach was in charge of the Ridgeville Township roads and kept them clear with the town's road grader. During one snowstorm, the snow was so high on Barres Road that the grader could not push it. Stoney Ridge Road resident Ralph Smith got his tractor, attached a long tow rope, and between the two men, the road was cleared. Soon after, however, it began to snow again. (Courtesy of Lois Sullivan.)

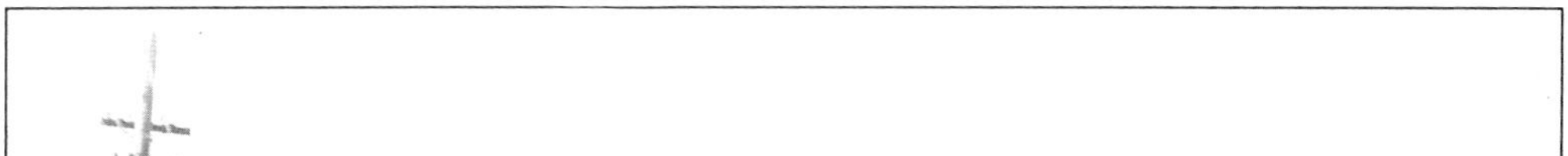

A streetcar siding, an extra track that allowed a car going one way to stop until a car from the opposite direction passed, is shown in front of the St. Peter Parish grounds. There was a single track out of Elyria that ran along the south side of Center Ridge Road to just east of the present Pitts Boulevard and then east across the fields, coming out on Lorain Road near Barton Road. It then followed Lorain Road into Cleveland.

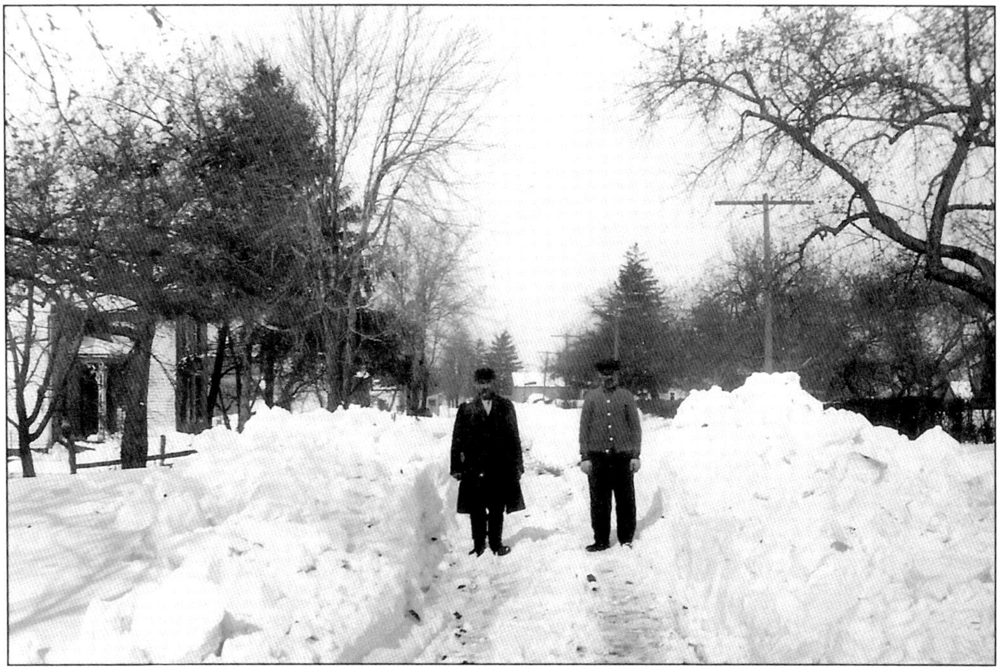

These two men, a Mr. Schneider and Joseph Myers, appear to be standing in the middle of Center Ridge Road following a very heavy winter snow. The snow is so deep it was probably considered best to walk rather than use a horse and buggy or any other vehicle for traveling.

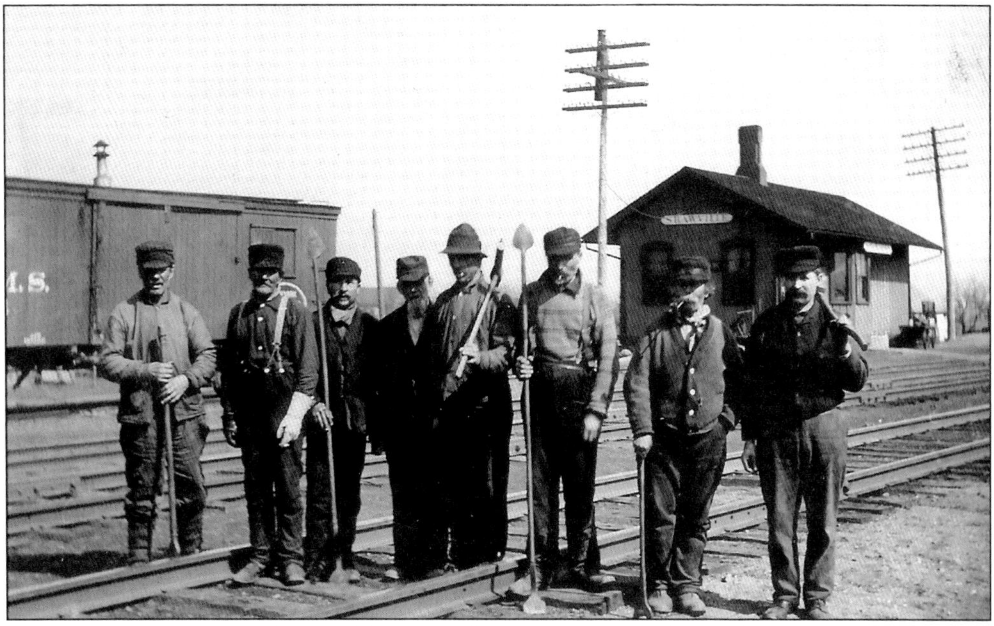

After many German, English, and Irish people came to Ridgeville in the 1840s and 1850s, the small community known as Shawville developed, complete with a general store and post office, in the vicinity of the railroad crossing on Avon Belden Road. It was named for the Shaw family that lived nearby, and Zimri A. Shaw was station master for 45 years. Shown is a section gang at the railroad tracks.

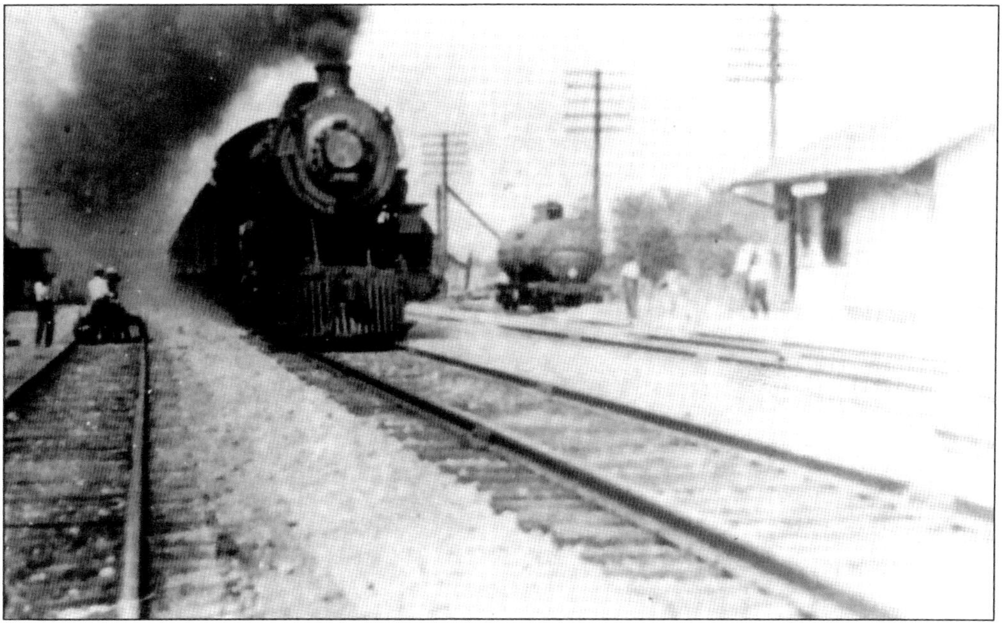

In 1853, the railroad through Ridgeville Township was completed. It was later called the Lake Shore and Michigan Southern Railway, then the New York Central Railroad, and more recently, Conrail/Amtrak. A passenger and freight station was first called Ridgeville station and, after 1890, Shawville. Shawville Station was in regular use until 1947. The building was moved to Elyria in the late 1950s. (Courtesy of Tom Guggenbiller.)

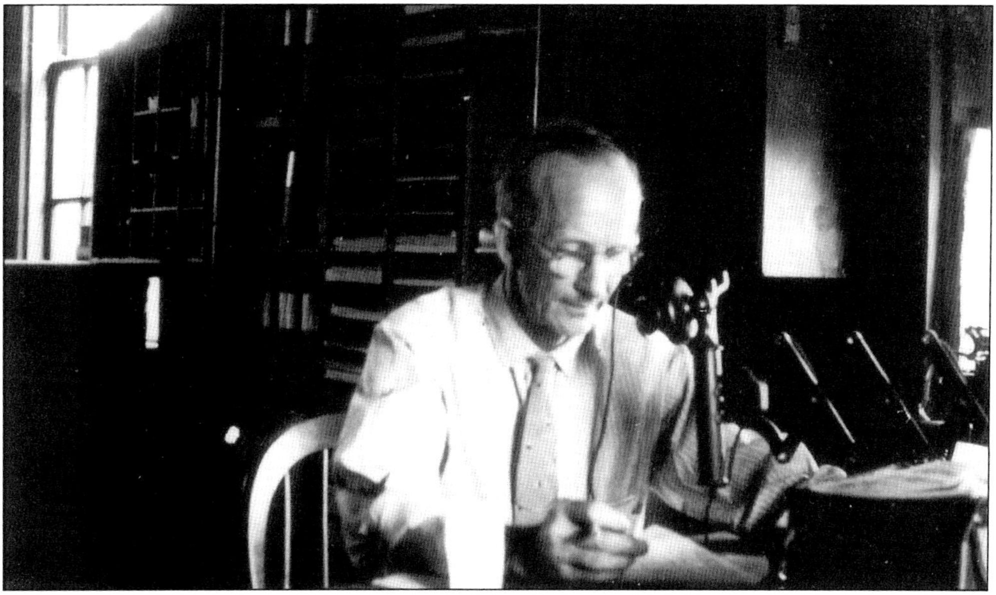

Between 1852 and 1950, there were only three men who served as permanent telegrapher and station agent for Shawville Station, where the Lake Shore and Michigan Southern Railway and the New York Central Railroad crossed present-day Avon Belden Road, then called Station Road. The first was Shaw, and the last was Robert Nuhn. The second Shawville Station agent was the man seen here, Ezra M. Knowles, who was born in 1885. In this 1920s photograph, he is using his "extension" candlestick telephone. (Courtesy of Tom Guggenbiller.)

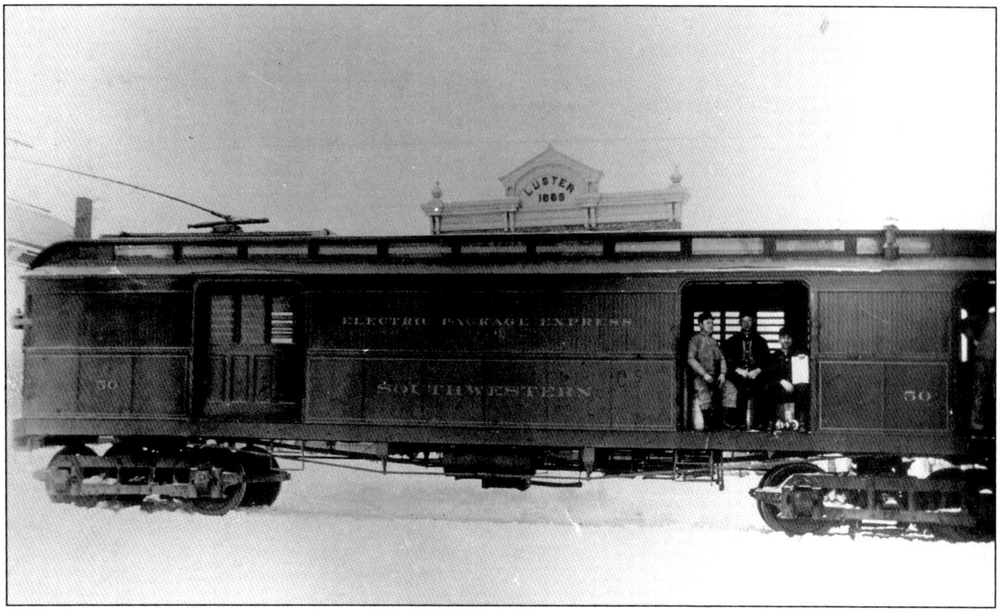

The Cleveland and Southwestern electric trolley line, called the Green Line, served Ridgeville Township from 1895 to 1931. The tracks ran from Lorain Road and Butternut Ridge, near the North Olmsted line, westward through fields and woods to a point on Center Ridge near Pitts Boulevard. From there, the tracks continued along the south side of Center Ridge Road to Elyria and beyond. Baggage or package cars like this one transported local farmers' milk east to Kamm's Corner on Lorain Road. Alex Brewster, the ticket agent for the Cleveland and Southwestern Electric Railroad Company, the Green Line interurban, is shown standing in front of the ticket office near the southwest corner of Center Ridge and Avon Belden Roads, despite the deep snow.

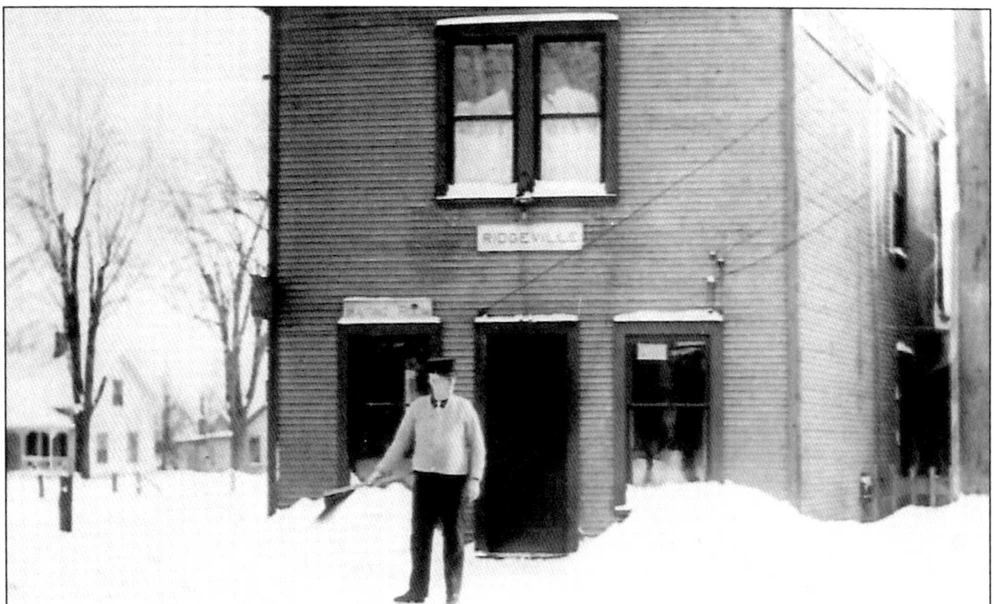

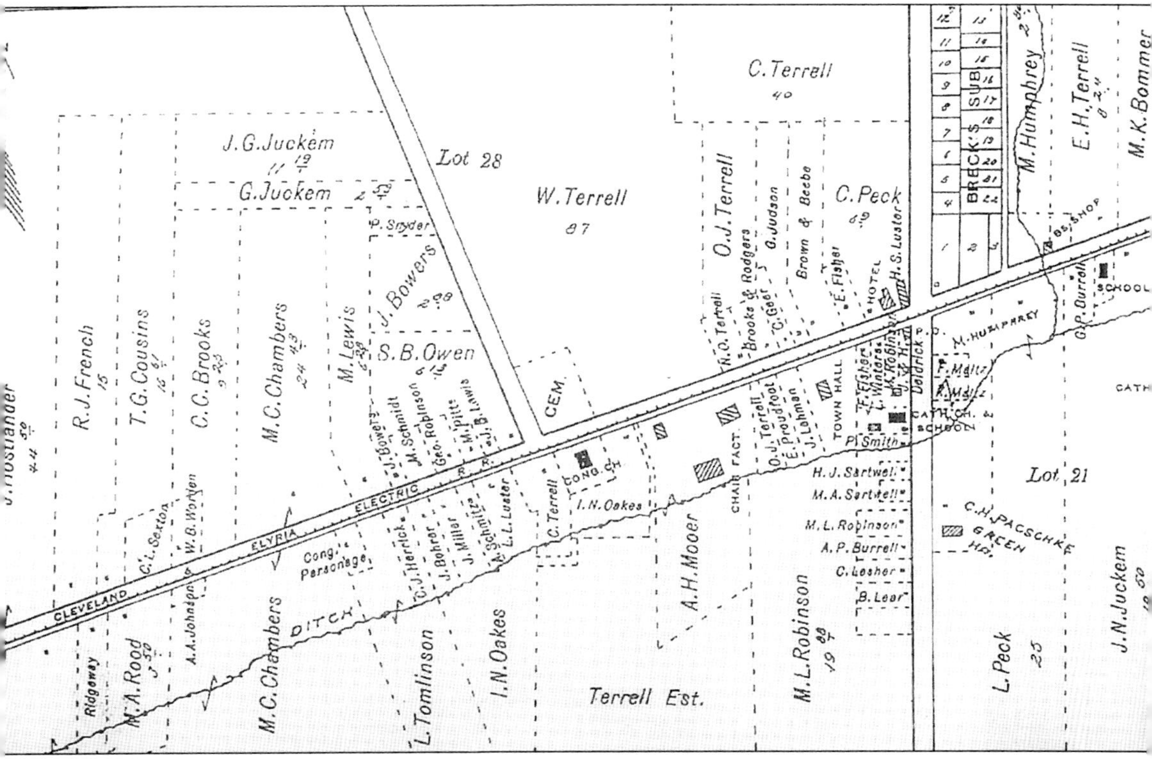

Seen in this 1896 map, Ridgeville Township's downtown section was known as Ridgeville Center. It covers the area from Maddock Road in the southwest to about where Ridge Plaza Drive is today in the northeast. Center Ridge Road runs east and west. Avon Belden Road, now Route 83, at one time had two names. To the north of Center Ridge Road it was known as Center Road. The portion south of Center Ridge was called Station Road. Stoney Ridge Road goes northwest near the middle of the map. The Green Line trolley tracks run along the south side of Center Ridge Road. The Mooers Chair Factory and the town hall are also on Center Ridge Road. The Ridgeville Cemetery is across from the Congregational church near the middle of the map, and the two-room District No. 1 school and St. Peter's Catholic Cemetery are at the far right.

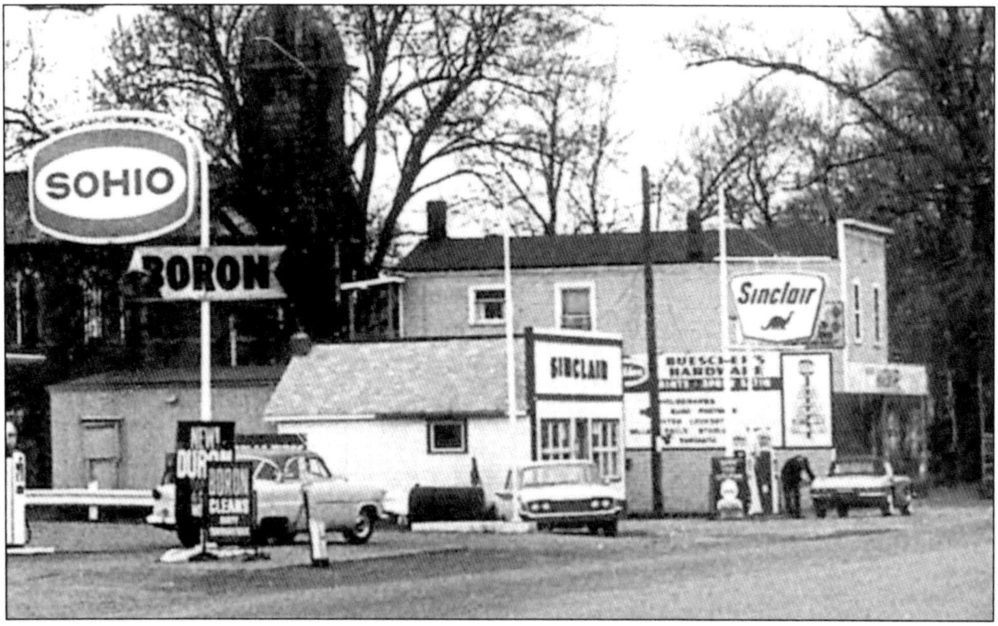

John D. Rockefeller cofounded the Standard Oil Company in Cleveland in 1870. Through the years, Standard Oil added a number of subsidiaries to its company, including Boron Supreme, which was introduced in 1954. This photograph shows Charley Brown's gas station on Center Ridge Road west of Avon Belden Road. Buescher's True Value Hardware Store can be seen in the background. (Courtesy of Tom Guggenbiller.)

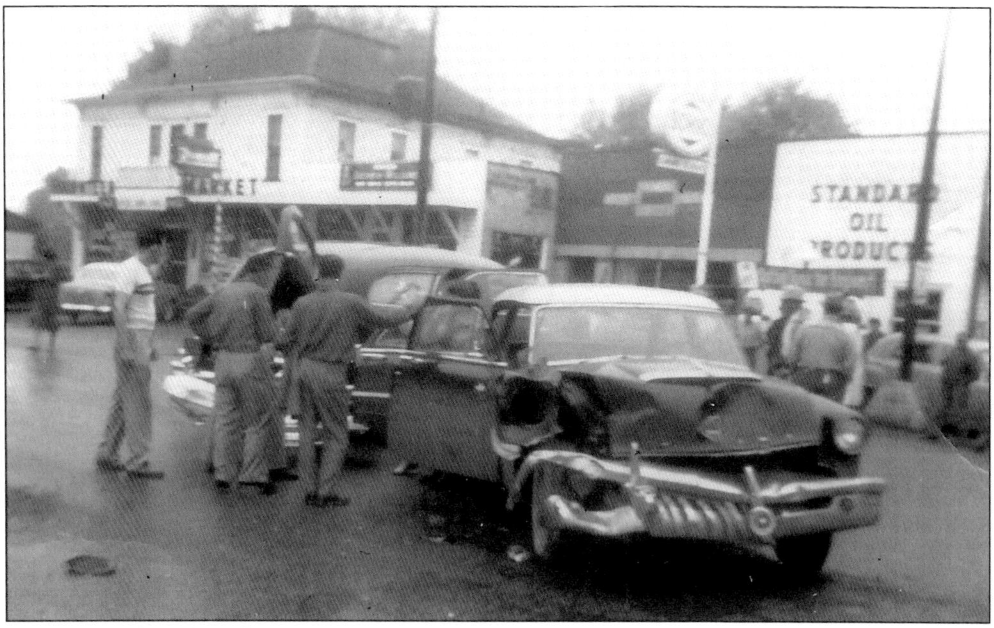

Even in North Ridgeville's early days, accidents happened. This photograph from the mid-1950s shows an automobile that had a mishap on Center Ridge Road (Route 20) at Avon Belden Road (Route 83) in front of Brown's gas station. The post office and Spitzer's Store can be seen in the background. The building left of the Standard Oil Company station is presently Ridge Cleaners. (Courtesy of Bob Gilder.)

Six

Remembering People and Places

There were many people who helped shape North Ridgeville through the decades, but the names of two families and their descendants are always remembered whenever the community's history is discussed. The Terrells and the Beebes were among the 17 pioneers who came from Waterbury, Connecticut, and first settled in the area. Three of the 17 served in the Revolutionary War, and 80-year-old Oliver Terrell was a soldier in the French and Indian War. Not long after the first group, Electa Wilmot Terrell arrived and was the only woman. As time went on, other names became familiar to the residents, such as Peter Meyer, who was recognized as a very successful man and in 1900 built the large Victorian house on Avon Belden Road south of Center Ridge Road, which still attracts the attention of passing motorists. The names Diederich, Pitts, and Worcester are familiar even today because many members of these families continue to live in the area. Some of the early structures remain in North Ridgeville, although they have gone through changes in ownership. The Century Tavern on the east end of Center Ridge Road and the Cahoon House on the west end of Route 20, now owned by the R. W. Beckett Corporation, are two of the oldest buildings in the town.

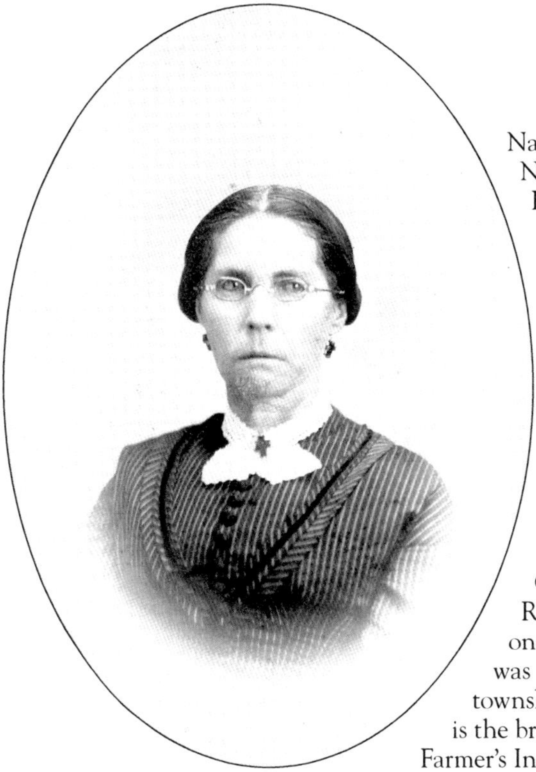

Nancy Beebe was born on April 18, 1812, in North Ridgeville, the daughter of David and Belinda Hodge Beebe. She is recognized through the community's history as the second pioneer child born in Ridgeville Township. On September 27, 1834, she married Mark Humphrey of North Ridgeville. They owned and operated the Farmer's Inn Tavern and stagecoach stop, later called Humphrey's Inn, on the northeast corner of Center Ridge Road and Center/Station Road, now called Avon Belden Road. Nancy died on February 26, 1872. The white frame hotel in the photograph stood on the north side of Center Ridge Road just west of Avon Belden Road. It had been operated by the Terrells, one of Ridgeville's pioneer families. This hotel was one of several once located throughout the township. Beyond the gas station to the far right is the brick building that formerly was known as the Farmer's Inn and Humphrey's Tavern.

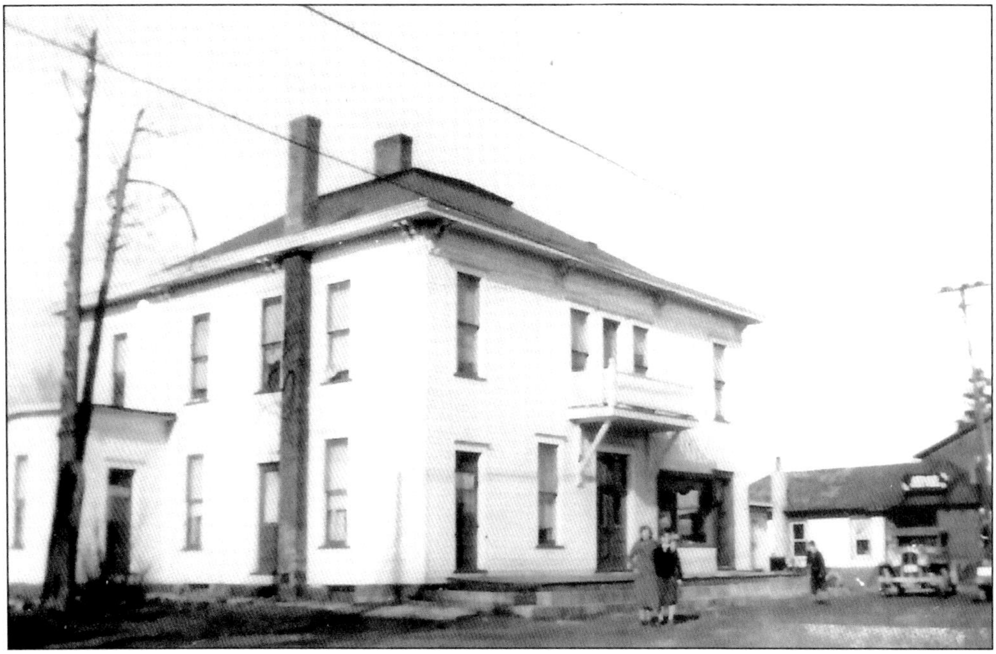

Peter Bauer was born in 1848. He was a farmer who lived on Stoney Ridge Road, which was probably the place where he was born. He always carried a basket with him to pick up elderberries, blackberries, or whatever he came across. One day in late autumn of 1925, he was standing in front of the cemetery at the northeast corner of Center Ridge and Stoney Ridge Roads waiting for an interurban car to take him to see his brother in Amherst. Suddenly an eastbound automobile on Center Ridge Road crossed the center line and struck and killed him. He died on November 22, 1925, at the age of 77 and is buried in St. Peter Cemetery.

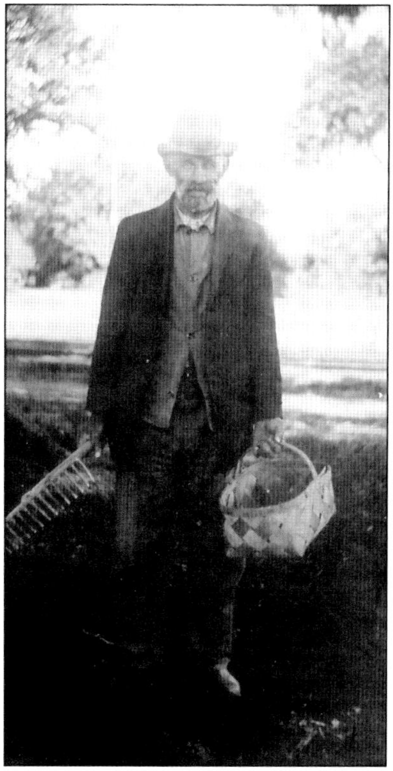

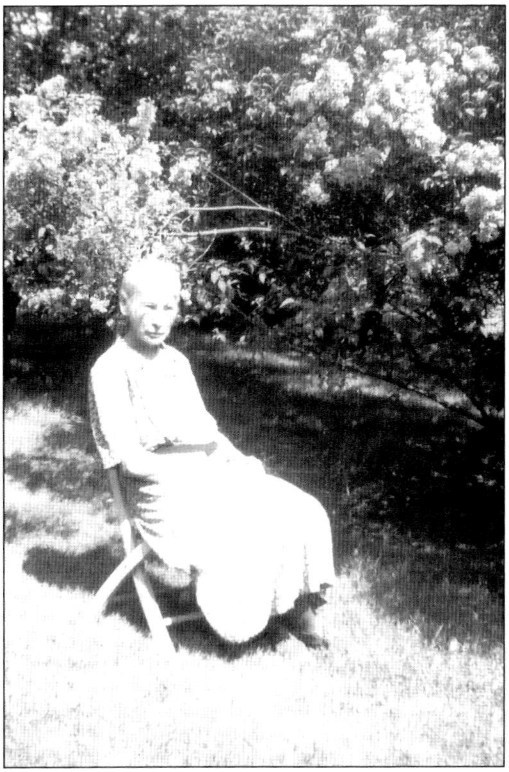

Mary Pitts, the sister of former North Ridgeville police chief Ronald Bauer's grandmother Theresa Pitts Barnes, lived on the north side of town. Pitts was born in 1881 and died in 1957 at the age of 76. In this photograph, she is sitting in the yard enjoying the sunshine. (Courtesy of Ron Bauer.)

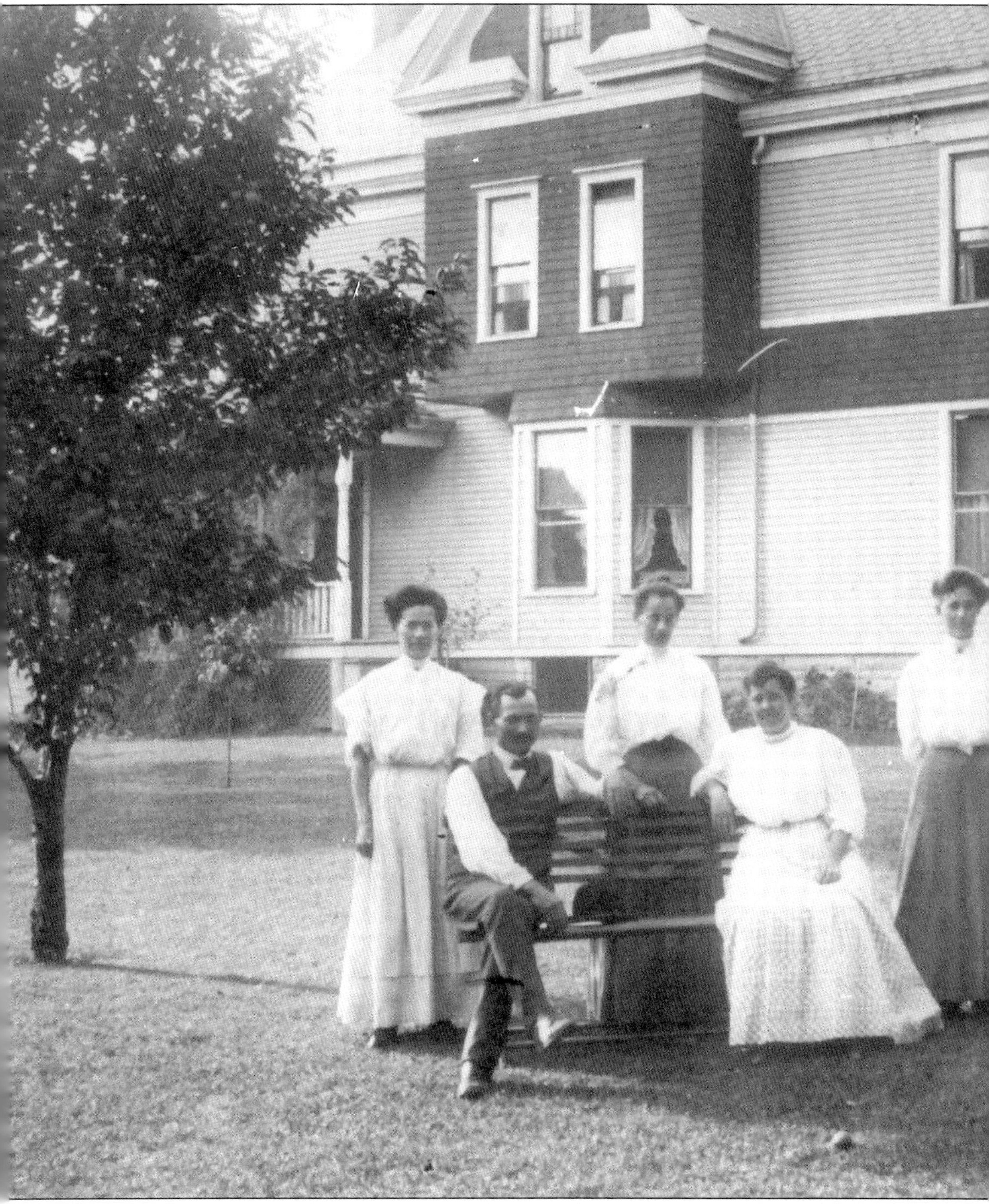

Peter Meyer was born in Bavaria in 1844 and came to America two years later with his parents, Andrew and Mary Catherine Meyer. The family sailed in 1846 from LeHavre, France, landing in New York Harbor after a voyage of 48 days. The Meyers settled in Ridgeville Township, where Andrew and Mary Catherine lived until 1871 before moving to neighboring Elyria. Peter served in the 107th Ohio Volunteer Infantry from 1862 to 1865 during the Civil War. He was slightly

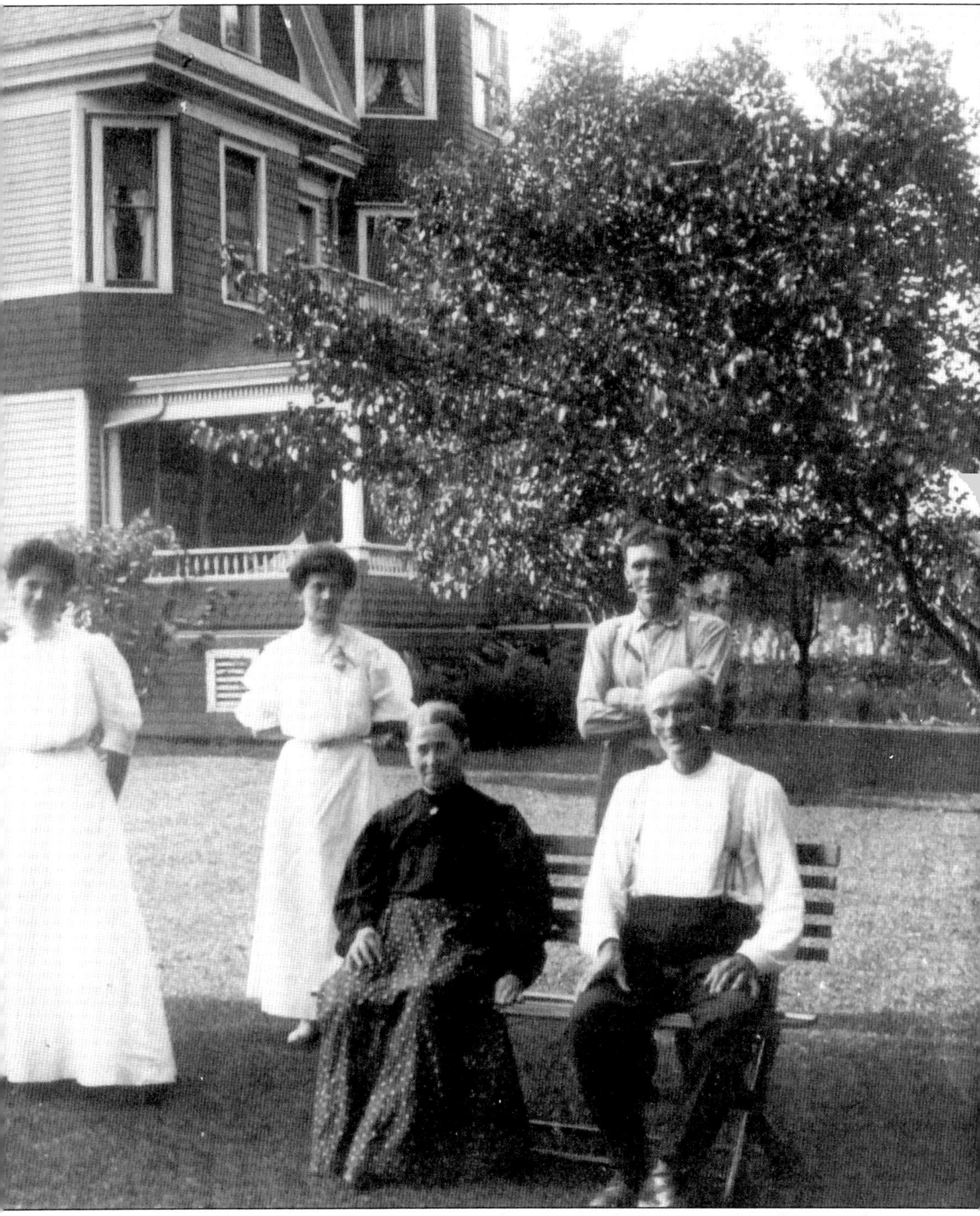

wounded at the Battle of Gettysburg. He returned to the family farm in Ridgeville Township, and in 1872, he married Catherine Stander. They raised a family of 12 children. In 1901, Peter built a large Victorian-style home at 5656 Avon Belden Road (Route 83). The house is pictured soon after completion. It is still occupied and remains in good condition today.

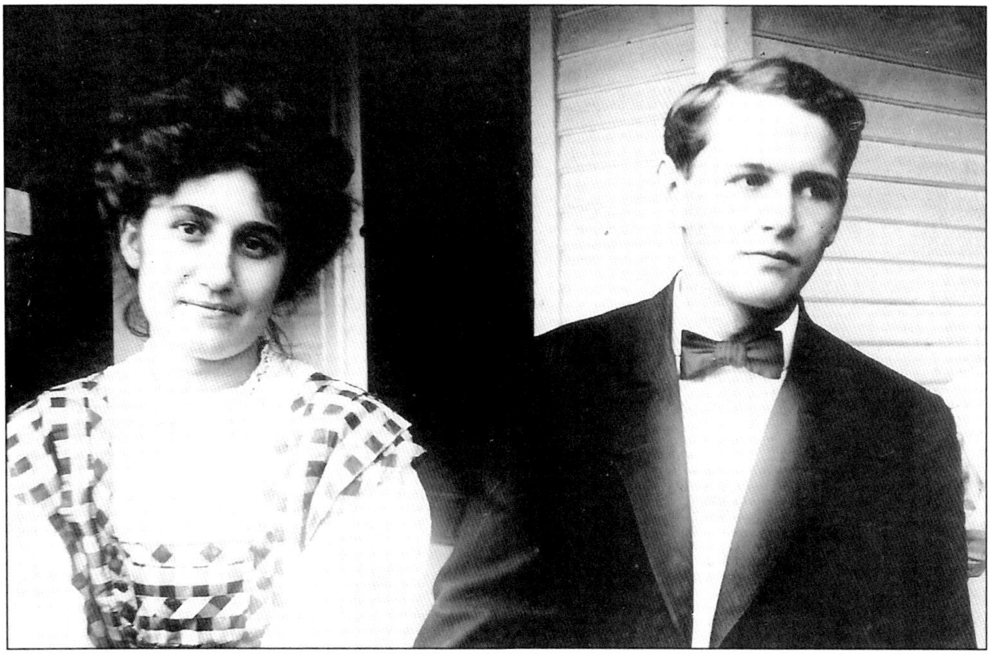

North Ridgeville's landmark, the Old Town Hall, had a theater on the second floor, complete with a stage and upholstered seats, where people enjoyed various performances. The unidentified man and woman in this photograph from the 1800s were two of the actors who once visited the theater and entertained audiences. (Courtesy of Marge Lesnick.)

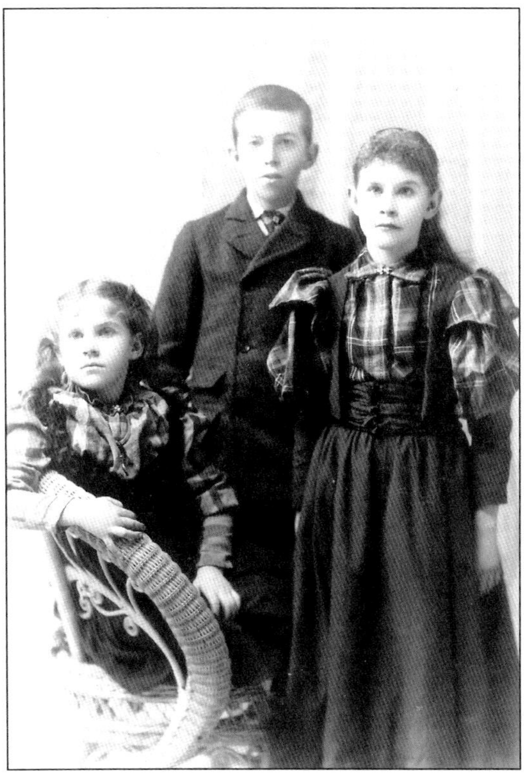

These are the children of George E. Hill, who was born in 1852, and Evalyn Terrell Hill, who was born in the summer of 1853. Evalyn was the daughter of Eleazer Homer Terrell. From left to right, the children are Ella Evalyn Hill, who was born on January 21, 1888; Raymond Irving Hill, who was born on June 14, 1881; and Mary Jane "Mayme" Hill, who was born on January 23, 1884. Ella married Rudolf F. Goecke, and Mayme married Robert S. Davies.

The Reverend Joseph Trapp was pastor of St. Peter Parish from 1909 to 1920. He was interested in people and how they lived, and his interest in photography provided the vehicle for a pictorial documentary of North Ridgeville. He developed and printed his own photographs. Following his death in 1942, Gertrude Worcester, a niece living in North Ridgeville, received his album. Worcester decided early in 1980 to give the collection to the North Ridgeville Historical Society.

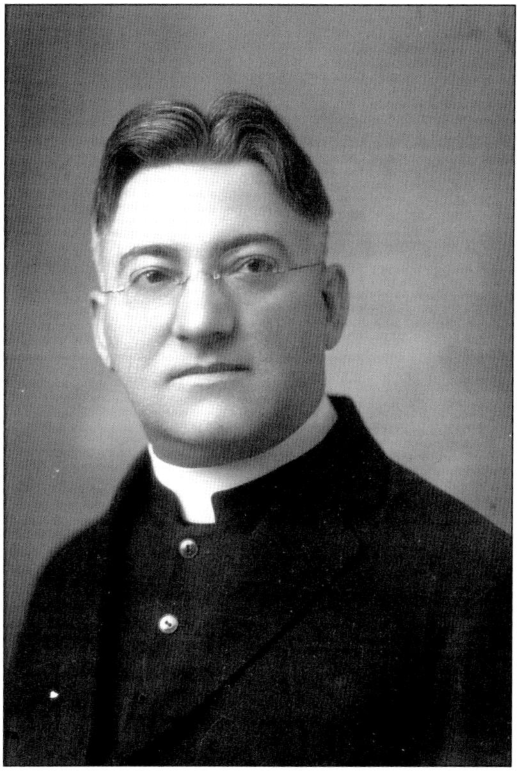

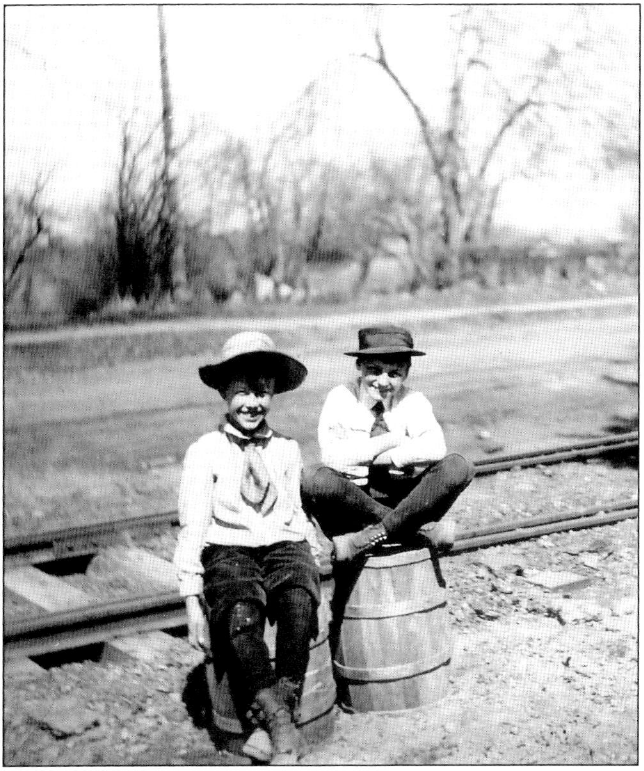

These two little boys rest on a couple of wooden barrels next to the railroad tracks. Walter Horwedel (left) was a twin, and Alfred Trapp, was the nephew of Joseph, the reverend. Alfred was the oldest of nine children and often visited his uncle Joseph. (Courtesy of Marge Lesnick.)

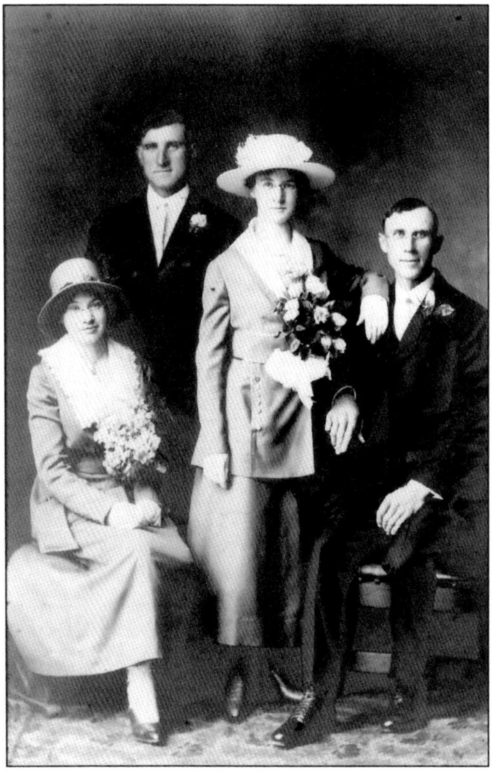

In the early 1900s, some couples enjoyed having a formal photograph taken of their wedding day, as this couple did. William and Theresa Barnes exchanged wedding vows on April 17, 1918. The best man and maid of honor, who served as witnesses for the wedding, were Hank Barnes and Mary Pitts. (Courtesy of Ron Bauer.)

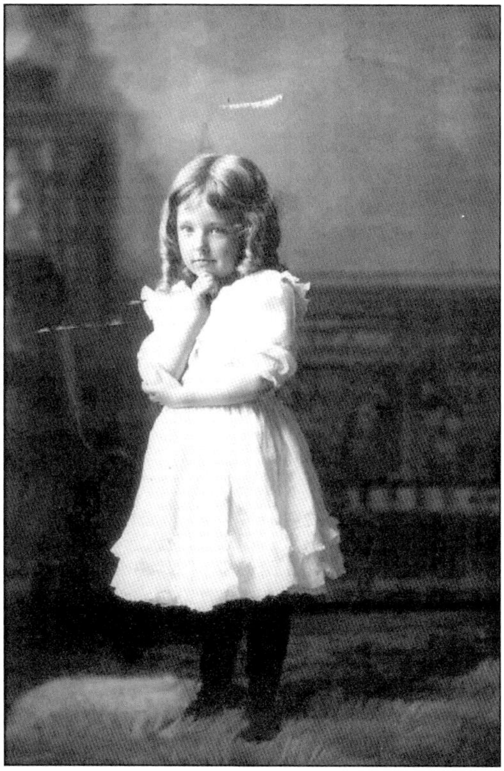

This photograph is of M. Beatrice Terrell Hall when she was four or five years old. She is the mother of William Hall, who presently lives in North Ridgeville. They are descendants of Electa Wilmot Terrell, the first pioneer woman to live in Ridgeville. (Courtesy of Bill Hall.)

The Barnes family owned a farm near Shawville, a little community built near the railroad crossing on the north side of the tracks. The family sometimes permitted hunters on its property, such as these two men, shown in this 1920s photograph. With their hunting dog and apparently proper attire, they were ready for a day in the field. (Courtesy of Ron Bauer.)

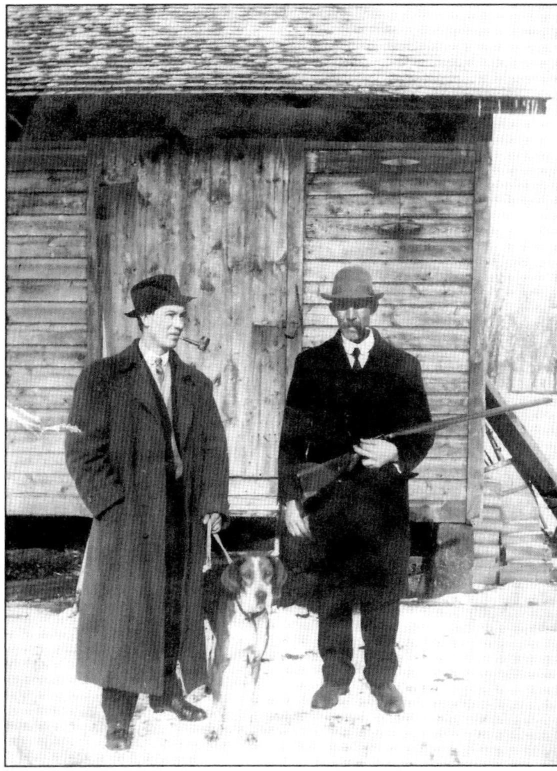

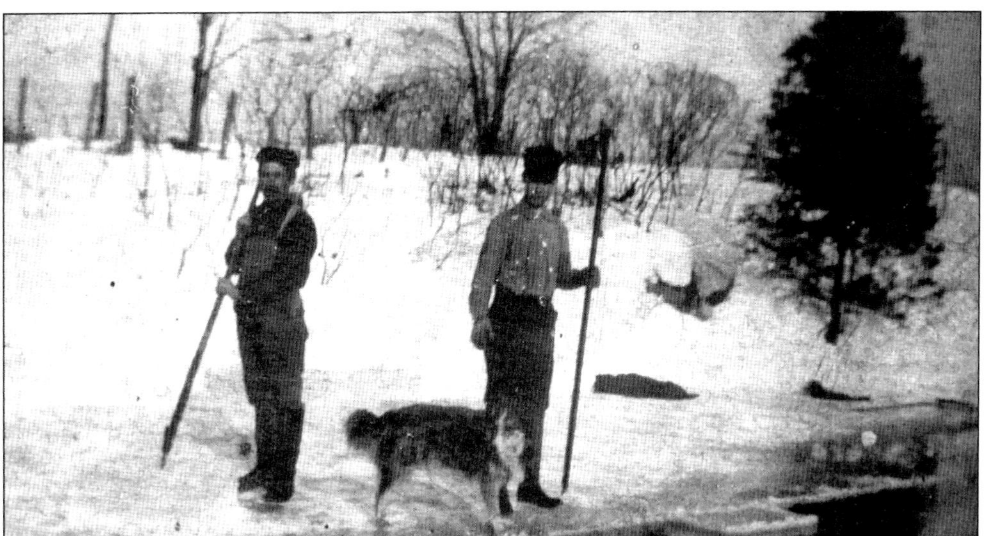

During some winters, the temperatures dipped so low that some of the creeks running through the township became frozen. This photograph, probably taken in the 1900s, shows Frank Sweet (left) and John Sweet on Root Road cutting ice, perhaps to do some ice fishing or maybe to collect ice to take home.

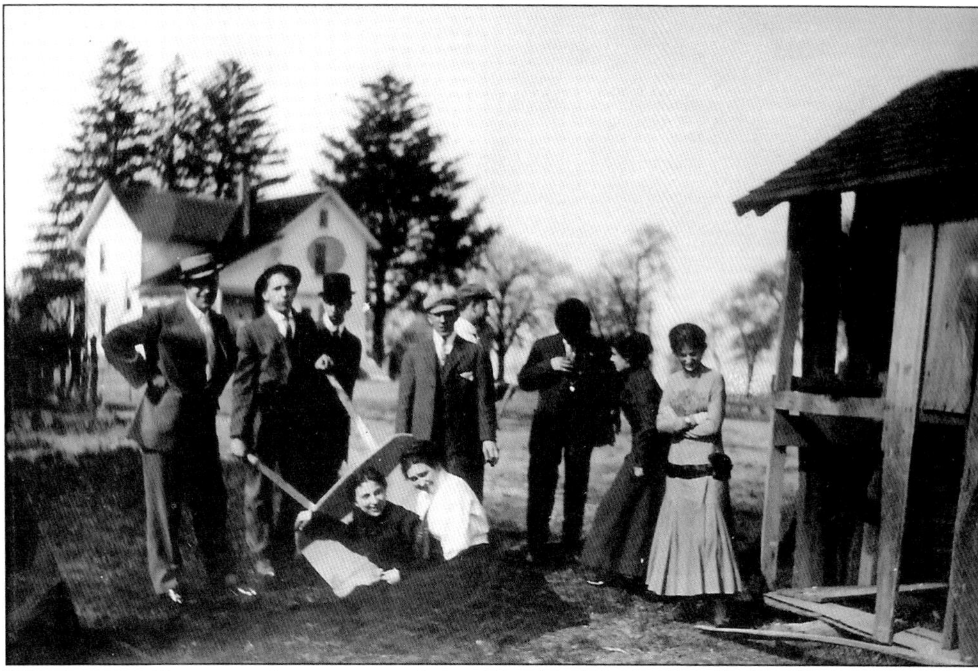

The Lyceum Players, a theater group from Cleveland, arrived in Ridgeville to present the production *Along Came Father* at the Old Town Hall. The play was held on April 11, 1915, for a benefit for St. Peter Parish. Before the play, members of the group had a good time outside upsetting a wheelbarrow with two actresses in it (above). The St. Peter Parish house can be seen in the background. In the photograph below, the entire cast of the play is seen gathered along the creek bank. Behind them is the School District No. 1 schoolhouse, located at the center of town.

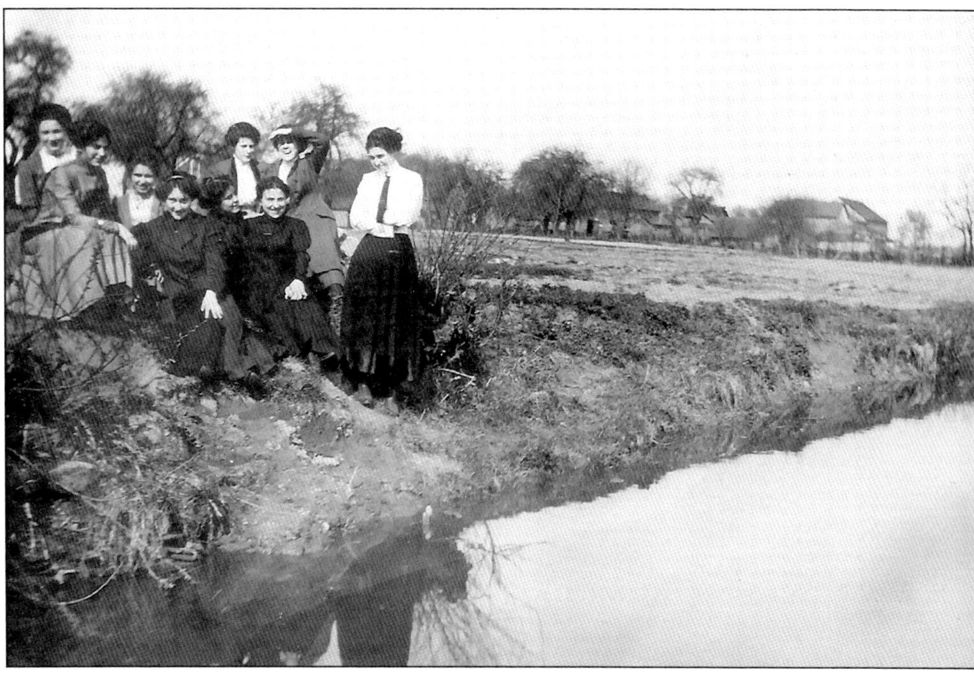

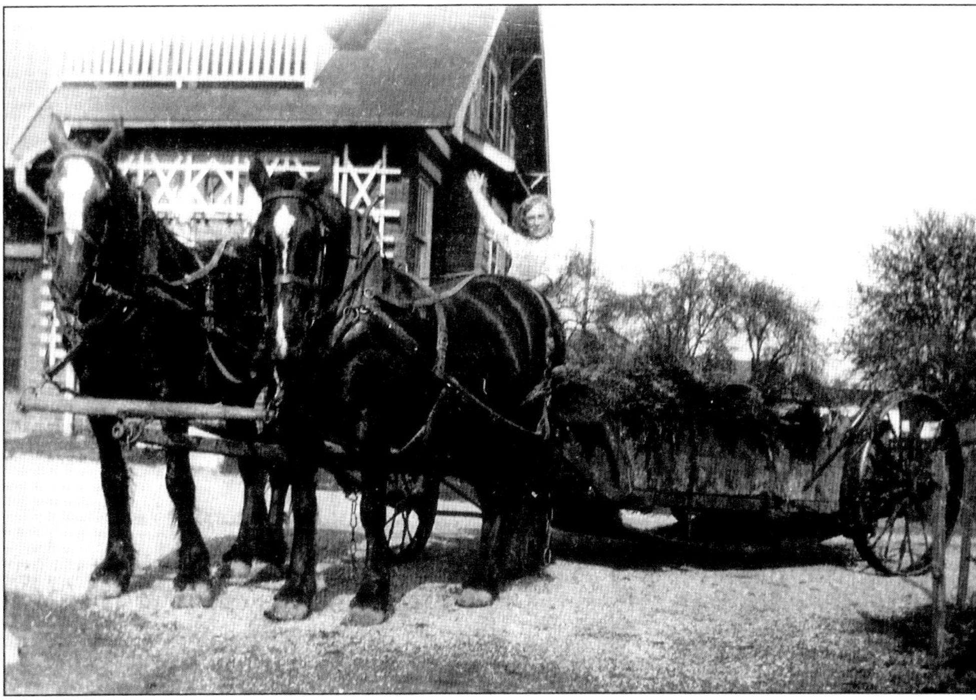

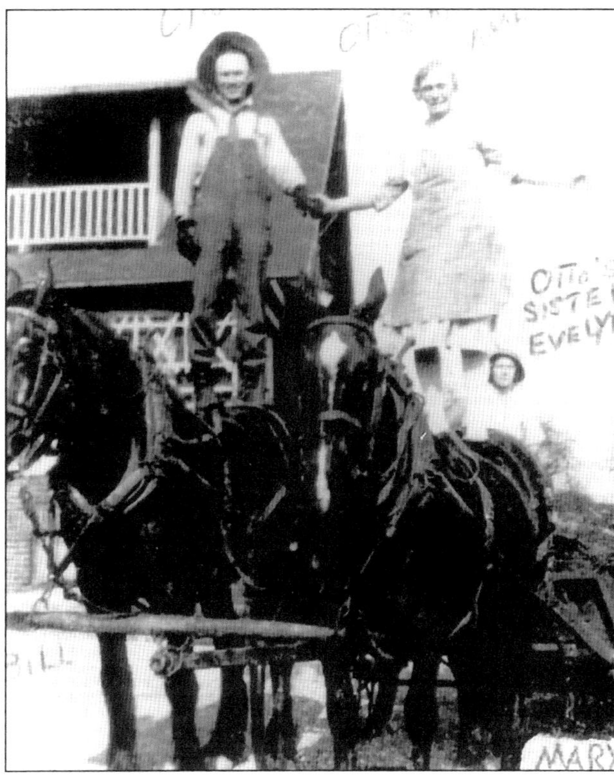

Otto Laubenthal's mother, Amelia Laubenthal, was a hard worker and an energetic lady who often could be seen driving a team of horses. In the 1930s photograph above, Amelia was at the Dudek home on Route 83, handling the horses named Bill and Mary while she was spreading manure. At right, Otto and Amelia climbed atop the horses and stood up like circus performers, probably scaring Otto's sister Evelyn half to death. Evelyn is pictured in the background looking on but apparently not ready to join the fun. (Courtesy of Bill Laubenthal.)

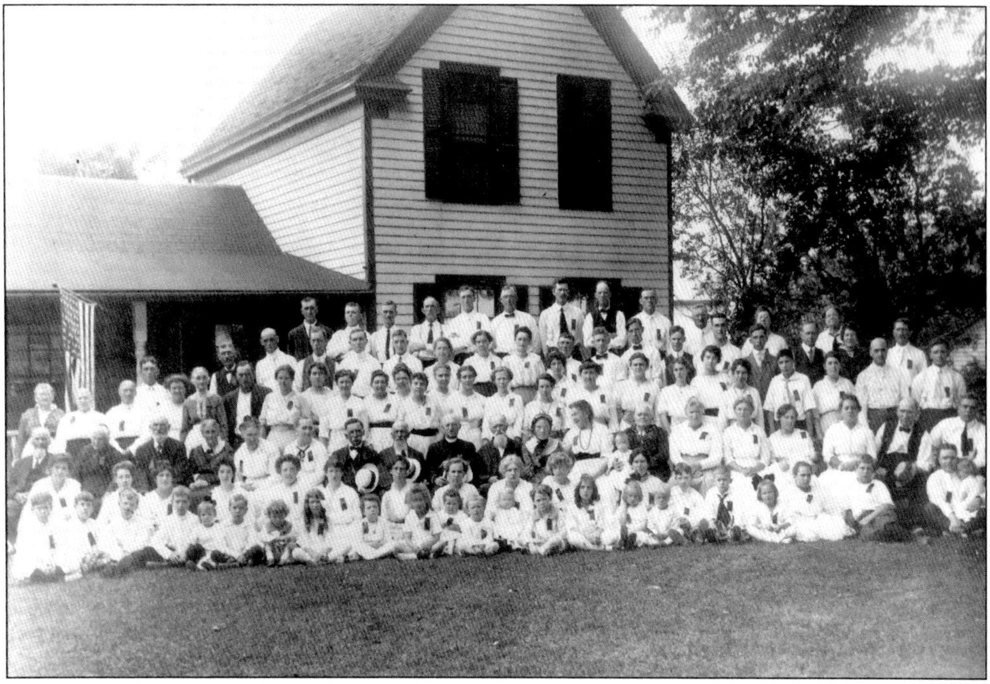

Diederich family members, including mothers, fathers, grandmothers, grandfathers, and a large assortment of grandchildren and great-grandchildren of all ages, gather at the family farm on Center Ridge Road to celebrate the golden wedding anniversary of Frank and Katherine Diederich in this 1915 photograph. Each guest at the party wore a ribbon commemorating the occasion. The Diederichs were married on July 25, 1865, at St. Teresa's Catholic Church in Sheffield Village. (Courtesy of Loyola Diederich.)

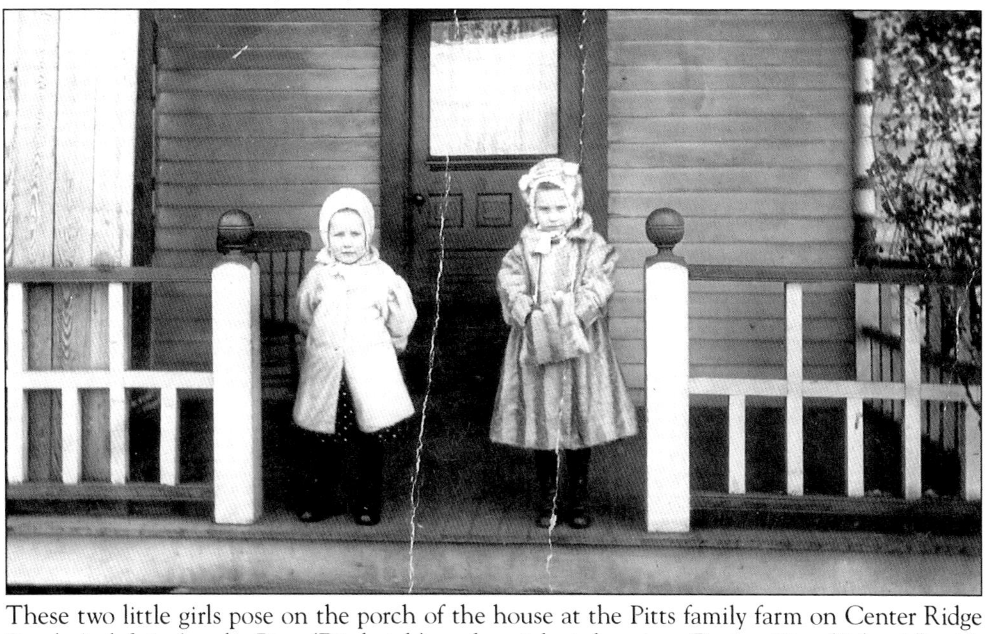

These two little girls pose on the porch of the house at the Pitts family farm on Center Ridge Road. At left is Aurelia Pitts (Diederich), and at right is her sister Regina Pitts (Schneid) with her hands tucked inside her muff to keep warm. (Courtesy of Loyola Diederich.)

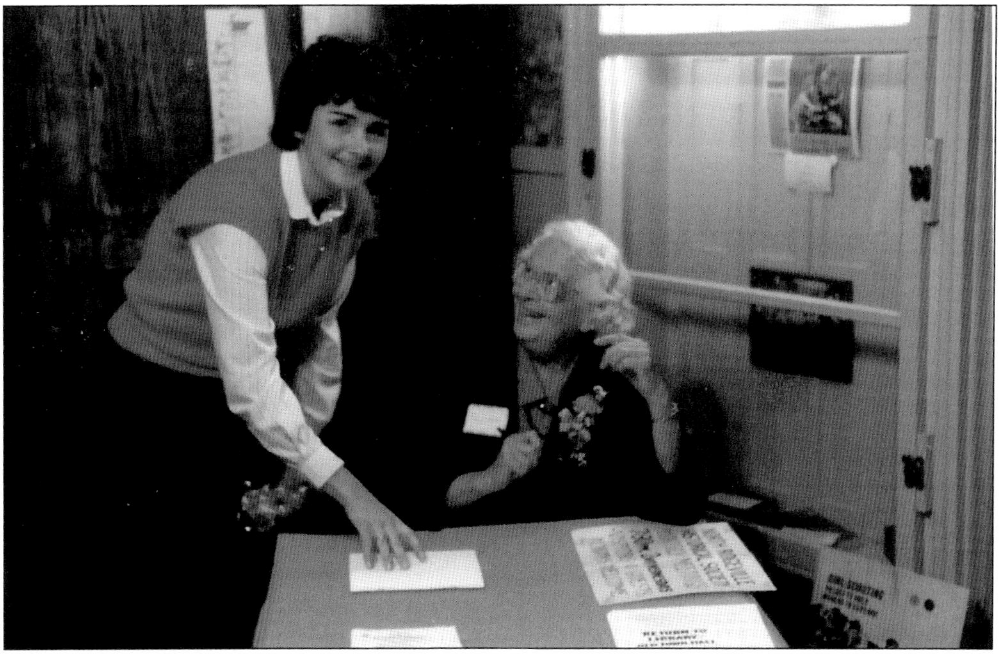

A North Ridgeville historian, the late Frances Smith penned the book *The Elm Tree Talks*, in which she recalled events from the town's past from the viewpoint of an old elm tree that stood in the yard of the family home. Smith is shown autographing a copy of the book for her niece; the book was published in 1985 in conjunction with the 175th anniversary of the first settlement in Ridgeville. The age of the elm tree pictured is unknown. Smith said her mother, who was born in 1880, recalled that it was a big tree as far back as she could remember and stood as an umbrella to shade the house and yard. (Courtesy of Lois Sullivan.)

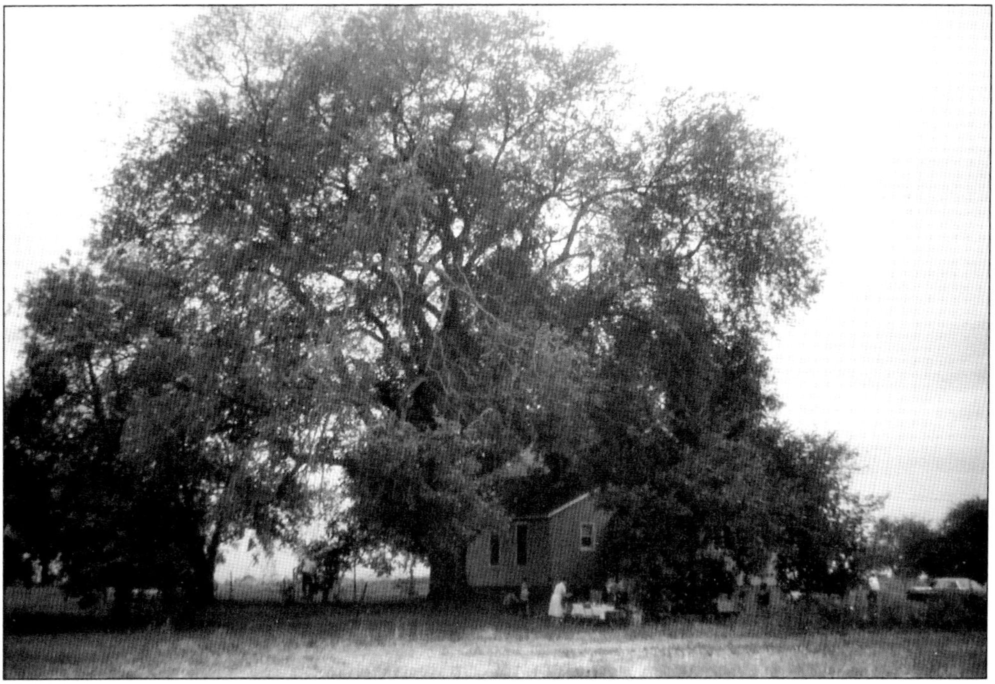

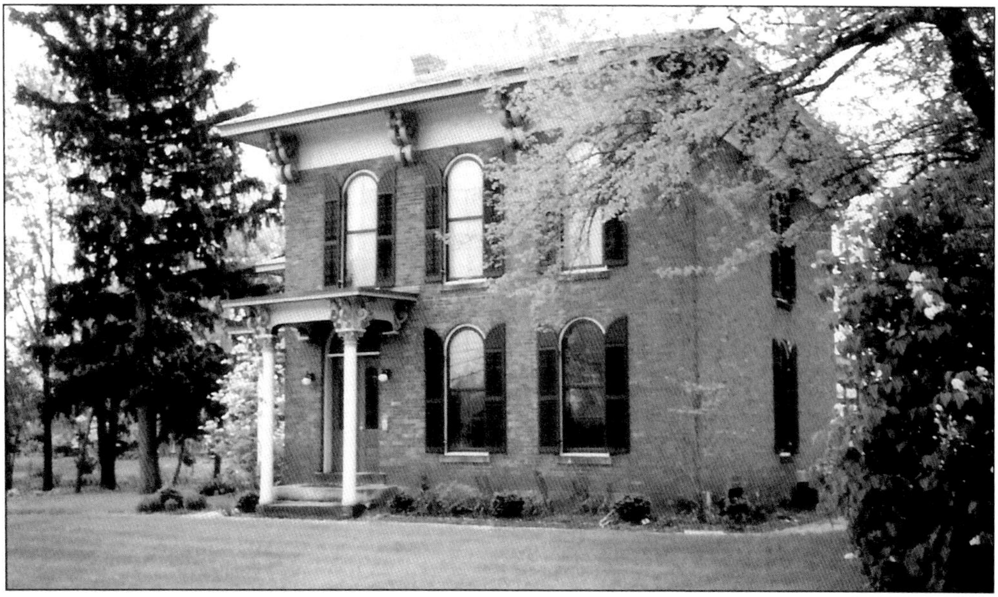

Samuel C. Cahoon, born in 1787, was a pioneer farmer and merchant who built the original log and frame house on this Center Ridge Road property in the 1820s and 1830s. In 1849, he sold the home to his son, John Barnum, who built this brick home in the classic Italianate or Tuscan villa style about the mid-1850s. The bricks for this were all made on the farm. John Barnum manufactured and sold farm implements here. In the 1940s, members of the Amidon family, who at the time owned the property, discovered an opening under a piece of sandstone while renovating the house. It is believed that it hid slaves who were making their way to freedom in earlier years. Antique and craft shops were located in the home in the 1960s and 1970s. The North Ridgeville Historical Society Museum was housed in the home from 1977 to 1986. It was restored in the late 1980s by its owner, the R. W. Beckett Corporation, for business use.

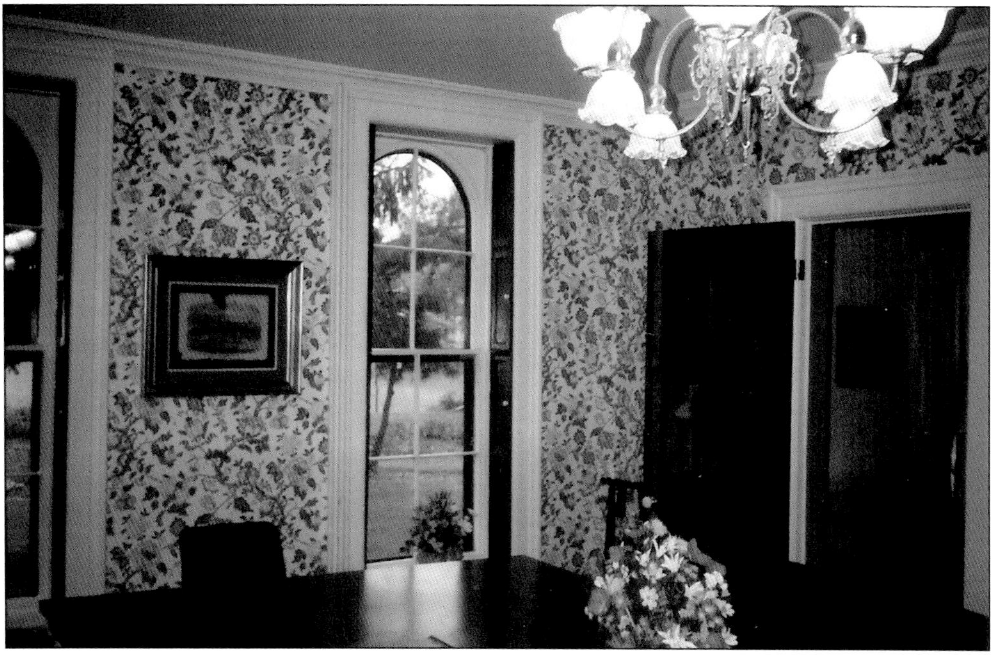

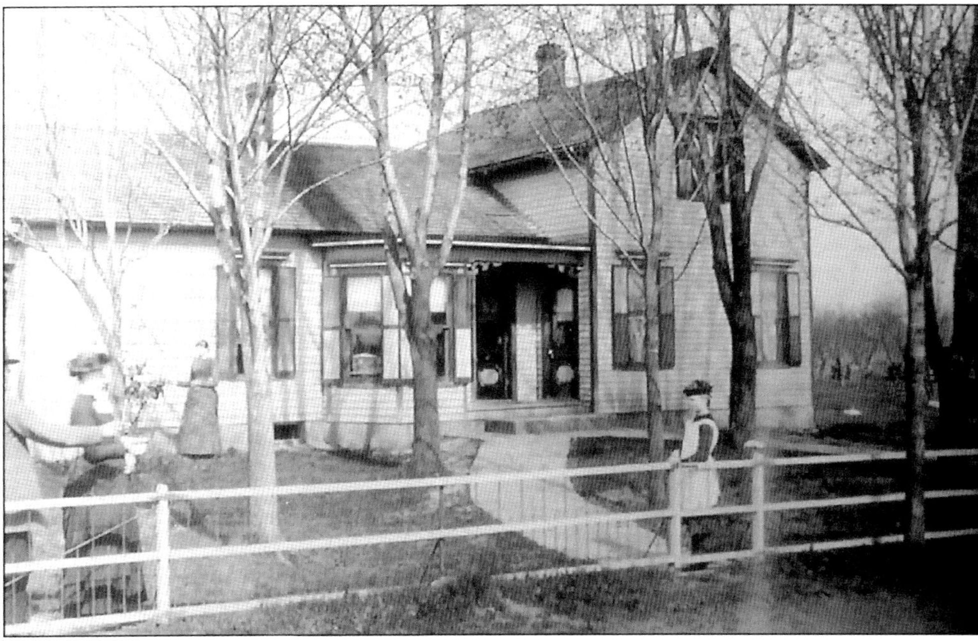

This is the Samuel Horatio Shaw home in Shawville. He was born in Bristol, New York, on April 9, 1829, and moved to Ridgeville Township in 1851. He was the father of Zimri Alpine Shaw, the first and longest-serving station agent and telegrapher at the Shawville railroad station. Samuel served as a township trustee and the school director. He and his wife, Julliette Wiley Shaw, are on the left side of the photograph from about 1890. The child is Lola Shaw, and the second woman is Lola's mother, Lizzie Lucinda Shaw. (Courtesy of the Lorain County Historical Society.)

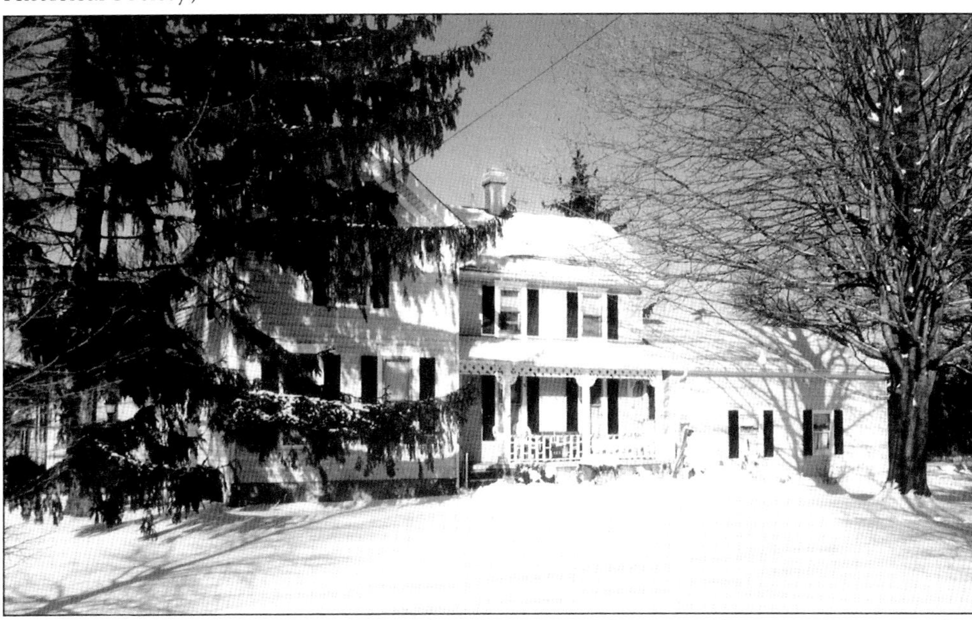

This house, built in about 1870, is located on the curve of Otten Road just past Barres Road. It is presently known as the Wences Rak family home but in earlier times was owned by the Adam Barres family. An old corncrib stands behind the home. (Courtesy of Andrew Rak.)

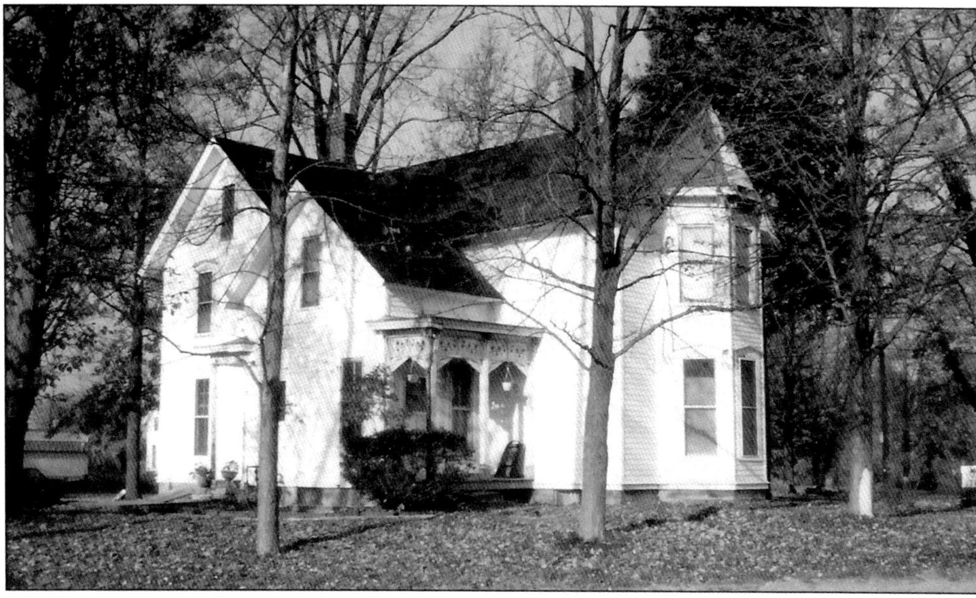

This large Victorian home is situated on the southwest corner of Chestnut Ridge Road and Route 83. It has been home to many families over the years and was even home to the well-known comedian Martin Mull, who spent a few years of his childhood in the house. In 1987, Mull was the marshal of the Corn Festival Grande Parade and also did a live television show from the community. During the 1950s, his father, Harold Mull, served briefly as overseer of the Ridgeville Grange.

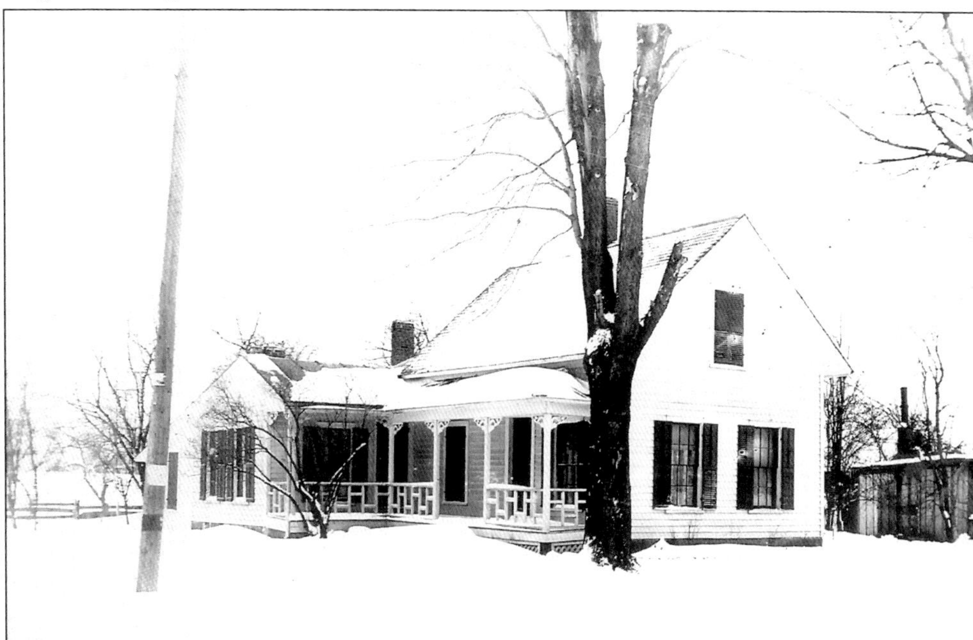

Structures in Ridgeville were very often relocated from one part of town to another, and it was not unusual to see a house being moved from its original site, such as the Frank Moltz home, which was originally near what was referred to as "the Center." Later the white farm-style house with black shutters was relocated farther south on Avon Belden Road near the railroad tracks.

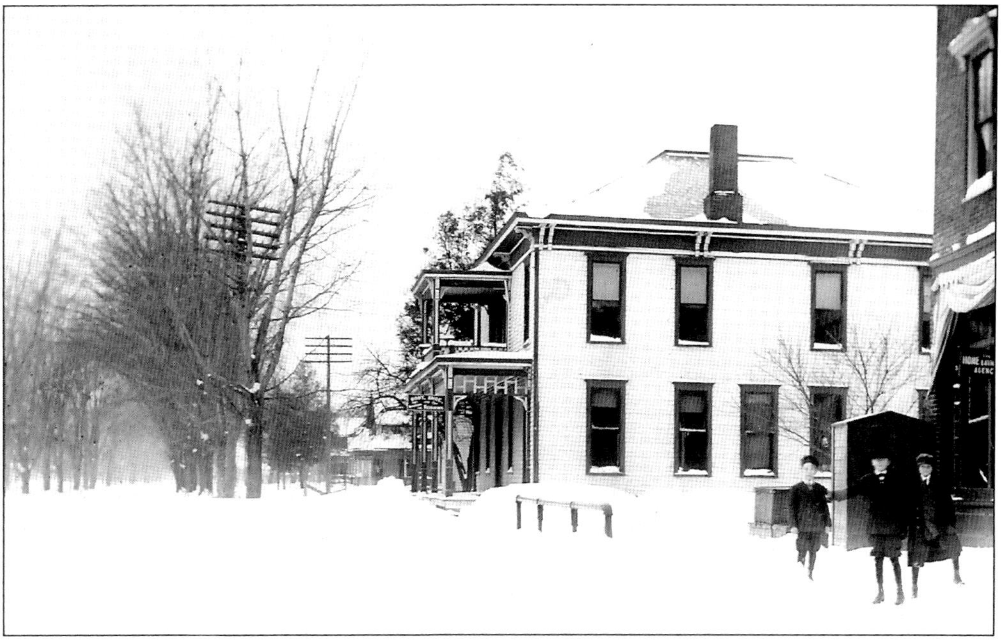

Since Ridgeville was located on Center Ridge Road, which was one of the many prehistoric lake ridges that crossed through Lorain County and the location of many of the first settlers' homes, it was the appropriate site for a hotel to welcome people as they traveled through town, heading either east or west. The old hotel was situated on the north side of Center Ridge Road, looking west from Avon Belden Road.

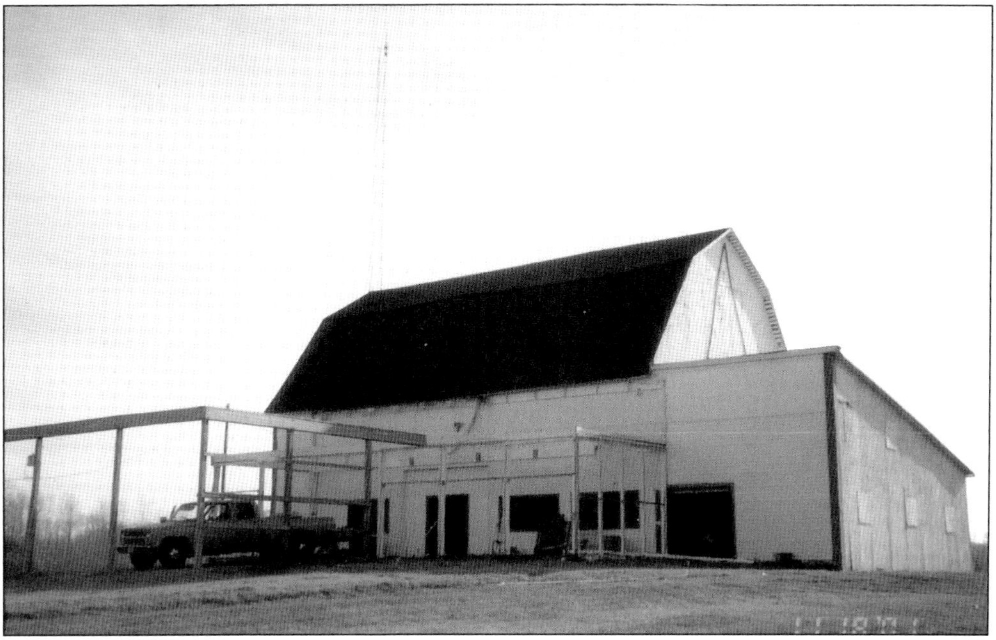

This barn and large house were located on Center Ridge Road at Lear Nagle. At one time, they belonged to the Faulkner family, but both structures were torn down a few years ago to make way for the now-closed Tops Market. Prior to the supermarket, the land had been the site of the Emerald Valley Garden Center.

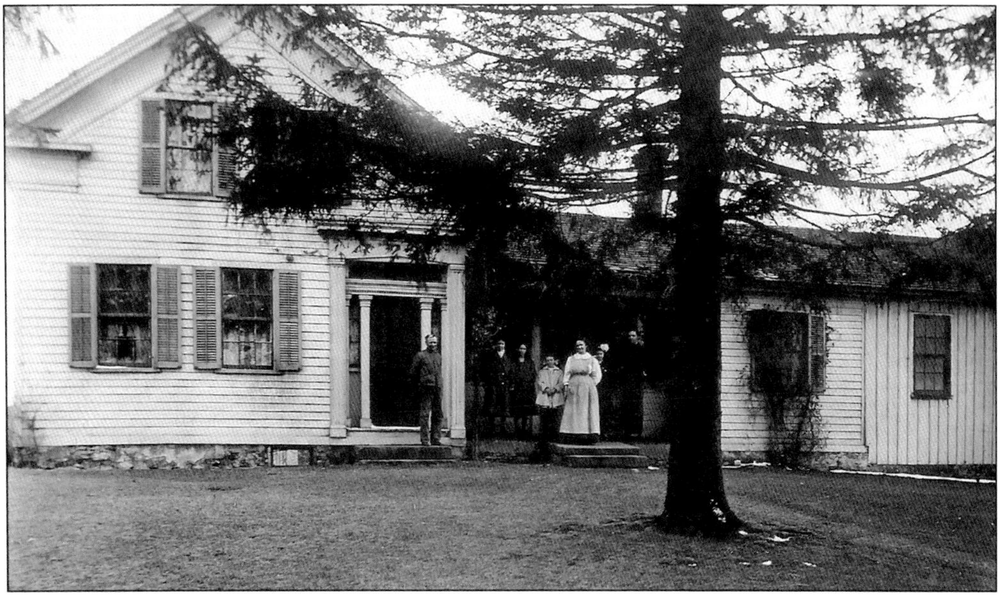

This home, belonging to the Pitts family, was built in the mid-1800s and initially was located on the south side of Center Ridge Road east of Jaycox Road. Later the family homestead was moved farther west on Center Ridge Road across from where CVS is presently located. (Courtesy of the Don Pitts family.)

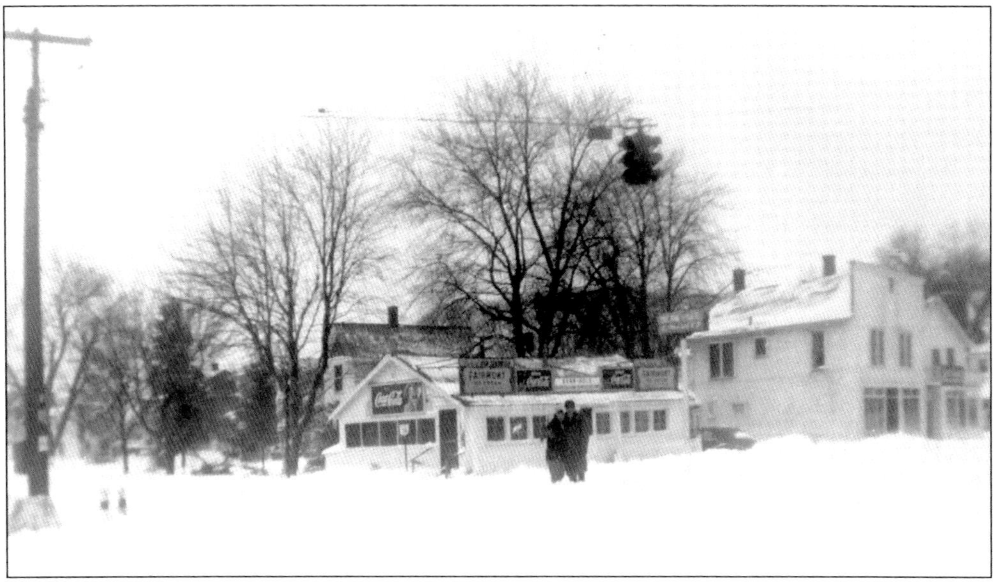

This photograph is of the intersection of Center Ridge and Avon Belden Roads, looking southwest. The Bean Hole, a well-known place to eat for many years, was built in the 1920s by Jim Curran. It was well known for its baked ham sandwiches and baked beans. The original building was enlarged and operated by Jim and his wife, Margaret (Ritsko) Curran, until it closed in 1957. The Green Line ticket office can be seen in the background.

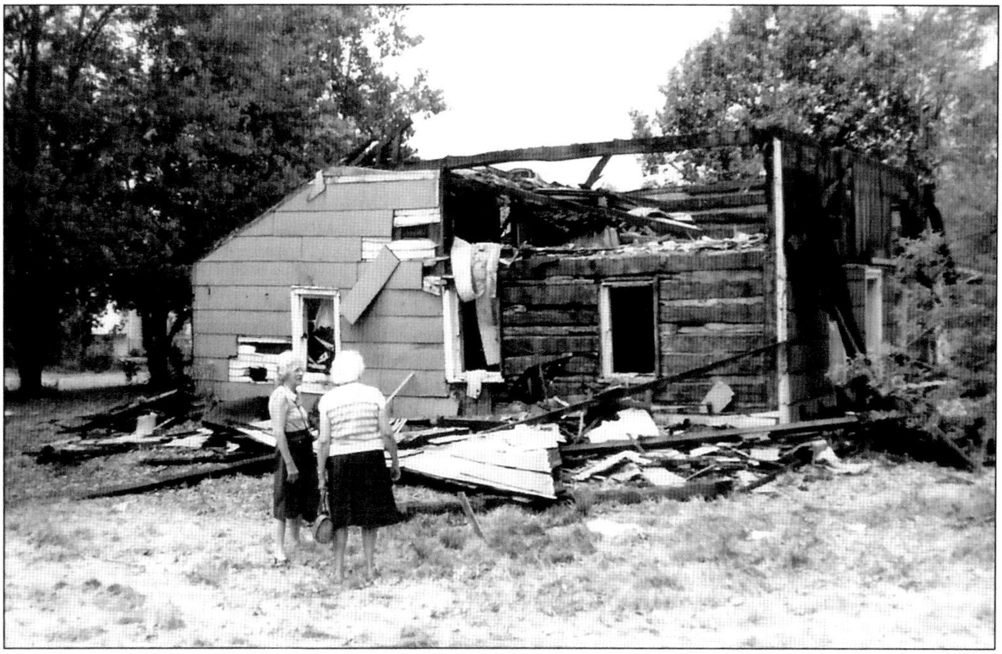

When the early settlers arrived in Ridgeville, they immediately began building log cabins to provide living quarters for themselves and their families. Most of the wooden structures were eventually replaced with houses of brick or clapboard; however, in the 1980s, when an aluminum-sided house on Jaycox Road, formerly owned by Alvah and Jean McVeigh, was being demolished, it was discovered that underneath the modern structure was an old log cabin. The structure eventually was dismantled and replaced with a modern house, and the old logs were sold and taken to Cleveland where they were used in a new structure. Lois Sullivan and her sister Frances Smith study the log cabin that was hidden by the siding. (Courtesy of Lois Sullivan.)

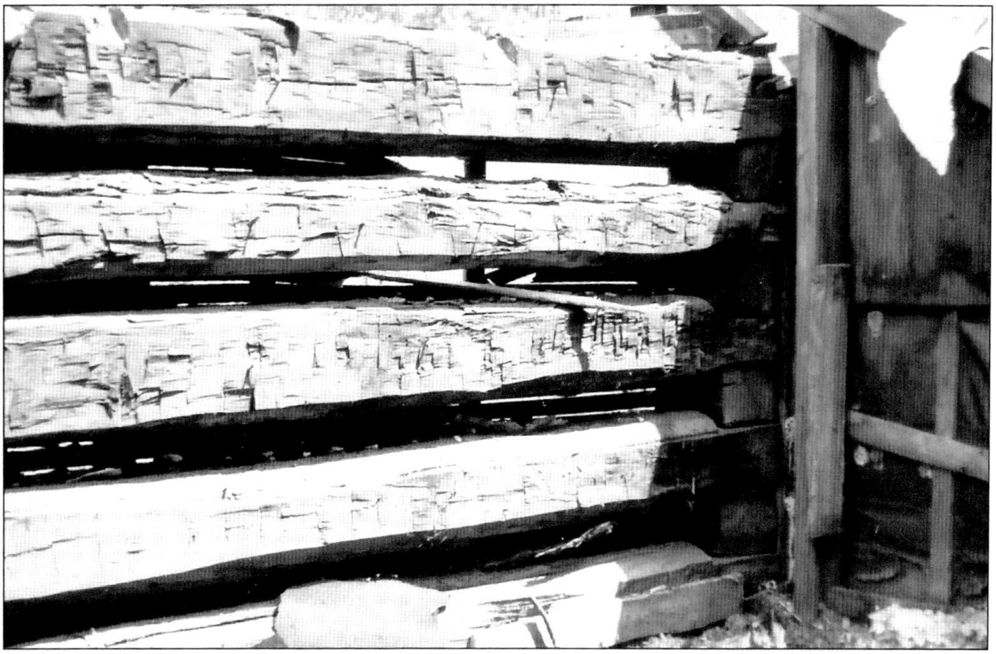

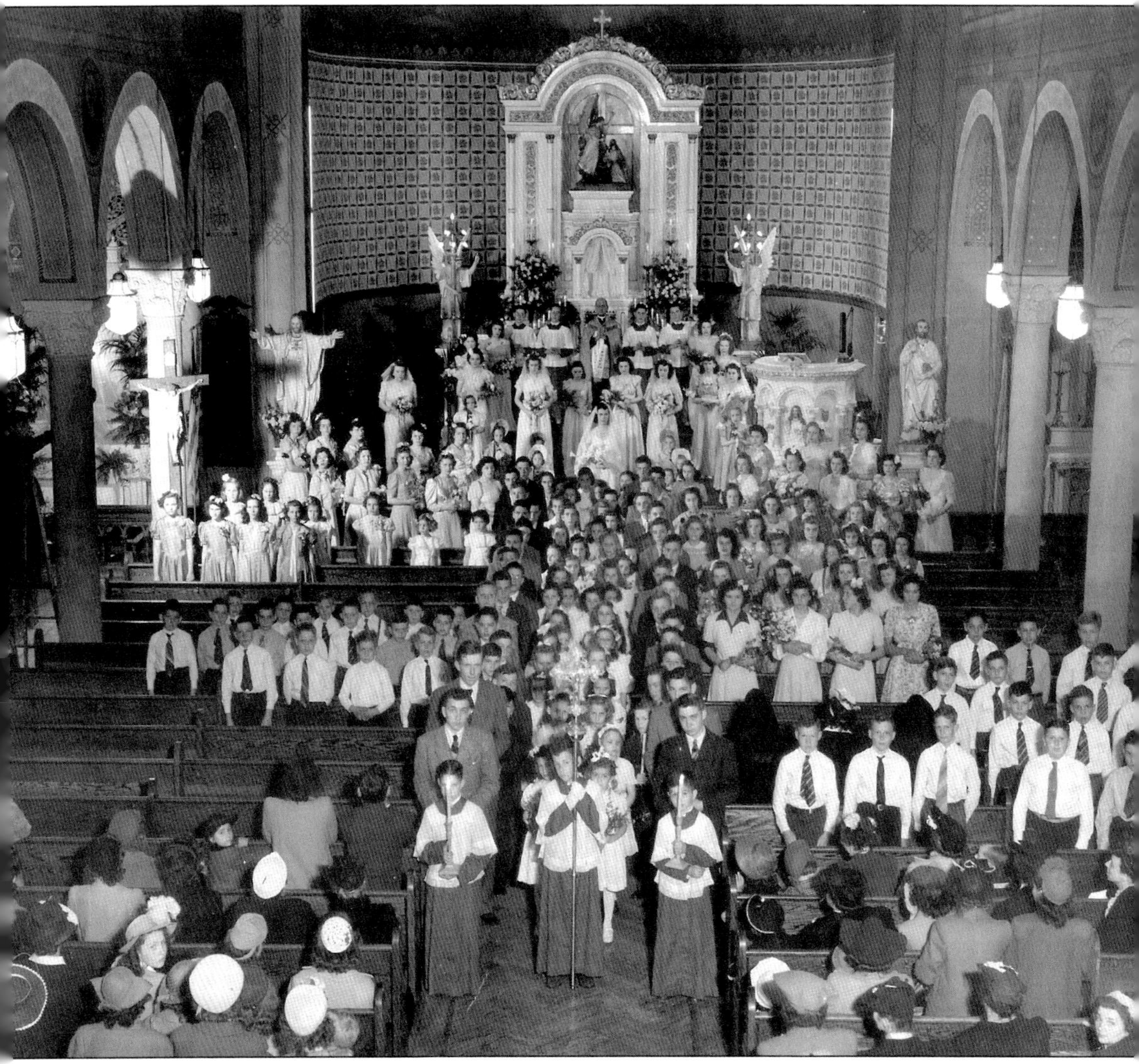

The entire congregation gathered in St. Peter Parish each May to participate in the annual May crowning. It was held in church and was a great honor. Many young girls in the parish often wished they could be chosen to be the May queen. In this 1944 photograph, Loyola Wensink had the honor of being the May queen. Other May queens included Marian Schneider (1940), Aileen Pitts (1942), Marie Gilgenbach (1943), Mary Holtwick (1945), Betty Pitts (1946), Velma Wakefield (1947), Ursula Schneider (1948), Ruth Zacharias, (1949), Jean Cummins (1950), Mary Hass (1951), Loyola Diederich (1952), and Janet Cummins (1953). (Courtesy of Loyola Diederich.)

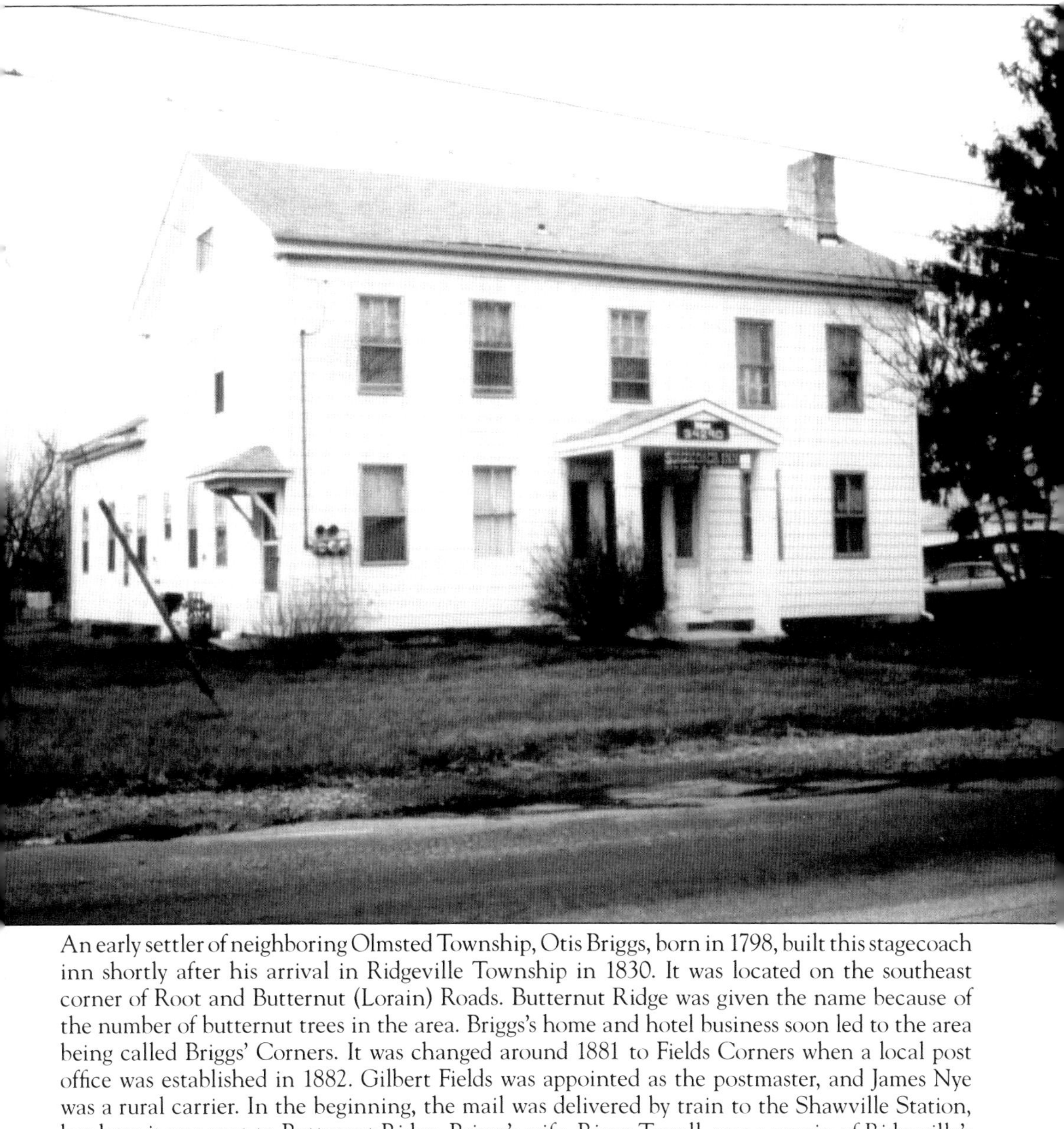

An early settler of neighboring Olmsted Township, Otis Briggs, born in 1798, built this stagecoach inn shortly after his arrival in Ridgeville Township in 1830. It was located on the southeast corner of Root and Butternut (Lorain) Roads. Butternut Ridge was given the name because of the number of butternut trees in the area. Briggs's home and hotel business soon led to the area being called Briggs' Corners. It was changed around 1881 to Fields Corners when a local post office was established in 1882. Gilbert Fields was appointed as the postmaster, and James Nye was a rural carrier. In the beginning, the mail was delivered by train to the Shawville Station, but later it was sent to Butternut Ridge. Briggs's wife, Rispa Terrell, was a cousin of Ridgeville's founding family. The former stagecoach inn has been in the Worcester family for many years.

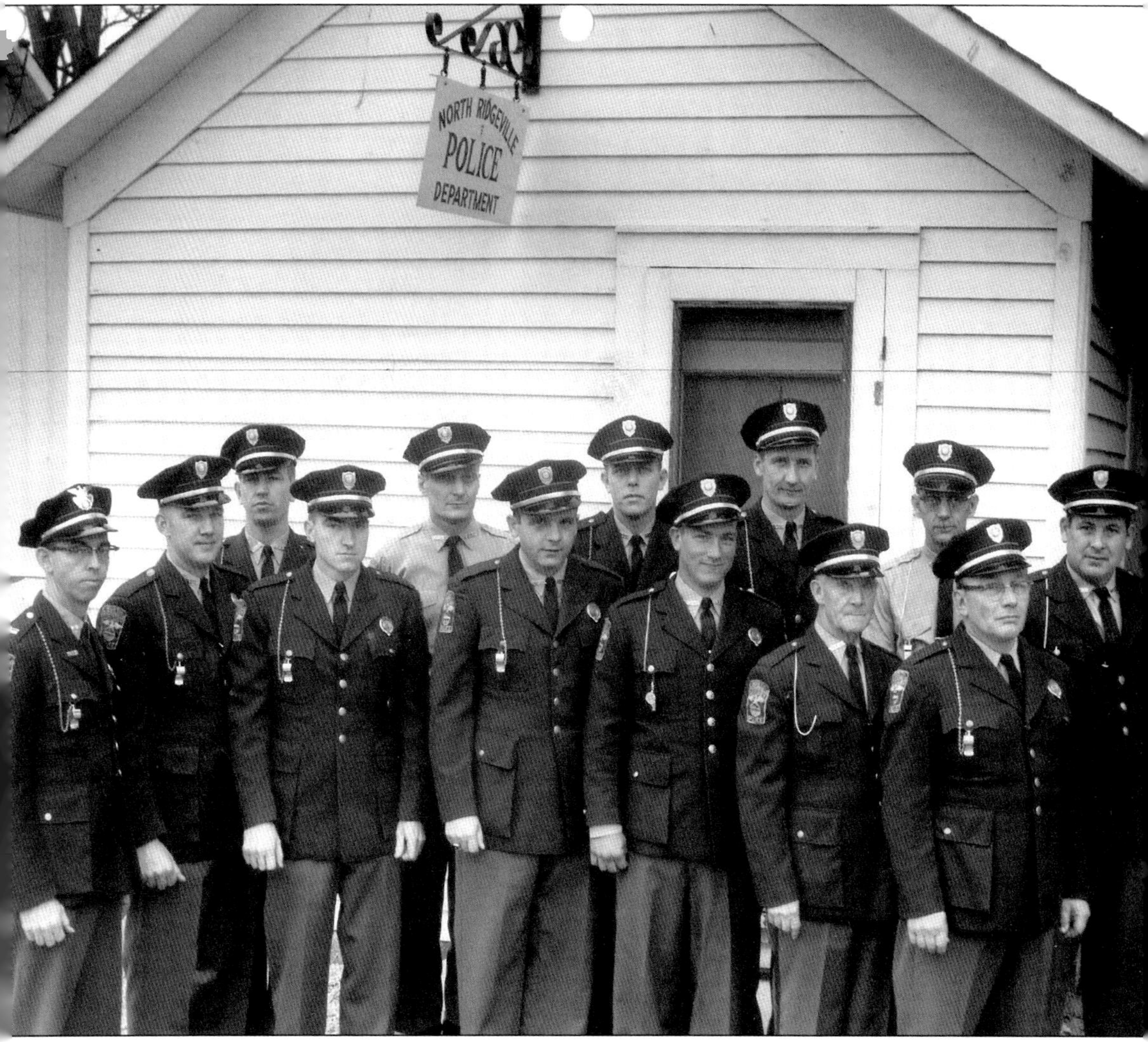

Members of the North Ridgeville Police Auxiliary are helpful to the regular police officers in the community. In this 1961 photograph, the members who served in the auxiliary at that time are standing in front of the old police station, which was housed in a former township voting booth behind the Old Town Hall. From left to right are (first row) Capt. Robert Shaffold, William Yonkof, Thomas Sigsworth, Albert Prebis, Harold Lovell, Jesse Whalen, and John Osbun; (second row) Harvey Jarvis, Frank Mancuso, Clarence Firestone, Charles Morris, William DeVault, and Ronald Wysocki. (Courtesy of the North Ridgeville Police Department.)

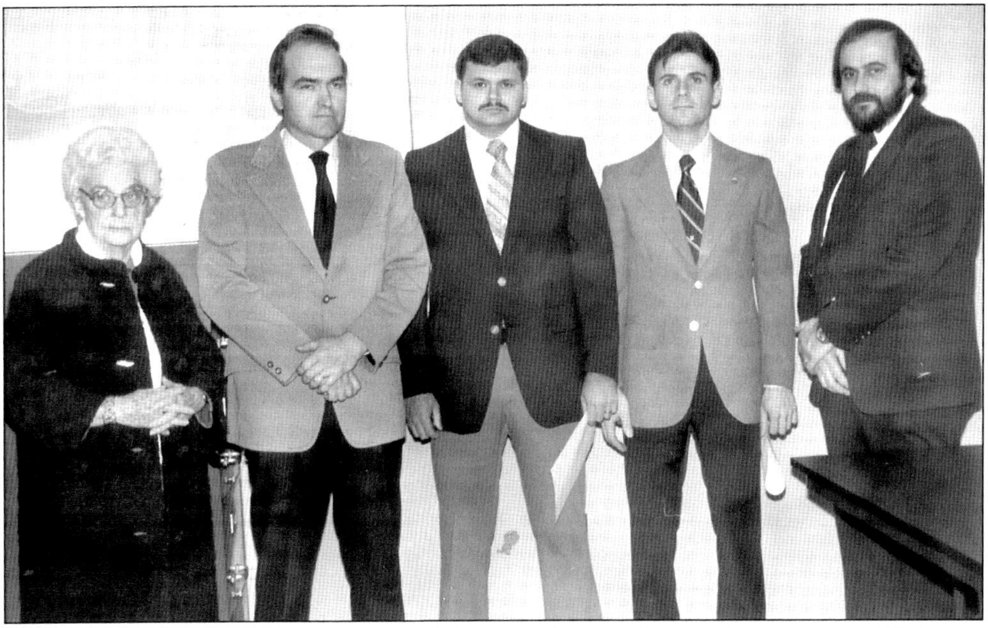

During Richard Carje's term as mayor of the city of North Ridgeville in the mid-1970s, two men were hired as members of the North Ridgeville Police Department. Pictured from left to right after the swearing in are councilwoman Leota Mitchell, Chief Thomas Sigsworth, Richard Thomas, Barry Accorti, and Carje. Thomas is presently the chief of police. (Courtesy of the North Ridgeville Police Department.)

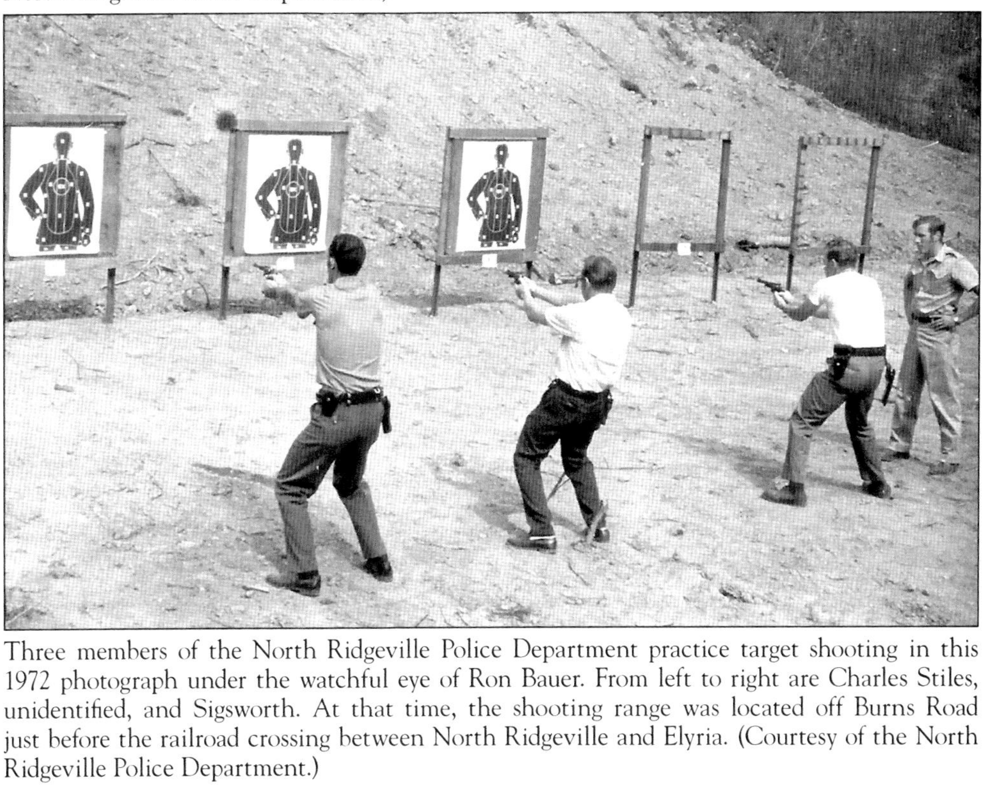

Three members of the North Ridgeville Police Department practice target shooting in this 1972 photograph under the watchful eye of Ron Bauer. From left to right are Charles Stiles, unidentified, and Sigsworth. At that time, the shooting range was located off Burns Road just before the railroad crossing between North Ridgeville and Elyria. (Courtesy of the North Ridgeville Police Department.)

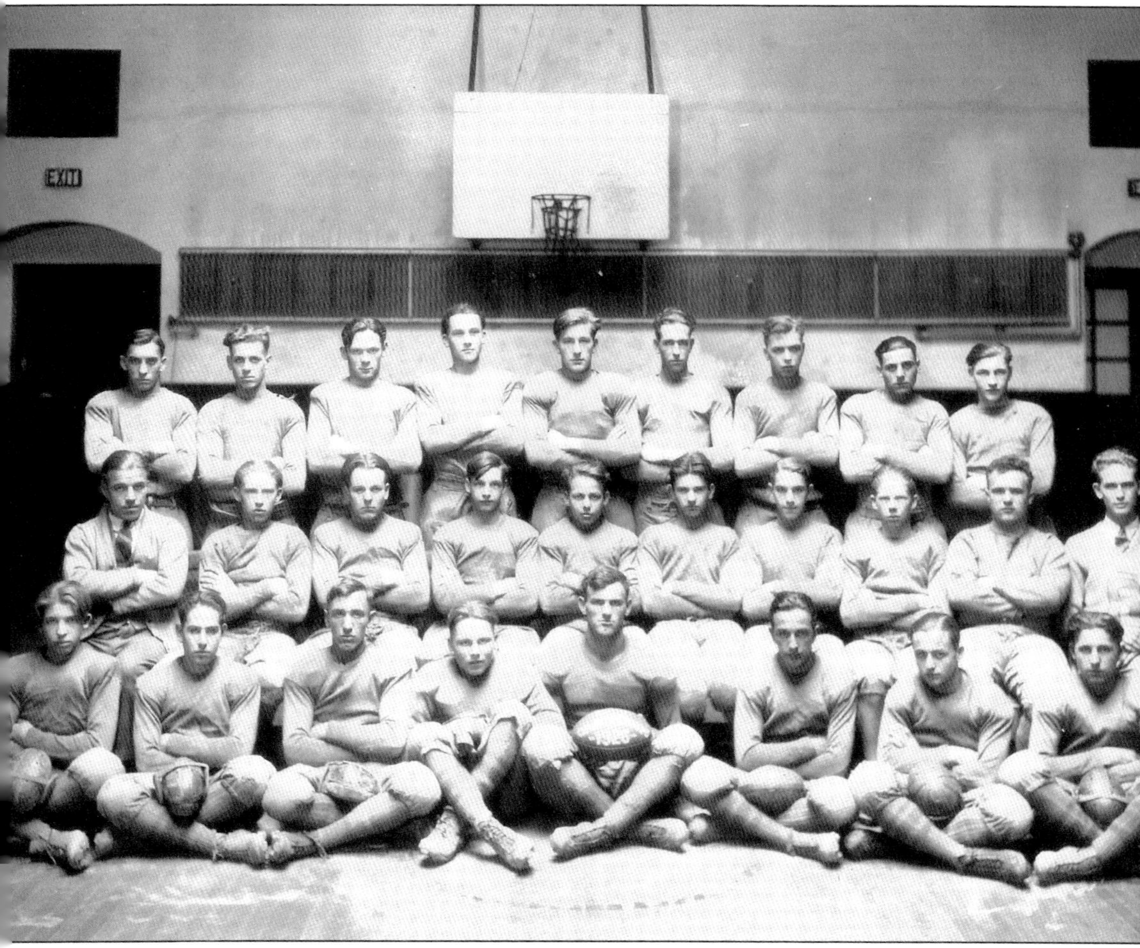

Members of the 1926 Ridgeville High School football squad were Lorain County champions after winning all four league games. The team is pictured in this photograph; however, they are identified by last names only and in no particular order. The coach was Ralph K. Reed, and the captain was Herb Myers. The first team included Bartter, Cheesman, Hadaway, VanWormer, Krugman, and Mills. Playing backfield were Limpert, Kotysbar, and Gibbons. The ends were Diederich, Schmittgen, and Myers. Playing tackle were Walker, Rauh, and Hopp, with Mastick as center. Substitutes for the 1926 team were Hopp, Bitzer, Smith, Lang, Perkins, Fortune, Wiley, Yost, and Wilford. (Courtesy of Kathy Bly.)

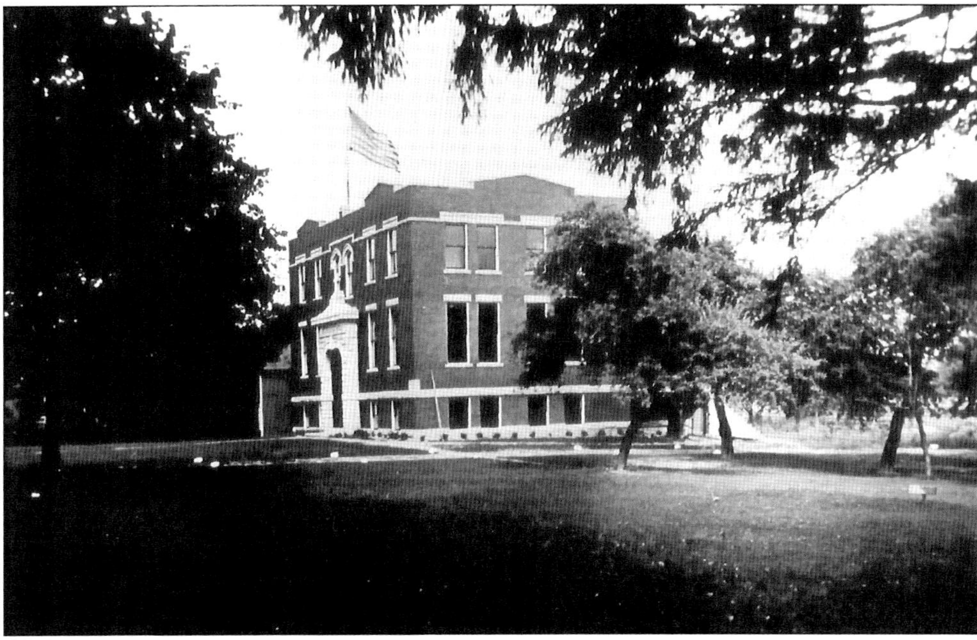

In 1910, St. Peter parishioners wanted to have a strong parochial school taught by nuns. The Reverend Joseph Trapp, with his councilmen, hoped to gather funds for a new school building. They succeeded in collecting $3,335. Building began in the beginning of July, and on September 25, 1910, the cornerstone was laid. When the school opened, the enrollment was 86 students.

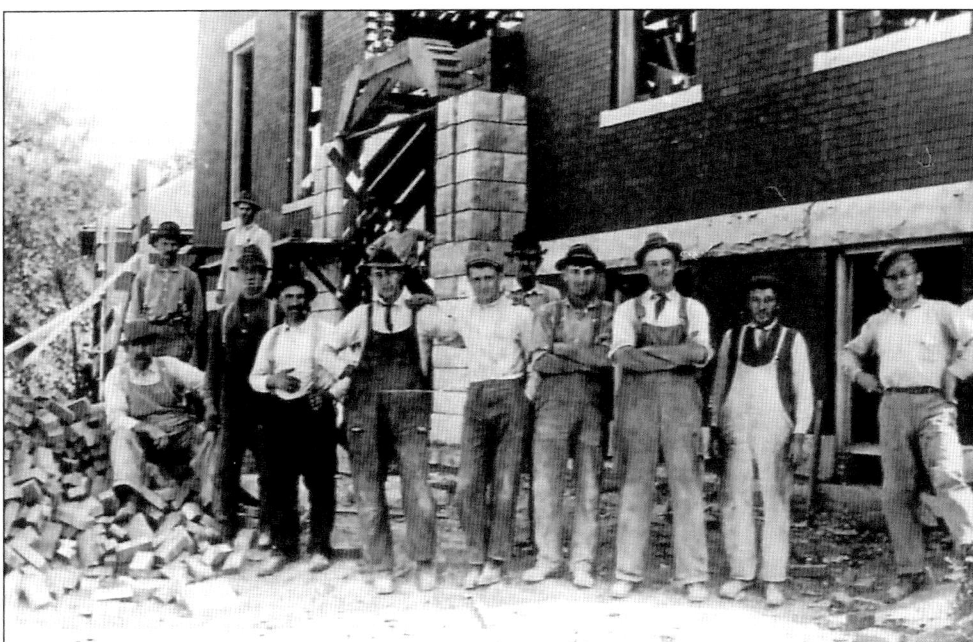

These are some of the workmen who helped build the first St. Peter School in 1910. The building was torn down in July 1964 and replaced by the current school building, located on Center Ridge Road next to the parish church. (Courtesy of Thomas Guggenbiller.)

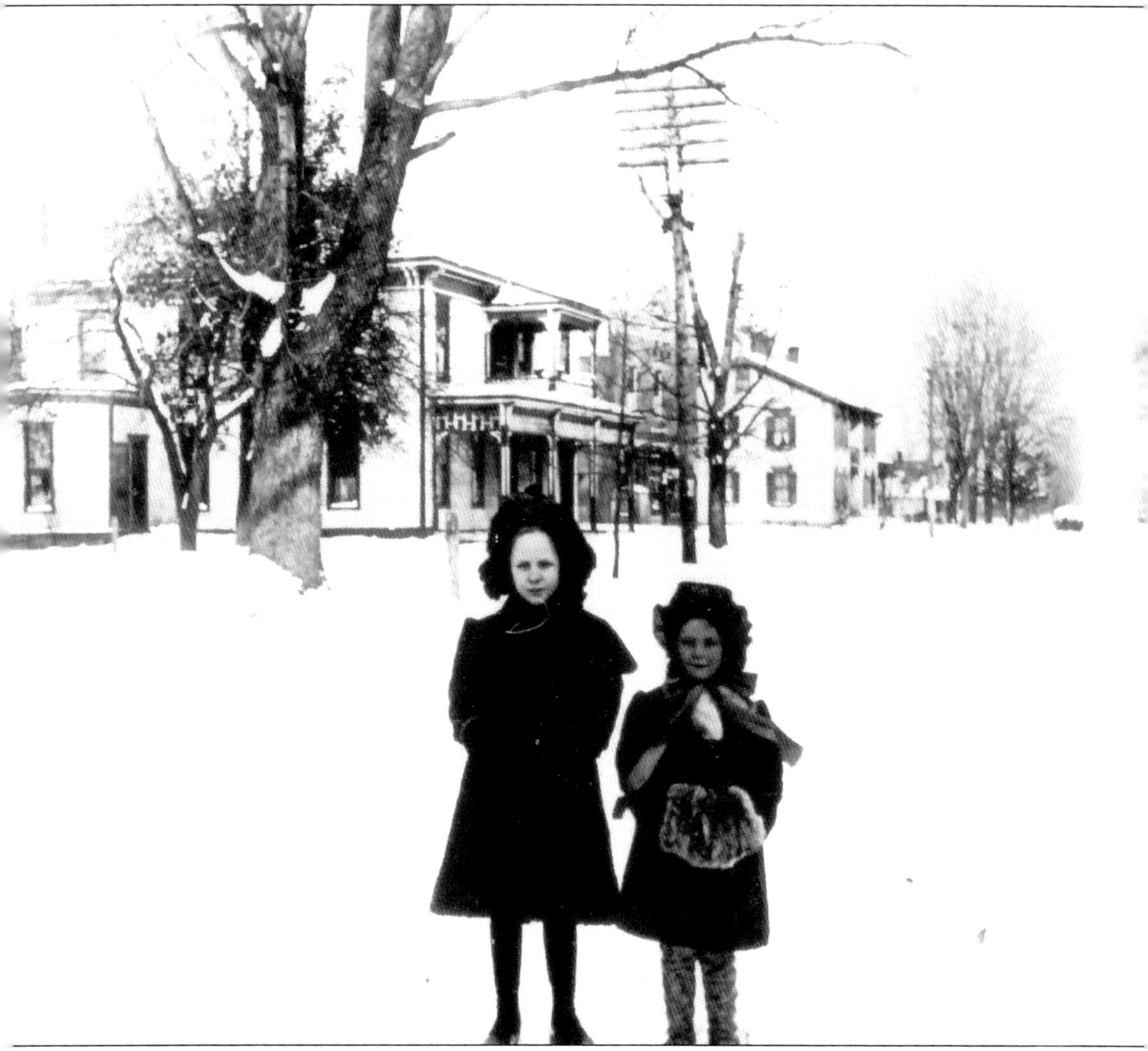

Irene and Viola Loescher, pictured here around 1908, were the adopted daughters of Henry and Rose Loescher of Center Ridge Road. In January 1922, the girls were returning home in a friend's automobile after attending a party at Fields Corners, which was located in the area of Root and Butternut Ridge Roads. The Root Road grade crossing was especially steep, and the vehicle they were riding in had to wait while two freight trains passed each other. At that time, the young people thought it was safe to cross; however, a fast passenger train they did not see struck the vehicle the sisters were in, and they, along with the driver, were killed. Irene was 20 years old, and her sister Viola was 17.

Ron Bauer's grandmother Theresa Pitts Barnes and her brother Edward Pitts are standing in front of the Barnes house in the Shawville community in this 1940s photograph. Edward Pitts died in 1967. (Courtesy of Ron Bauer.)

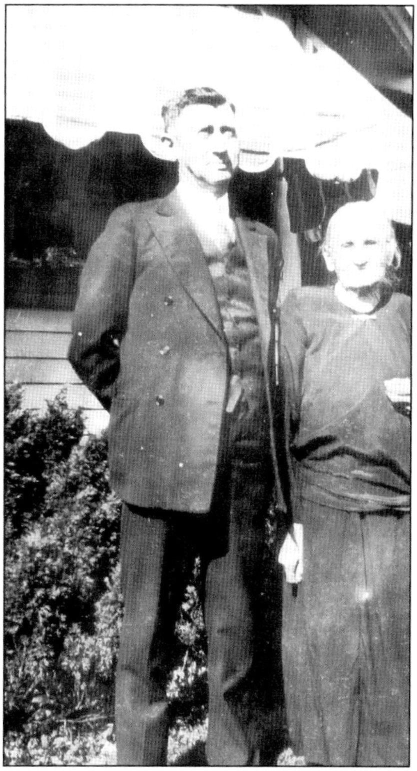

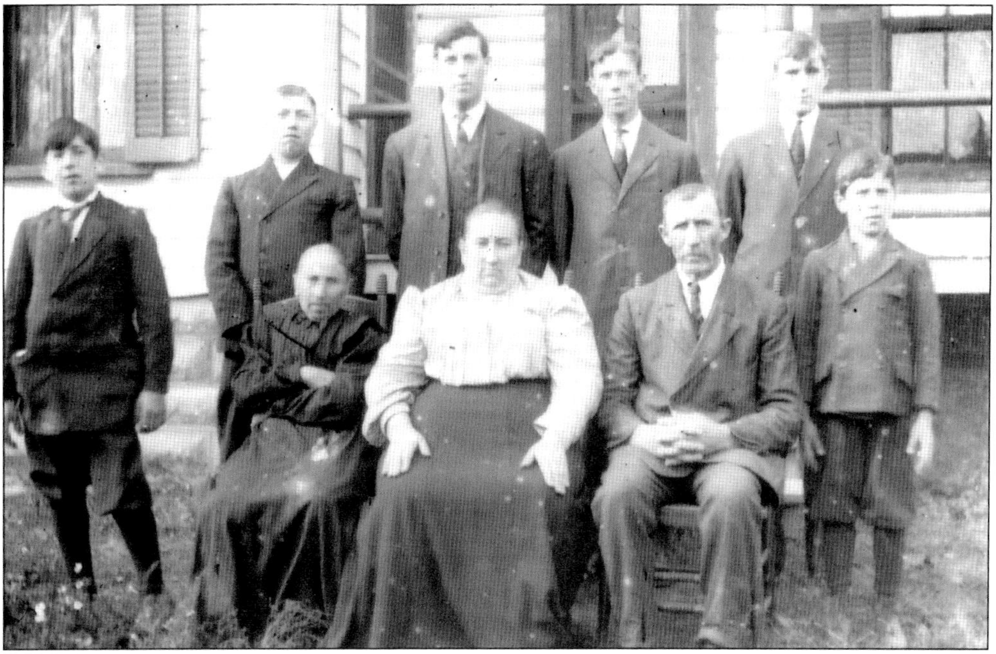

The Barnes family lived in the second house in from the railroad on Avon Belden Road in the early 1900s. From left to right are (first row) a woman identified as "mother-in-law," Gertrude Barnes, and Joseph Barnes; (second row) Sam (Bernard), Frank "Fatty," Jacob (Jake), William (Bill), Henry (Hank), and George. (Courtesy of Ron Bauer.)

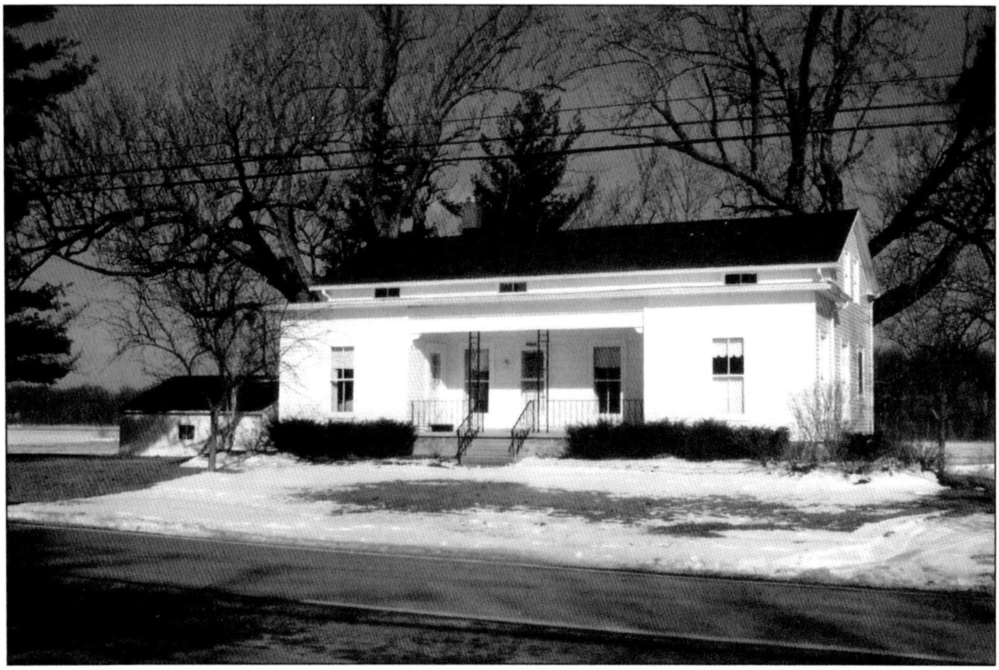

Although some of them have been remodeled or updated, North Ridgeville has a number of old structures still standing in the community. This house on Sugar Ridge Road is known as the Baxter house and is said to be more than 100 years old.

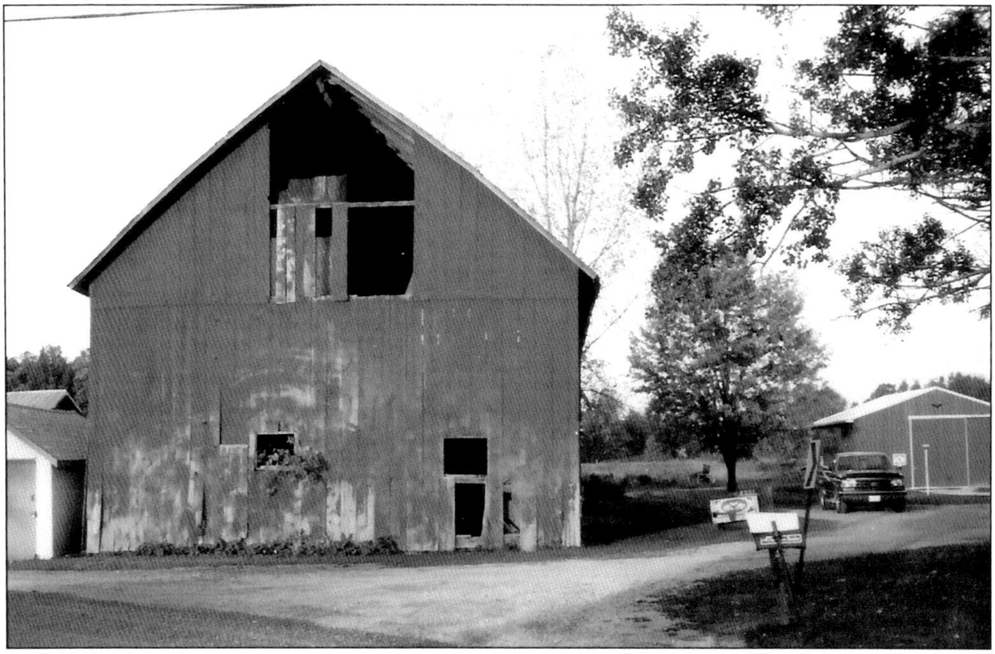

Because North Ridgeville was a farming community from its earliest times, barns could be seen along the highways and were considered a part of the landscape. Even today, barns still stand here and there; however, most of them have disappeared in the name of progress and to make way for modern developments.

Seven

HEROES OF YESTERDAY

Surviving in the face of many adversities made North Ridgeville's pioneers unsung heroes, perhaps especially Electa Wilmot Terrell, the only woman in the band of colonists who trekked from Connecticut westward to Ohio and the first white woman to settle in the area. She and her husband, Tillotson Terrell, brought three children from their home in Waterbury, Connecticut, and the couple had eight more children during their lives in Ridgeville. There have been many heroes in North Ridgeville's history, including those who served in the military in the Revolutionary War, the Civil War, World War I, World War II, and any of the other conflicts throughout the years. Each Memorial Day, North Ridgeville residents come together to honor the community's war heroes with a parade along Center Ridge Road, followed by speeches in the football stadium and services at the cemeteries.

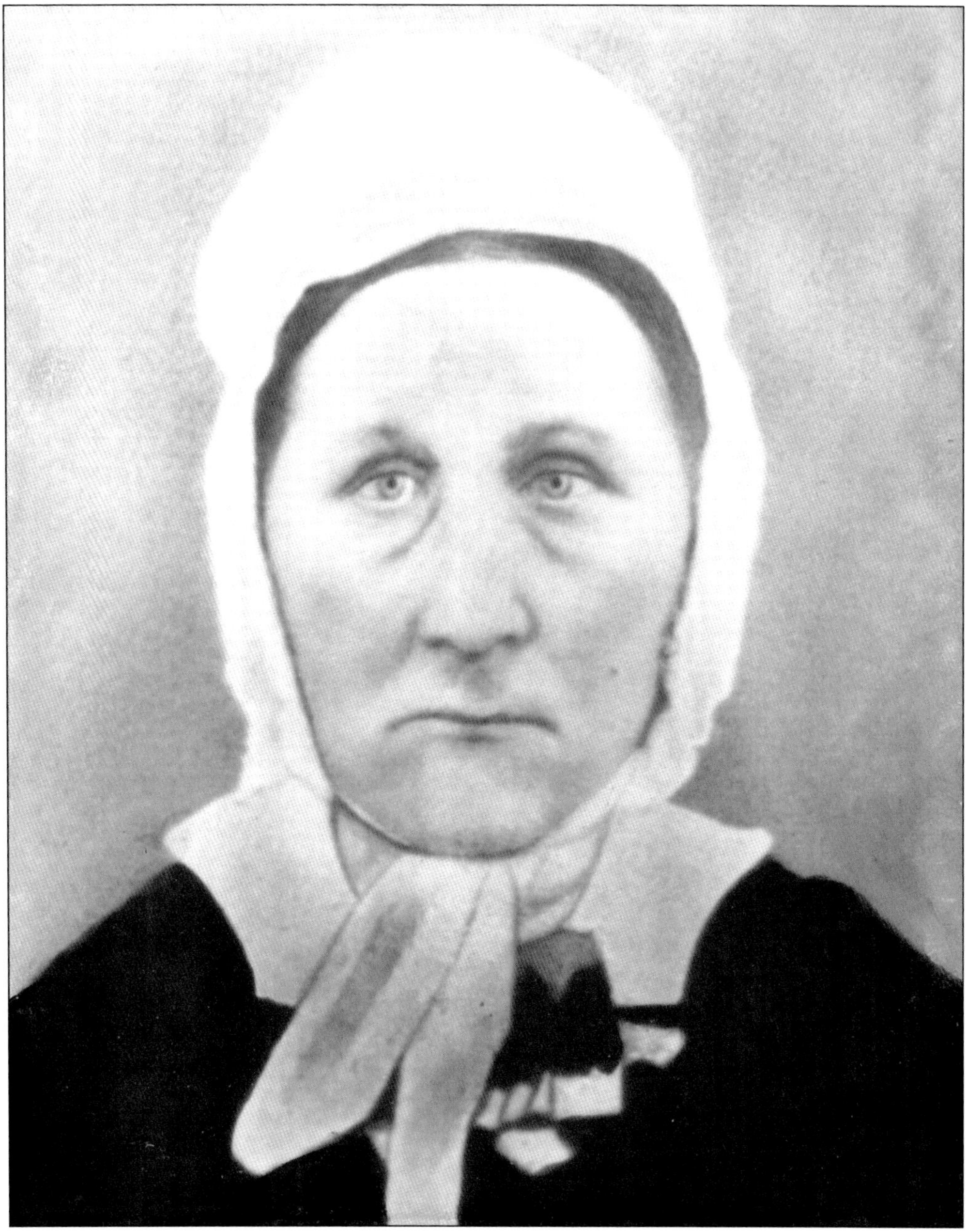

Electa Wilmot Terrell, the first pioneer woman to settle in Ridgeville Township, arrived from Waterbury, Connecticut, in July 1810 with her husband, Tillotson Terrell, and their children. They originally came to Columbia Township in 1809 and moved to Ridgeville the following year, becoming the town's first family. Tillotson's brothers and cousins arrived earlier with the first group of 13 settlers in May 1810, and two months later, he brought Electa to Ridgeville. She was the only woman living in the township from July to October 1810. Electa and Tillotson had a total of 11 children, including Horatio, Eliza, Alonzo, Lucinda, Andrew, Esther, Harriet, Tillotson Jr., Marcus, Pauline, and Lovinus. Electa was born in 1776 at the start of the Revolutionary War and died at age 85 in 1861, the first year of the Civil War.

Tillotson, born in 1775, was among the original 13 men who settled Ridgeville Township in May 1810. The following July, he returned to Connecticut and brought back his wife, Electa, and the first 3 of their 11 children. Tillotson was accidentally shot while hunting and died on December 23, 1838. The couple's gravestone, along with the markers of many other Ridgeville pioneers, is located in the Ridgeville Cemetery on Center Ridge Road at Stoney Ridge.

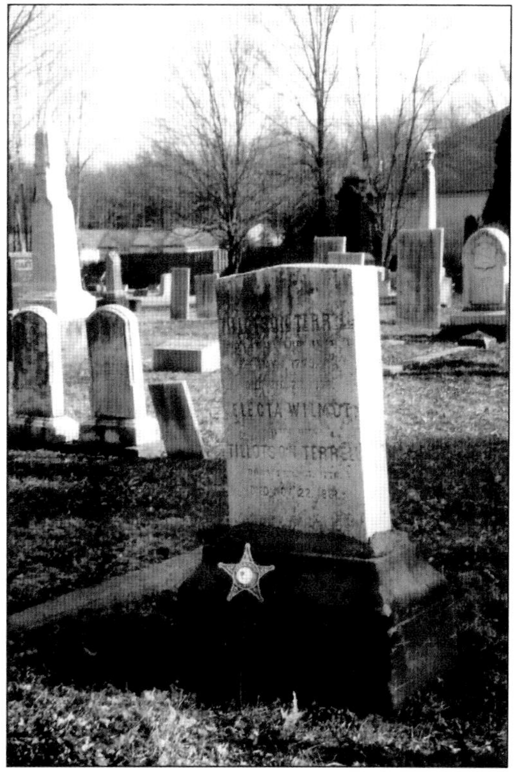

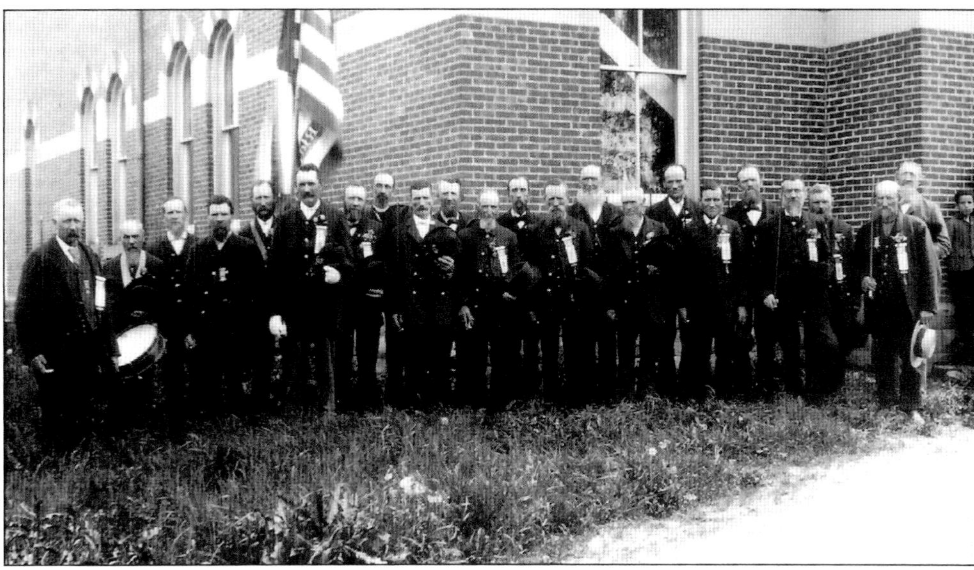

These Civil War soldiers from Ridgeville were members of the Wesley Kibbie Post 708 of the Grand Army of the Republic (GAR). They are pictured in front of the Ridgeville Township Hall. From left to right are James Spriggs, Theodore Bauldinger, William Zeman, Tom Andrews, Charles Warner, John D. Cole, John Brinker, Morris Frisbee, Charles H. Blake, John Schneider, ? Bradley, Rollin Emmons, ? Johnson, Jonethan Taylor, Adam Barres, Peter Meyers, James Nye, Frank Diederich, Anson Owen, ? Lett, Matthia Nuhn, and Joe Cutler. The boy is unidentified. (Courtesy of the Lorain County Historical Society.)

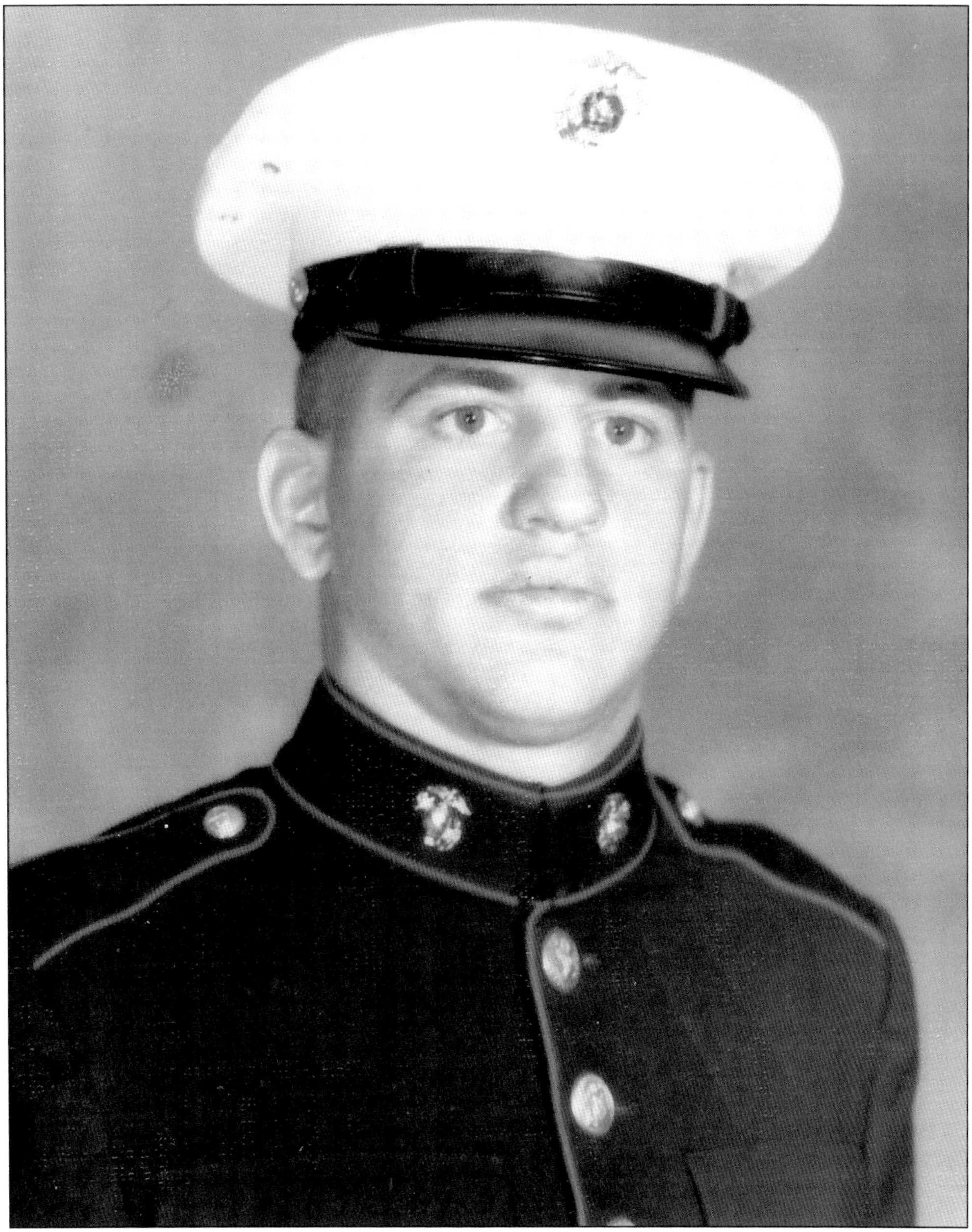

Lance Cpl. Raymond J. Baldauf, a rifleman with the 3rd Marine Division, was killed by enemy fire while on patrol in Mai Loc Quang Tri Province in the Republic of Vietnam on February 14, 1969, just two years after his graduation from North Ridgeville High School. Flags in North Ridgeville were flown at half-mast in honor of him. Mayor Dick Noll issued an official proclamation asking that residents and business places join in the gesture of respect. He was the son of Harold and Marcella Baldauf. Each year, his mother is honored as a Gold Star Mother during North Ridgeville's annual Memorial Day observance. Raymond was one of five North Ridgeville soldiers who died in the Vietnam War between 1966 and 1969. The others were Michael L. Brundage, Charles D. Flood, Gaylord D. Kerr, and James D. Smith, all members of the U.S. Army. (Courtesy of Marcella Baldauf.)

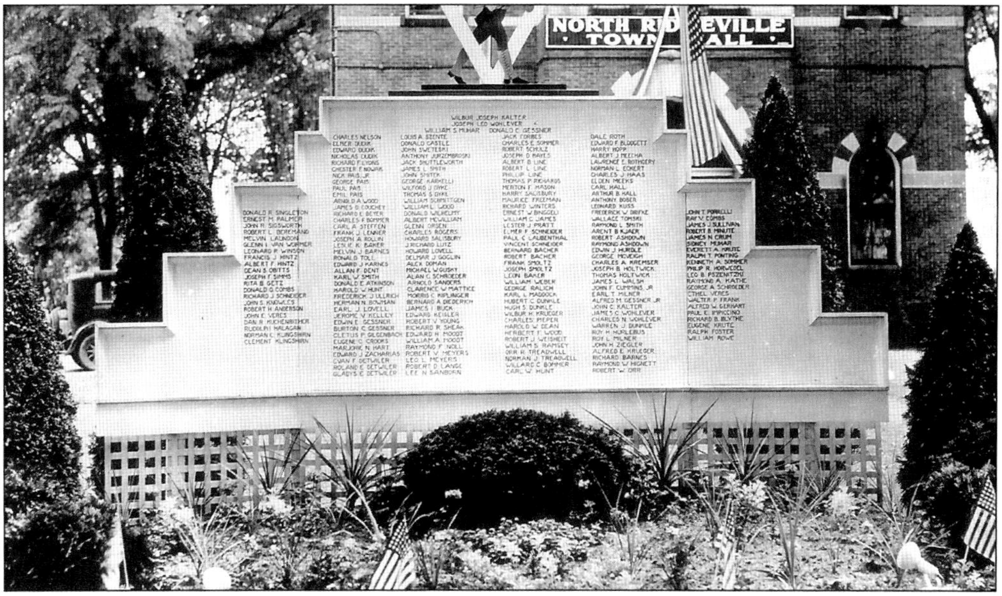

During World War II, a large, white, wooden service roster board was displayed in front of the town hall. The hall had served as District No. 5 of the Lorain County Draft Board, handling the wartime inductions of dozens of township servicemen. Several years after World War II, a memorial stone replaced the service roster and was dedicated to the memory of the 16 Ridgeville Township soldiers who had given their lives during the war. The single Ridgeville casualty from World War I was included as well.

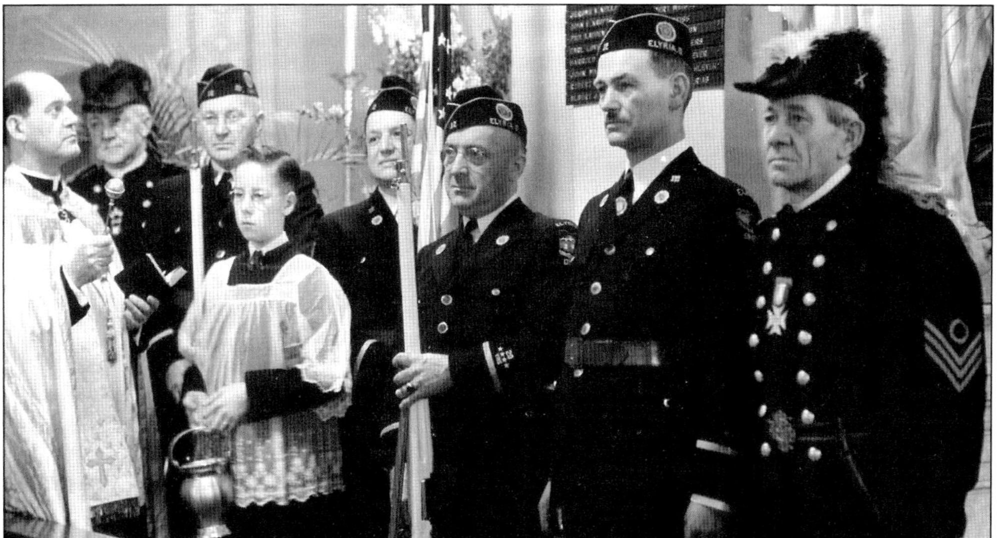

On February 22, 1943, the Reverend Francis Brucker, pastor of St. Peter Parish, held a blessing of the honor roll ceremony to honor those in the parish who served in the armed forces. It was a religious and patriotic ceremony. The honor roll, made of simulated bronze, contained the names of 88 men and one woman. It also included the name of Sidney Muhar, an aviator who lost his life in Egypt. Dale Wakefield is the pastor's server. George Noll, at far left, and Henry Zacharias, at far right, are members of the Knights of St. John. The other men in uniform are unidentified.

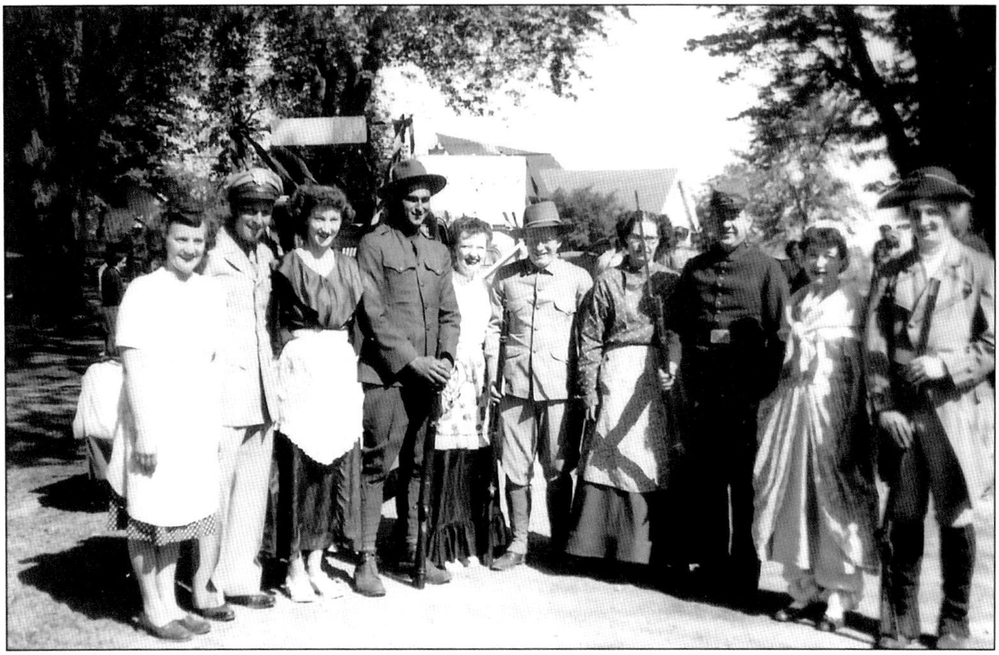

When the Ridgeville Township held its Memorial Day parade, it honored the local men who had served in the nation's wars. On May 30, 1951, some residents dressed in costumes representing the times of different battles. The women pictured above are not identified, but several of the men are. From left to right are Bob Minute, dressed in a World War II uniform; Ernie Bingelli, representing World War I; an unidentified man in a uniform from the Spanish-American War; George Clark representing the Civil War; and John Fritz in the uniform of the Revolutionary War. In the photograph below, men who were in various branches of the military at that time marched in the parade, carrying the U.S. flag.

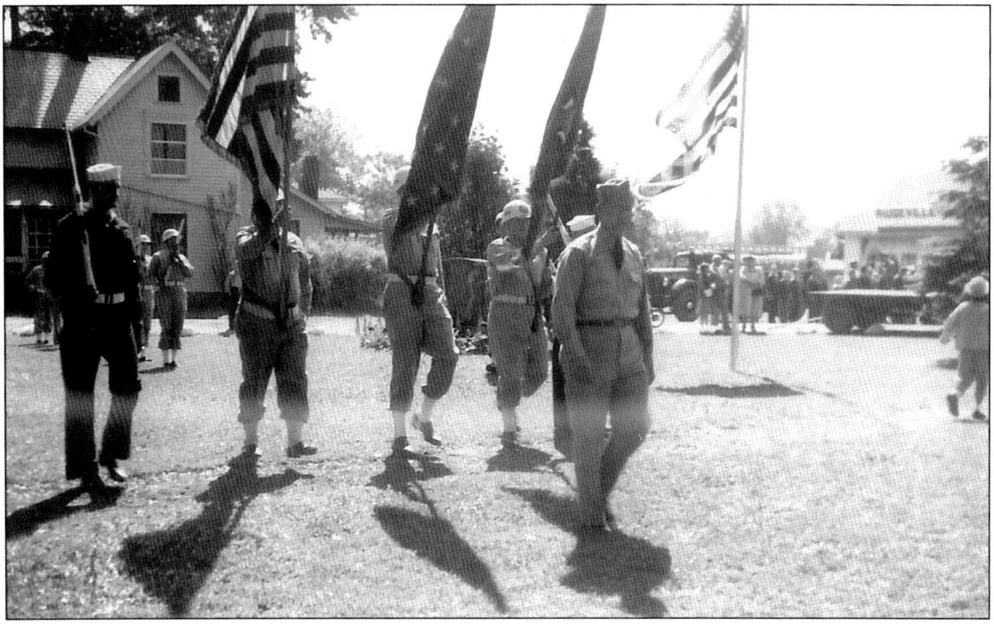

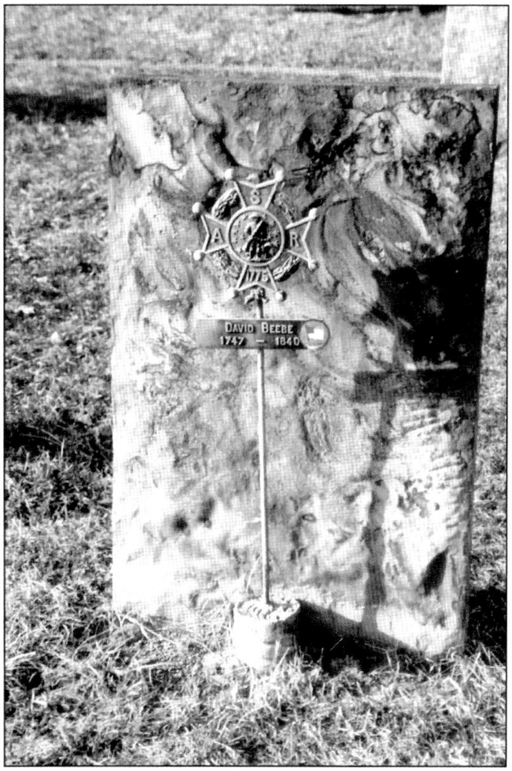

The historic Ridgeville Center Cemetery, located at the intersection of Center Ridge and Stoney Ridge Roads, is the final resting place of many of North Ridgeville's earliest pioneers, including well-known family names like Beebe and Terrell. In addition to the very old tombstones in the cemetery, with some so worn that it is difficult to decipher the names, several of the graves have special markers, denoting that person's service in the military. The cemetery is not difficult to locate and is situated on the north side of Route 20 across the street from the First Congregational United Church of Christ.

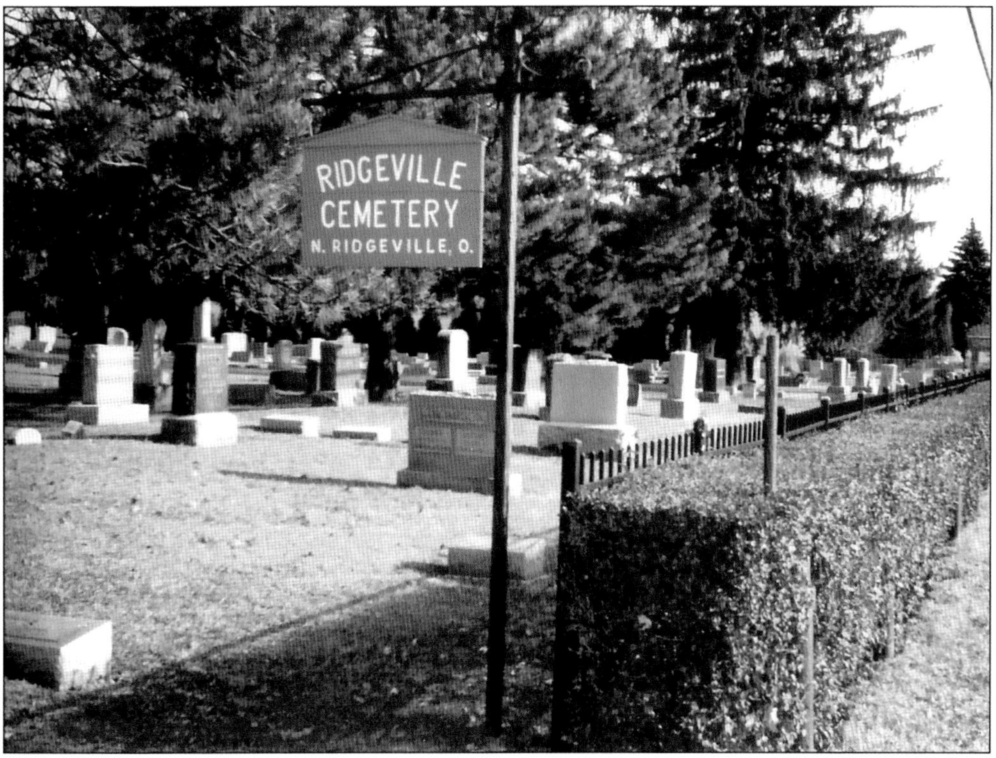

Discover Thousands of Local History Books Featuring Millions of Vintage Images

Arcadia Publishing, the leading local history publisher in the United States, is committed to making history accessible and meaningful through publishing books that celebrate and preserve the heritage of America's people and places.

Find more books like this at
www.arcadiapublishing.com

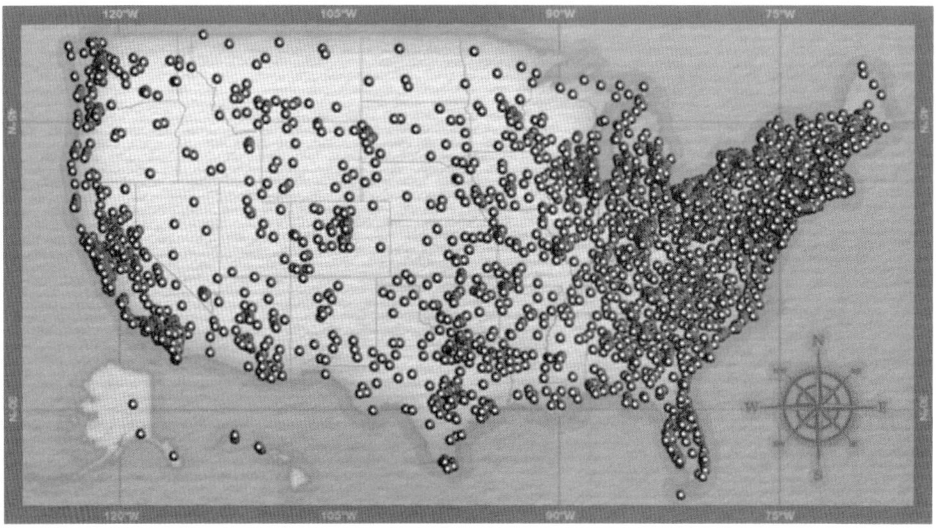

Search for your hometown history, your old stomping grounds, and even your favorite sports team.

Consistent with our mission to preserve history on a local level, this book was printed in South Carolina on American-made paper and manufactured entirely in the United States. Products carrying the accredited Forest Stewardship Council (FSC) label are printed on 100 percent FSC-certified paper.

MADE IN THE USA